IMAGES OF THE CHURCH
IN THE NEW TESTAMENT

IMAGES OF THE CHURCH
IN THE
NEW TESTAMENT

by
PAUL S. MINEAR

THE WESTMINSTER PRESS
Philadelphia

LIBRARY OF CONGRESS CATALOG CARD No. 60–11331

PRINTED IN THE UNITED STATES OF AMERICA
5 6 7 8 9

To
GEORGE L. MINEAR (1868–1924)
OLIVER J. HOFFMAN (1875–1959)

Acknowledgments

I wish first of all to recognize a massive debt to my colleagues on the Theological Commission on Christ and the Church who have furnished many fresh insights into the character of New Testament ecclesiology. A second word of gratitude is due to those who made so enjoyable a year's study in the Netherlands, where this manuscript took shape. Especially helpful were Professor Willem C. van Unnik of the University of Utrecht and Dr. Johanna J. van Dullemen of the U.S. Educational Foundation in the Netherlands. Still another vote of thanks goes to two schools where various chapters were used as lectures: the Theological Institute held by the Nanking Board of Founders in Singapore in 1959; the Perkins School of Theology in Dallas in 1960. Above all, a salute must be given to my wife, whose help, from first draft through the last, has been phenomenal.

PAUL S. MINEAR

February, 1960

CONTENTS

I

THE SCOPE AND METHOD OF STUDY

EVERY READER is entitled to know at the very outset the central objective of this study. Briefly stated, it is the fuller comprehension of the many ways in which New Testament writers thought and spoke about the church. Less succinctly but more precisely stated, it is the examination of the varied meanings of the image of the body of Christ within the context of all the other pictures of Christian community. This objective determines the schedule of exploration. First we will sift out and give brief attention to the less significant analogies (Chapter II). Then we will survey somewhat more fully the views of the church reflected in more important images (Chapters III to V). Then we will examine at still greater length the basic associations of the body image (Chapter VI). And finally we will trace the networks of thought that bind the major images together (Chapter VII).

Why should such a study be worth undertaking? Many answers could be given and perhaps each could be contested. Here it may suffice to rely on the historian's method of telling why by reconstructing the order in which things have happened. This study is the result of work assigned to the author by a theological study commission in 1954. This commission, under the title Theological Commission on Christ and the Church, was established by the Faith and Order Department of the World Council of Churches as an outgrowth of the Third World Conference on Faith and Order, which met in Lund, Sweden, in 1952. At that conference a vigorous demand was voiced for studies that would explore not so much the formal doctrines of the church, concerning which the several Christian communions are deeply divided, as the inner relationships that link the church to Jesus Christ and to the Holy Spirit and which therefore bind the various communions together even in spite of themselves. In response to this demand, one commission was set up in America and one in Europe, under the following terms of reference: "To study the nature of the church in close relation both to the doctrine of the person and work of Christ and to the doctrine of the Holy Spirit." Since 1954 these commissions, composed of representatives selected from different communions, have held annual consultations and have circulated and discussed essays dealing with numerous aspects of the one theme. Over the years several books and many articles have been written by commission members, each of whom has thus carried forward his share of the mutual task.[1] This present book represents an effort to complete its author's share and is therefore initially intended to contribute to the continuing discussions within the Faith and Order Movement. A secondary intention, however, is to enable a wider circle of readers to take part in this complex yet constructive conversation. During recent years the earlier segments of the study, which have circulated in mimeographed form, have elicited such a vigorous discussion that the author has been encouraged to believe that this larger constituency would welcome such participation.

This account of how the study originated may convey to the reader the circumference of our concern. The overarching motive is that of advancing the unity, the renewal, and the mission of God's people. Such an advance presupposes and produces the need for a more adequate comprehension of the nature of the church. But all recent explorations of the nature of the church have made it clear that the church does not have a nature that can be readily defined simply by looking, no matter how directly, at the church itself. Its life springs from, is nourished by, and is oriented toward the fullness of glory of the Triune God. If we would glimpse even the barest outlines of the church, we must take full account of the activity of the living Christ and of the Holy Spirit. A valid understanding of this activity, according to the testimony of many contemporary theologians, requires in turn a new perception of the depths of meaning in the Pauline description of the church as the body of Christ. Yet the effort to understand this description, although altogether necessary, may quickly become an obsession, blocking rather than building comprehension, unless the employment of the phrase in the New Testament is rightly assessed. Our best defense against infatuation with our own theological jargon will be to set this one picture of the church among all the other pictures. The New Testament has an extensive gallery of such pictures, many of which effectively delineate the essential links between the life of the church and the diversely hidden workings of God.

This sketch of the total range of concern, gradually narrowed until it brings into focus the terms of reference for this study, intimates several limitations which the reader must anticipate. This study must concentrate solely upon those church images which appear in the New Testament and not elsewhere. Moreover, we must give priority to those implications which are relatively clear in terms of particular contexts within the New Testament. We cannot attempt a completely detailed and adequately documented history of any single image. Volumes have been written about each image, and more should be written, even though none of these can be wholly definitive. In this study we will not trace the historical development of each image but will chart the range of connotations conveyed by the image in this particular stage of that development. Moreover, we disavow the intention of providing a formal, systematic treatment of the doctrine of the church. That task also remains for other pens. By the same token, this survey of the varied pictures can offer no thorough analysis of the many ways in which the living Christ and the Holy Spirit operate in and through the community of faith. We will not, of course, ignore these wider horizons of concern; but there are some types of study — and this is one — where, unless the student sets and observes certain boundaries, he will never complete the task. The objective that has been set and stated, narrow as it is, will more than tax the resources of both author and reader. What follows, then, is merely a rough initial survey of all the church images in the New Testament, with a view to disclosing their more certain connotations and tracing their mutual interactions.

So far as I know, there has been no similar effort within one volume to review all the Biblical pictures of the church and to examine their interdependence. Most ecclesiologies concentrate upon the more prosaic doctrines of the church. When they venture into the realm of images, they do so by way of selecting only a few. Such procedures are to be expected. The range of images is in fact too extensive, too fluid, too variegated, to encourage a systematic survey of them all. A venture like ours, to be successful, must therefore recognize and observe certain limits. As we have already indicated, we cannot pursue the history of any image backward toward its hidden origins in the cultures of the ancient world. Nor can we carry its history forward into the centuries of subsequent Christian usage. We cannot even explore all the subtler rays of light that an image may emit in its circulation within the New Testament. We must concentrate upon those texts in which a reference to the Christian community can be affirmed. And where a given image bears directly or indirectly upon the conception of the church, we must be content with stating those connotations which are most tangible and probable. This book is not the proper place to advance a whole medley of hypotheses concerning possible or marginal inferences that might be drawn from each successive Biblical text. If we were to do that, we would have to include carefully reasoned and heavily documented arguments for each hypothesis, buttressed by extensive quotations from contemporary scholars. And where a particular interpretation is contested (and few there are that remain unchallenged) we would need, in fairness to the reader, to give the evidence for all the major alternatives. We must be content, rather, with reporting for a nonprofessional constituency the more obvious lines of interpretation on which we might find broad agreement among historical and theological interpreters. No doubt there will be many points on which the conclusions of the author will seem all too arbitrary and dubious. But his intention is that of presenting a comprehensive body of deductions on which a wide consensus might be reached.

At the present time, of course, this consensus could hardly be called very broad, and there must be no dishonesty in ignoring the extent or the depth of disagreements. Nevertheless, a consensus of judgments, and nothing less, remains the goal. We would diminish the chance of reaching this goal unless we adopt an ecumenical starting point, an ecumenical perspective, and an ecumenical method. Probably no individual scholar can measure up to such conditions, but at the very least he can seek to free himself from the more parochial biases of his own relatively modern ecclesiastical tradition. He can read with empathy the interpretations of the Bible that have been offered by the best representatives of other traditions. He can discuss his work with such representatives, learning as much as possible from their reactions. What is still more important, he can seek to employ methods which, on the one hand, will be congenial to the thought world of New Testament writers and which, on the other hand, will be generally viable in the contemporary Christian world.

This last sentence raises a most difficult matter indeed. Our objective would be much easier to accomplish if there were a genuine congeniality between the New Testament thought world and the contemporary Christian thought world. But such congeniality is, to say the least, both minimal in extent and problematic in content. Many scholars will deny that there is a unity of perspective within the New Testament itself, especially with regard to doctrines of the church. Any rejection of their denial must be supported by evidence that the early Christian community had received from Christ a unity that was manifested at least in the consciousness of New Testament authors and that was not destroyed by their diversity of gifts. In similar manner, many scholars deny the existence of any significant unity of perspective within contemporary Christendom. Again, those who reject their denial must present evidence of a genuine unity in Christ which permeates the diverse modes in which the churches think and pray and work. There is yet a third denial that must be dealt with: the denial that any substantial congeniality obtains between the two thought worlds, that of the first-century church and that of the twentieth-century church. In this case the contrasts between the two centuries loom up so sharply that it is difficult indeed to affirm the existence of a kinship that effectively explains those contrasts. Yet the difficulty in making this affirmation does not diminish its importance or its truth. In fact, a Christian communion makes this affirmation whenever it expresses its self-consciousness as a church. The Christian theologian makes the same affirmation when he defends the unity of the church as an " ecumenism in time," to use a phrase of Father Georges Florovsky. Certainly one hears on all sides and in many forms the assertion of an essential continuity between the church of the apostles and the church of their latter-day successors. Yet the evidence that supports an opposite conclusion is abundant and cogent.

One must confess that the distance between the two communities, a distance of nineteen centuries when measured in time, is magnified twentyfold when measured in other terms. Some find it most difficult to recognize any kinship whatever to the wandering band of Jesus' disciples in the modern church as a powerful and prosperous social institution, whether or not it appears in the form of a state religion. For others the distance becomes even greater when one contrasts that ancient society, whose ethical and social behavior was articulated in the radical pacifism of the Sermon on the Mount, with modern churches whose employment of power politics and reliance on public relations betray its identity with " the world." Still others detect the most extreme anomaly in the realm of internal organization, where the leadership of laymen, who pioneered an unstructured movement hostile to the temple clique, has been replaced by a priestly hierarchy whose monopoly over church life exceeds anything dreamed of in ancient Israel. Or should we locate the greatest contrast in the forms of worship, where an initial simplicity, informality, and rejection of cant, cloth, and custom have been replaced by elaborate ceremonies by robed priests, in which the efficacy of the ritual requires an exact observance of the proper formulas? Or is the distance still greater when measured by the archaic mythology of the New Testament with its fantastic concepts of heaven, the angels, the demons, and hell — all repugnant to the scientific world views of modern churchgoers? There is little to be gained in defending one of these anomalies against the other, but it may be well to grant that there is much evidence to validate them all. For our purpose we must begin by recognizing the existence of tremendous contrasts in three related areas: in the shape of the church's life, in the doctrines formally espoused by the church about its own nature and function, and in the images by which the Christian imagination articulates its self-understanding.

It is the recognition of these contrasts which poses the difficult problems of method to which we have referred. If we adopt methods of study that are fully appropriate to the mind of the New Testament church (a way of thinking dominated by pictures, analogies, and images), not only will we appear to be dealing with a community wholly different from the modern church, but we will also seem to be using a language that is foreign to any contemporary audience. If, on the other hand, we adopt methods fully congenial to the mind of the modern church, we may be quite unable to shake loose from the tendency to justify and to exalt its own self-image. In this case our language would become quite unintelligible to Christians of the first century. In stating the dilemma thus, we are describing only one side of the picture: the radical discontinuity between the mind of the New Testament and our own mind. Much could be said about the other side. Yet it is well to be alert to the difficulty. To focus attention on images may alleviate the difficulties, since they sometimes transcend changes in forms, concepts, and practices better than does the more prosaic language. On the other hand, they may enhance the difficulties, since they are peculiarly subject to changes in content which are hidden behind continuity in sound.

Changes in content are, of course, due to changes in the structure of the imagination[2] as well as to changes in conceptual thinking. Processes of communal imagination lie deeper than the images. The images of the church are rarely the clever concoction of one person to suit his own purposes. They have been produced out of a common stock of images preserved over the generations by a living community. Their use presupposes a shared life of the mind. Produced from the collective subconscious, they speak to the collective subconscious. In them the imagination of the community is reflected and nourished. Transferred to another community where the processes of imagination are very different, they fail to speak with their initial clarity and power. The recovery of that clarity and power, therefore, often requires the conversion of the communal imagination. Each image manifests its vitality and exerts its power only within this imagination. What makes a genuine recovery of Biblical images so difficult is the fact that the church's powers of creating and using such images must be restored before the picture language of another century begins to make sense. This fact holds true especially for New Testament images of the church. It is not enough for the historian to state their meaning, always an impossible task because the image *is* the meaning; only when Christian imagination is active in the use of the image does the image come alive. The very discussion of the intrinsic meaning of an image indicates that *rigor mortis* has set in, and that full rapport between the eye and the picture has been lost.

In our day this has happened not alone with regard to the separate pictures that were indigenous to early Christian thought, such as the Holy City or the bride of Christ. It has happened to the whole facility for thinking and speaking in images. When dealing with vital matters we instinctively prefer nonfigurative language. As a result, many questions are raised by any serious effort to rehabilitate the use of figurative language. Let us examine a few of these questions. We will not attempt to answer them now, but we may return to them at the close of our survey. Even so, it may prove helpful to state such questions now because each question throws light upon the "apperceptive mass" of modern readers in their response to the use of ancient images. The problems are as native to our own minds as they were foreign to the minds of New Testament Christians. The form of each question therefore becomes something of an index to the distance between the two worlds of vision.

1. What is it that makes a word recognizable as a figure? How may we identify what is and what is not an image? The posing of the question indicates the desire to separate imagistic and nonimagistic forms of thought. Figurative expressions are one thing; nonfigurative expressions are quite another. We assume that clarity in thought and precision in expression demand that we discriminate sharply between the two. But this demand is quite absent from the New Testament. There it is impossible to separate the figurative words from the nonfigurative. Such terms as " dispersion," " circumcision," " temple " may illustrate the point. Very often the same word is used both as a basic image and as a nonfigurative geographical or medical reference. What is even more baffling, the very writers who use the word in both senses may do nothing to indicate when one or the other connotation is dominant. Often a word that in one stage of its history was clearly figurative (a possible example here is the basic word *ekklēsia,* church) develops a quite nonfigurative use. But the opposite development is also to be traced; a nonanalogical word (e.g., slave) becomes a basic and necessary image. Someone has observed that the whole history of Biblical interpretation might be told in terms of the process by which certain key images have, during successive periods in the history of thought, moved from the realm

of relatively marginal metaphors into the realm of central and decisive concepts. Moreover, the opposite movement has always been in operation: a concept once deemed essential has moved toward the periphery of thought. The extreme poles of these two tendencies may be represented by the New Testament period itself and by nineteenth-century rationalism. In the earlier period, priority was given to images, so much so that words that were quite factual in denotation became filled with figurative meanings that virtually displaced the nonfigurative (e.g., sonship). In the later period the whole weight of concern was placed upon substituting for figurative words those concrete terms whose meanings could be given a fixed weight. Men today are becoming more alert to the values that inhere in the figurative use of all words, but they are still eager to separate the factual from the figurative and to reduce the figurative to a hard core of meaning. The question we have posed, then, is very much alive for many persons; they become baffled and confused by the difficulties in distinguishing picture words from fact words.

2. Given a term that has both literal and figurative meanings, how can these meanings be disentangled? Must we not first separate them before we can use the word accurately? This question is always difficult to answer because almost every important word bears a so-called literal reference and yet many of its meanings should be classified as figurative. The word "temple," for example, may refer to a specific building located in one place and one time, and, simultaneously, to the divine-human traffic that takes place there. The building does not become a temple apart from the actualities of that traffic, nor can that traffic be wholly separated from a particular assembly of men at a specific place. The so-called figurative and literal meanings are inseparably woven together in the activity of men and gods, in the meeting of heavenly and earthly potencies. Before they can be separated, the persons who separate them must be absolutely clear in their own minds concerning the precise criteria by which they define the literal as literal and the figurative as figurative. By what measurements do they establish the fact that a temple is literally a temple? Do they do so by reference solely to space, solely to time, solely to external visibility, solely to the standards of those who do not worship in the temple or to the judgments of those who do, solely to a current human definition of what constitutes true wor-

ship, or solely to the verdict of the God who is presumably the judge of what constitutes such worship? All this leads into a quandary in which it becomes extremely difficult to define the terms "literal" and "figurative." The definition of what is literal and what is figurative reveals more about the world view (ontology, cosmology, epistemology) of the definer than it reveals about the term with which he is dealing. From this quandary we draw two quite simple deductions: (a) it is useless in evaluating the full meaning of an image to insist that the first step must take the form of separating the literal components from the figurative; (b) it is wise to expect that vital figures of speech will have a more literal referent than is at first apparent and that apparently literal terms will have a larger cargo of figurative meanings. Living words are channels, rather than receptacles, of thought. Where thought is absorbed with realities that intrinsically fuse God's activity with man's and that therefore combine heavenly and earthly components, there this thought, together with its channels, will more often than not ignore any inflexible earth-bound distinction between the literal content and the figurative. Such thought will use without embarrassment images around which a whole galaxy of meanings revolves in orbit.

3. How can we determine the ontological weight of a particular figure of speech? This question has been raised with increasing urgency in recent discussions of the body image.[3] The heat of this debate often crystallizes two positions, neither of which is tenable. Those who defend the metaphorical element are cast, sometimes against their will, in the role of repudiating the ontological realism of the image. Those who defend the latter are often impelled, also against their will, to deny to the image that flexibility of figurative nuance which appears so richly in the Biblical uses. Something is basically wrong with posing the issue in terms of a choice between the metaphorical and the ontological. The very formulation of the question reveals a poverty of imagination. Inevitably an issue wrongly stated produces premature and distorted answers. In concentrating on this aspect of the problem the question begs a dozen other questions that should be given priority. It ignores the metaphorical character of all language and forgets the degree to which all theological speech must rely on analogies.[4] It begs the question of whether the body image is in this respect decisively different from

all other images that the New Testament applies to the church and whether, if this selected term is "more than metaphor," the others may not also be more than metaphorical. It assumes that a metaphor cannot, without ceasing to be a metaphor, convey an ontological message. In short, it introduces into our perceptions of New Testament confessions a polemical either-or which as a product of modern philosophical debate plays havoc with the ancient modes of thought. It deflates the truth value of one kind of image by inflating the value of another. It replaces patient exploration of the subtle nuances in all the images by arbitrary claims for the unique ultimacy of one. It tends to make one segment of the New Testament — the Pauline letters and especially Colossians and Ephesians — normative and determinative, and to twist the outlook of other authors into arbitrary conformity with this one.

I cannot on my part believe that decision on this issue should precede the careful unprejudiced survey of all the images, and I hold that this survey should be conducted without an effort to sift out in advance those which convey a clear word on the ultimate ontological structure of the church. As a preliminary attitude I commend to the reader the remarks of an able Anglican scholar:

Much depends on our understanding of the necessarily symbolical character of all theological language. It would surely be wiser to say that such a phrase as "the body of Christ" (meaning the church) is used realistically, ontologically, and *therefore* metaphorically or symbolically or analogically.[5]

And I suggest the adoption of a similar attitude, at least until the results of thorough study convince us otherwise, toward the other pictures of the church in the New Testament.

Behind the three questions that we have mentioned lies the same modern thought world where priority is normally given to prosaic, apodictic, propositional definitions and where other forms of speech (parables, riddles, pictures, images, allegories) circulate only under a heavy discount. In this thought world the accepted functions of metaphorical language are severely limited.[6] It was not so in the thought world that we shall seek to enter along the roads of symbolic and analogical forms. In that earlier world the very priority that we instinctively give to nonmetaphorical language was instinctively given to metaphorical. Nor is this priority merely a matter of choosing between one or another tool for communicating thought; it is far more a matter of the forms of apperception and of reflection. It is well, therefore, to ask one more preliminary question, not in order to answer it at once, but in order that the reader may find his own answers in the course of the survey.

4. What are the basic functions that may be performed by images? An entirely true but not too helpful answer is that language performs no function that cannot and has not in some place or period been performed by mental and verbal pictures. It may be more to the point here to suggest three specific functions that may be assigned to picture language.

a. Images may serve as tools of rhetoric, designed to help men describe and convey an impression concerning something that is already adequately known. A boy knows his father — who he is, what he does, what he is like. He may express this knowledge by calling him an old fossil or a powerhouse. In each case the image gives color and accent to the thought even though it does not change the thought. Similarly the defender of the church may term it the fortress of honor and its critic may call it a den of thieves. Both assume that they know what the church actually is; both use picturesque language to impress their knowledge on others, usually out of a desire for others to share their conviction. Figurative language has always served thus as an effective rhetorical device for widening the circle of praise or blame. Often the repertoire of available similes and metaphors does no more than this. As such it is quite right that the rhetorical use of images should attract to itself such labels as sentimental, exaggerated, naïve, baroque, or " *merely* metaphorical." The rhetorical figure is tested by its power to attract attention, to carry conviction, to evacuate phlegm or pride. We may often admire its pungency while denying its accuracy, for it does not really describe the character of its object. But behind these rhetorical uses of pictures lies the assumption that the speaker knows the person or object prior to and apart from his picturesque description. If this is so, he can, given a degree of mental flexibility and linguistic versatility, find other epithets to replace one that may previously have seemed apt. No single picture is necessary to his perception of this reality or to the communication of that perception. It is, I think, true to say that current skepticisms concerning the validity of imagistic thought stem in a large part from the use and abuse of the rhetorical function. If this were the only function of images, the person who wished to be accurate and honest would be fully justified in fighting shy of their use. It is therefore quite right to test one's rhetorical use of images by asking: is this the most effective and the most accurate way of saying what I have to say, of describing the entity at which I am looking? On applying this test, a person often learns that his choice of metaphor has been neither so effective nor so accurate as he has supposed.

b. Images, however, often serve a quite different function, that is, as a mode for perceiving a given reality, especially where this reality is of such a nature as not to be amenable to objective visibility or measurement. Any reality that is inherently a mystery will demand for its perception the awakening of the imagination. So will any reality whose existence is a sign, however ambiguous, of the operation of invisible demonic or divine forces. The same is true of those realities which are of such proportions as to extend beyond the range of human manipulation or organization. Realities of this order may easily elude our attention, our perception, and our comprehension. Perception of this unknown " x " often proceeds by analogy: a person compares it with things that can be more readily perceived. If he describes it for others, he will have recourse to those analogies which have stimulated his own perception. If this communication becomes effective, both narrator and listener will accept the analogy into the working vocabulary of their imagination, since both have been helped by the image to perceive a reality that thus far had eluded the nets of discourse. Images of this sort will not often arise from the acute insight or the clever tongue of one individual alone, for even the greatest poet relies upon a poetic tradition. More often will they be the possession of a community whose commerce over the centuries with the given reality has produced an extensive repertoire of effective images. To determine the weight that an individual image carver has assigned to his product requires one kind of procedure. But quite a different kind of procedure must be adopted to appraise a picture that has magnetized the mind of a community for generations. In this latter case, one must reconstruct the multilayered contexts within which the image has exerted its greatest magnetic power. I have in mind such contexts as an ancestral scripture, a hallowed liturgy, a contemporary crisis, and the release of new creative vitalities. In such contexts, the society's traffic with the invisible realm may increase. Its imaginative powers may flourish. Becoming freshly aware of a story that lies beneath and behind its own story, this society will adopt its inherited language of metaphor to meet the need of pointing to a cluster of forces which otherwise would escape notice.

c. A third function of images is that of advancing self-understanding, whether by an individual or by a society. Every person carries about with him a gallery of self-images. He views himself as a rebel or a rock of stability, as an inventor or a destroyer, a genius or a nitwit. His achievement of integration and his sense of direction will derive to a large extent from the inner acceptance of one of these images as dominant, as the mirror of his authentic self. Once he believes firmly that a picture is right for him, he will shape his emotions and actions accordingly. And much will depend on whether the picture *is* authentic, and dependably so. The same principle applies to any primary community. Its self-understanding, its inner cohesion, its *esprit de corps,* derive from a dominant image of itself, even though that image remains inarticulately imbedded in subconscious strata. If an unauthentic image dominates its consciousness, there will first be subtle signs of malaise, followed by more overt tokens of communal deterioration. If an authentic image is recognized at the verbal level but denied in practice, there will also follow sure disintegration of the ligaments of corporate life. The process of discovering and rediscovering an authentic self-image will involve the whole community not only in clearheaded conceptual thinking and disciplined speech, but also in a rebirth of its images and its imagination, and in the absorption of these images into the interstices of communal activities of every sort.

At best, this is always a painful process because the perennial tendency leads in the opposite direction. It is all too easy to allow the earth-shaking volcanic action at the depths of reality, an action that gave a pristine radicalism to the authentic self-portrait, to simmer down into tepid surface water, disturbing no one, and least of all the church. In their New Testament form, these symbols reflected "that level of experience . . . where man is made and unmade, where the world is shaped and reshaped, where the bondage of necessity or social and psychological patterns is dissolved."[7] The recovery of the images is ultimately dependent upon recovery of that level of experience.

One function of a church image is to satisfy this need. For example, we may consider the blunt, prosaic injunction: "Let the church be the church." Such a slogan implies that the church is not now fully the church. It implies that the true self-image is not at present the effectual image that it should be. But what is the church when it allows itself to become the church? Do we know? Yes. And no. We who stand within the church have allowed its true character to become obscured. Yet we know enough concerning God's design for the church to be haunted by the accusation of the church's lord: "I never knew you." So there is much about the character of the church to which the church itself is blind. Our self-understanding is never complete, never uncorrupted, never deep enough, never wholly transparent. In every generation the use and re-use of the Biblical images has been one path by which the church has tried to learn what the church truly is, so that it could become what it is not. For evoking this kind of self-knowledge, images may be more effective than formal dogmatic assertions. This may well be one reason why the New Testament did not legislate any particular definition of the church and why Christian theology has never agreed upon any such definition.

We may also note that those images which are most central to a true self-understanding are also the most misleading when used in a milieu alien to their native one. It is dangerous to detach one image from its initial rootage in one vocabulary and world view and to give it rootage in another. We can easily accomplish this transplanting without producing any decisive change in the community's perception of its intrinsic nature, i.e., in its capacity of imagination. This danger, however, is diminished when the church seeks to transplant its whole stock of images, for this can be done only by a continual transformation of its own capacities to see and to perceive. Therefore the church must perennially open its imagination to the wide panorama of New Testament imagery and especially to those images which may have temporarily lost their potency. At the very least the church should have constant recourse to the dominant pictures in the New Testament, not to use them as tools for rhetorical ingenuity or as mirrors for self-preening, or as weapons in ecclesiastical war-fare, but as modes of perceiving afresh that mystery of eternal life which God shares with his people, and as reminders of its neglected roles as the body of Christ and the fellowship of the Holy Spirit.

We have accented two convictions that will recur often in later chapters: the importance of rethinking *all* the images, and the rele-vance of these images to the self-understanding of the church. Now these two convictions, emerging as they do in a survey of more than eighty separate analogies, place the author in a quandary as he thinks about his literary responsibility. I know now what the reader will learn in the next few hours — that I am guilty of excessive repeti-tion. It is by viewing each image in its own context that I have tried to avoid prejudging what the texts say. Yet as a matter of fact, each major image points toward a perception of the character of the church that agrees, to an amazing degree, with the perceptions pro-duced by other images. In all their variety, they do not break out of the same magnetic field of thought and actuality. Because they often say the same thing, we must often say it also.

It may help the reader to endure this repetition, which by literary standards is inexcusable but which is nevertheless inescapable, if we compare our method of procedure with the map of the city of Am-sterdam, near which I am writing these words. The city is laid out in the shape of a huge semicircle with the railroad station at its center. From the center radiate the major streets, like spokes from the hub of a wheel. Much of the traffic is channeled along these streets, so that he who would study the city will follow some of these streets from the center to the periphery. But there is another series of transportation arteries, the canals that surround the center in concentric circles. On these, many homes and shops have their outlook and much commerce follows them. To learn to know the city well one must take a boat and trace out the labyrinthine ways of the canals. He will find that the canals intersect the major streets and that at the intersections he can look down the streets toward the center.

Now most treatments of New Testament doctrine adopt the plan of selecting certain streets and following their course from periphery to center. They follow the path provided in turn by different writ-ers; here is the Matthaean, here the Pauline, here the Johannine boulevard. They systematize the ecclesiology, first of one author, then of another. Each approach gives different views of the same area, each has its distinctive fascination, and each connects the same center, where unity is found, with outlying regions, where greater diversity is apparent. Our method, by contrast, is to use the canals, that is, those channels of communication provided by the major images and pictures of the New Testament. These all intersect the familiar ways, being used alike by Matthew and Paul and John. At such intersections one may get glimpses of the traffic of ideas along the street. The views of the city as seen from the canals are strikingly different, yet the view from each canal is authentic and representative and it contributes to a full knowledge of the city's life. Because the canals move around the center and cross under all the streets, there is much duplication and sameness; yet those very elements are useful in disclosing the homogeneity of the city's life. Some travelers find the canals more revealing than the streets; for others the reverse is true. In either case, no good map maker can omit either the canals or the streets from his chart. Most ecclesiologies of the New Testament guide the reader along the streets by foot or tram; we have chosen to explore the same area by boat. Though this means circling many times around the center rather than moving directly toward it, we may come in the end to a somewhat better conception of the entire area.

Some guidebooks to a city are designed for the tourist who can make only one hasty visit before hurrying on to the next, whereupon the utility of the guide ceases. Other guidebooks are designed for the interest of the more serious student who will want to make many trips through the area, noting first one aspect and then another of what he sees. What to the tourist is annoyingly repetitious detail may be welcomed by the student as helping him to absorb intangible textures of the city's life, both past and present. It is to be hoped that the chapters that follow will fall into the hands of the latter type of readers.

II

MINOR IMAGES OF THE CHURCH

Is it actually possible to grasp at once all the images in the New Testament that refer, in one way or another, to the church? Conservatively estimated, there are more than eighty of them, but this number might readily be increased to one hundred if the various Greek words were counted separately. Taking even the conservative estimate, it is quite impossible for one mind to deal simultaneously with so many disparate items. For the sake of comprehension we must therefore adopt the expedient of sifting out the less important pictures. The danger in such a process is that we may allow personal or confessional affinities to determine the mesh of our sieve. To guard against that hazard we have asked in the case of each image: How frequently does it occur in the New Testament? How many different authors show their acquaintance with it? Do the contexts in which the image appears suggest its power to dominate the Christian mind? Does the image serve to disclose a profound perception of the deeper levels of communal experience? It is only after asking such questions that we have sifted out some thirty analogies for quick review in this chapter. They are too significant to be ignored but not important enough to justify extended analysis. Some of them are like meteors that have no permanent place in any constellation (e.g., salt). Others are small stars that belong within larger galaxies (bread and wine). The former will not return to the substantive discussion in later chapters; the latter will recur more frequently in connection with kindred images. In either case we may be justified in including them in this section. Our initial desire is simply to indicate what light they cast on the nature of Christian community.

There is, however, a subsidiary intention. Any image, however peripheral in significance, may reflect the communal processes of imagination that gave it currency. These processes may be as important to us as the conceptual content of the images taken separately. This chapter may therefore give us an opportunity to notice traits of the mind which found the analogies viable. If we can do this when viewing the more casual pictures, we may thereby enhance our ability to interpret the major configurations of thought. With this double purpose, therefore, we begin our tour of some of the smaller "canals." To facilitate later consultation, we number the analogies in the order of treatment. (For a complete list, see the Appendix.)

Perhaps we should say here that there is no special reason for the order in this chapter. We could have begun with some other idea than " salt." Sometimes one analogy suggested another: " boat " suggested " ark." At times a chain of associations emerged: bread-loaf-table. By their heterogeneous character, however, the analogies resisted neat arrangement. In this there may be some virtue, since it accents certain traits of the New Testament imagination: e.g., the spontaneous and casual choice of metaphors, and the ease with which, once they had been used, they could be dismissed.

[1] The Salt of the Earth

In the Sermon on the Mount, Matthew reports Jesus as saying to his disciples, " You are the salt of the earth " (Matt. 5:13). Does this saying have an ecclesiological connotation? Almost certainly we must say yes. To be sure, there is no clear-cut assertion: " The church is the salt of the earth." But such formulas are extremely rare in the New Testament. Many undoubtedly ecclesiological sayings tend to take this form: Jesus, the Lord of the community of disciples, speaking directly to them, not as separate individuals but as a band of followers,[1] says, " You are . . ." This second person plural reminds us that the congregations that preserved and utilized this saying heard themselves being addressed by him who had called the church into being. Moreover, it is typical that in addressing his followers as a single unit he indicated their function in the world. The assigned function is essential to their existence as his people. This kind of formula (" You are . . ."), therefore, is an important characteristic of many ecclesiological images.

This saying illustrates other typical characteristics. The same metaphor which in one context (Matt. 5:13) must be judged as bearing a reference to the church may bear no such reference in other contexts (Col. 4:6; Mark 9:49); and in still others it may be difficult to establish any ecclesiological reference (Luke 14:34; Mark 9:50). This fact should discourage us from importing the ecclesiological connotations of a given image into all the places where that image appears. A given metaphor is capable of very diverse uses; the setting becomes as decisive for its meaning as the image taken by itself. On the one hand, this setting specifies the personnel involved (e.g., Jesus, the world, his disciples, the salt, in Matt. 5:13); on the other hand, the setting includes a particular literary sequence in ideas and this sequence in turn suggests the situation in the life of the church where the image exerts its meaning (e.g., in v. 13, the situation of suffering and persecution for righteousness' sake). In the interpretation of all images it is essential to observe these three interrelated contexts.

When we ask exactly what the image of salt connotes, in the light of these contexts concerning the function of this community, the answer is far from certain. In Luke 14:34 salt seems to signify the necessity for disciples to be ready to sacrifice everything. In Mark 9:50 it appears to express the harmony and peace required among those who are disciples, although it is also closely linked to the purging fire of that Final Judgment which Jesus announces, fire with which everyone must be " salted." If I were asked to paraphrase the Matthaean saying, this is one possible rendering: " You are those through whose persecution the earth [i.e., all men] will be seasoned, judged, purged, and preserved." But I would be quick to insist that this interpretation, although congenial to all the Beatitudes, remains very tentative. The extreme variety of interpretations, mostly homiletical, which this image has received over the centuries, indicates the absence of any decisive clue to its original meaning. We may conclude therefore that this picture of the earth's salt does not yield a dependable residue of meaning for instant application to theological needs.

One further comment is in order, an observation that will be found to be true of most images. The analogy of salt is not intended

primarily for praise or commendation. The motivation is not to exalt
the group or its members. The analogy is used as a warning, occasioned by the tendency of the group to lose its saltiness or to neglect
its assigned function. The worthlessness of the church apart from
its use for salting the earth is explicitly underscored. " It is good for
nothing. . . ." Thus the more seriously an image is used, the more
it may threaten the complacency of the group addressed.

[2]   A Letter from Christ

" You yourselves are our letter of recommendation, written on your
hearts, to be known and read by all men; and you show that you are
a letter from Christ delivered by us, written not with ink but with
the Spirit of the living God, not on tablets of stone but on tablets of
human hearts." (II Cor. 3:2-3.) This analogy is unusual in that it
appears only once. Also, it is virtually the only case in the New Testament where an extensive metaphorical construction is applied to
one congregation alone. Even so, the comparison betrays what Paul
might well have said to any congregation, or indeed to all congregations. The analogy of the letter specifies at least six points about
the Corinthian church: (1) the sender is Christ; (2) its delivery is
by Paul and others; (3) the ink is " the Spirit of the living God ";
(4) the words are inscribed on " tablets of human hearts "; (5) the
message is intended to be read by all men; (6) the substance of the
message constitutes a testimony to the authenticity of Paul's apostleship. The second and the sixth items might apply only to a congregation that Paul had founded, but the other items are applicable to
any congregation. The situation in Corinth is manifestly a heated
debate over Paul's authority, aroused by his earlier efforts to discipline these rebels. (Cf. II Cor., chs. 10 to 13.) The literary context is
Paul's extensive defense of his ministry. But there come to view,
through the allegory, Paul's thoughts on how a congregation comes
into existence and the purpose for which it is created. The analogy
accents the influential participants in the life of the Corinthian
church: Jesus Christ, the Spirit of the living God, the apostles (cf.
[30]), and the hearts of those who have been transformed by the
gospel. Moreover, the life of this church is not self-enclosed or
turned toward itself; the message written on its heart is " to be

known and read by all men." The analogy presents us not so much with a picture to be visualized by the eyes as with a continuing communal story in which all are engaged. Or, to put it in another way, the readers are invited, not to imagine a letter with its envelope and address, but to recall the forces that have been at work in their own hearts and to accept their resulting responsibility. The picture becomes a lesson in self-understanding, assigned to a community that needs it. It assumes that self-understanding may be restored by a lively sense of the purpose of God for the world to whom the church bears God's message.

[3] Fish and Fish Net

In scattered passages and in an elusive way Christians are compared to fish, and the church to a fish net. For instance, when Jesus called his first disciples to leave their boats to follow him he promised, " I will make you become fishers of men " (Mark 1:17; Matt. 4:19). If we identify these four disciples as the apostles of the church, it is but a short step to consider their converts as the fish whom they have caught. This step is clearly taken in the Lucan story of the marvelous catch of fish. (Luke 5:1-11.) The disciples had toiled all night without result. At the Lord's command they let down their nets again. The size of the catch amazed them. To the narrator of the story the business of an apostle was to fish for men and, with Jesus' help, to catch them.

The symbolic overtones become even stronger in the Johannine version (John 21:1-14), where it is the risen Lord who appears to the disciples and supervises their fishing. Here their experience of an abundant catch is related to their commission to " feed my sheep." We may also detect an allusion to the church in the haul of one hundred and fifty-three fish, successfully brought to shore without tearing the net. Each of these elements in the story bears a double significance: they suggest a subtle kind of dependence of the church on the apostles, and of the apostles on Christ.[2] Nevertheless, although most scholars recognize the presence of symbolic elements here, they are unable to agree on their exact definition. It is therefore hazardous to affirm any particular line of interpretation.

There is a similar ambiguity in the allegory of the fish net as recorded in Matt. 13:47-50, the meanings of which probably parallel those of the allegory of the weeds (vs. 24-30, 36-43). The net is probably, though not certainly, intended to represent a church that includes both good fish and bad. If so, the allegory suggests a contrast between the present inclusiveness of the Kingdom of Heaven and its final exclusiveness. The allegory may, like that of the weeds, convey a protest against premature efforts to purge the church of its evil members. In all these references the central interest seems to fall upon the relations between the fishermen (the apostles) and their master rather than upon the church itself. The number of occurrences is sufficiently great to indicate wide use of the image, but the meanings of the image are too fluid to be of much help to us. The image does, however, provide this clue to the process of imagination: it was not the fish or the net alone that were visualized, but rather the dramatic story of a man fishing with a net; included in that story were the fisherman's successive discouragements and triumphs and his reactions to his catch, whether large or small, good or bad.[3]

[4] The Boat

Some exegetes have discovered allusions to the church in the boat scenes of the Gospels, for example, the time when Jesus quieted the storm that had threatened to swamp the boat and that had frightened the disciples (Matt. 8:23-27). Is there an intended analogy between the boat in the storm and the church in the world? Or again, the story of Jesus walking on the waves to a boatload of disciples who were frantically fighting at night against a contrary wind. (Ch. 14:22-27.) Does this reflect the helplessness and the fears of a church left alone by its master to carry on its difficult mission? And does the boat-church analogy appear again in the postcrucifixion fishing of the disciples (John 21:8)? If this association of church and boat were certain, we might discern allusions elsewhere, as, for example, in those varied occasions when Mark pictures Jesus as teaching the crowds from a boat (Mark 4:1). It is probable that the first readers of the New Testament found multiple implications in all these episodes, but it is improbable that modern readers will ever agree on what those implications were. Though the stories suggest certain things about the church, it would be unwise for us to place much weight upon them.

[5] The Ark

The New Testament writers often drew their analogies from the Scriptural stories of events in the past. One such event was the Genesis account of God's destruction of the world at the time of Noah. Thus when Jesus compared the days of the Son of Man to the days of Noah he wanted to emphasize the suddenness, the unexpectedness, and the inclusiveness of God's judgment, along with the urgency of immediate and alert watchfulness. (Matt. 24:36-42; Luke 17:26-37.) Thus, too, The Letter to the Hebrews used Noah's preparation of the ark for a future emergency as an illustration of the character of faith. (Heb. 11:7.) For still another writer, the epic of Noah demonstrated that " God knows how to rescue the godly from trial " and how "to keep the unrighteous under punishment." (II Peter 2:4-10.) All these presuppose a far-reaching parallelism between modes of divine judgment and preparations for that judgment by the faithful. It is in I Peter 3:18-22 that this typology yields a clear clue to the church's situation.

God's patience waited in the days of Noah, during the building of the ark, in which a few, that is, eight persons, were saved through water. Baptism, which corresponds to this, now saves you.

Like the water, Baptism is a means of salvation; like the ark, the church carries the elect through the waters of eschatological crisis. This is because Baptism involves total reliance of the community upon Jesus' death and resurrection, through which the Messiah both "preached to the spirits in prison" and subjected to himself all angelic authorities and powers. This typological analogy was used initially to persuade Christians to rejoice in their sufferings with Christ (chs. 3:14; 4:1-2), but it also invited speculative extension. Later centuries provided such extensions in a profligate variety, but the New Testament itself is remarkably free from the vagaries of later typological phantasies. Here it seems that the experience of salvation in Christ suggested the basic points of similarity to the days of Noah; the Old Testament antitype had not yet received the power to dictate or to dominate thoughts about the church. So this analogy appears both rarely and marginally in the New Testament. Even this limited use, however, reflects a communal mind that could see itself in the multiple mirrors of Scriptural tradition.[4]

[6]   Unleavened Bread

The Christian community is never, in the New Testament, explicitly described as leaven. Early Christians normally regarded leaven as a symbol of corruption (Matt. 16:6). They knew how quietly, how unobtrusively, yet how pervasively the leaven acted in the dough. These aspects of leaven seem to be central in Jesus' parable of the Kingdom (ch. 13:33), in which some commentators discover a church reference. But this reference comes through more clearly in Paul's saying about unleavened bread: " You really are unleavened bread " (I Cor. 5:7). He calls upon the congregation to rid itself of the old leaven (i.e., the pervasive influence of malice, arrogance, and immorality) and to become " the unleavened bread of sincerity and truth." But this is far more than a simple metaphor. The analogy calls to mind the annual celebration in Jewish households of the Feast of Unleavened Bread. In this festival, bound closely, as it was, to the Passover, three symbolic actions were accorded dramatic significance: the riddance from each household of all leaven, the preparation of unleavened bread, and the sacrifice and consumption of the paschal lamb. These actions re-enacted the deliverance of Israel from Egyptian bondage; they dramatized the fact that Israelites remain pilgrims on this earth; they pre-enacted the promised Messianic deliverance at the end of the days.[5] The Christian congregation saw its own life as set within the frame of this festival; this made it possible for it to see itself as unleavened bread, and thereby to celebrate its deliverance in the Messiah. " For Christ, our Paschal Lamb, has been sacrificed." (V. 7.) It is this sacrifice which defined the status of this church as unleavened bread.

The passage at hand thus enables us to draw several inferences concerning this community. The adoption of this analogy related the church to the inner and ultimate meanings of Israel's life and worship. (Cf. [52]) It showed how the memories and hopes of the church were oriented toward the initial and the final deliverances from bondage. It suggested the continuing movement which, beginning with Christ's sacrifice, would encompass the sanctification of the whole world (Rom. 11:15-16). It preserved the dependence of the community on the sacrificed Lamb, yet at the same time articulated the contemporary participation of the community in the transformation of social relations which that sacrifice produced. For, after all, the cohesion of this group was provided by the unleavened bread of " sincerity and truth."

We may also discern in the analogy important clues to the kind of imagination that was at work. In this case, as in many others, the thought focused upon an event important to the historical consciousness of the people (the Passover), an event that had been celebrated in an annual festival but that now had become daily experience within the Christian community. At the same time, thought probed beneath the surface of Christian life to the substratum of social and moral relations (Paul had in mind the congregation's boasting over an individual case of fornication) and to the pervasive and cohesive elements in the structure of community relations. These elements, so subtle and yet so decisive, were viewed from the perspective of Christ's Passion, a perspective that, in turn, called into play the associations with the Passover as the central symbol of Israel's history. The image of unleavened bread thus bridged the new and the old, and at the same time articulated the eschatological character of the communal life. We may also note that the image was presumed to have imperative force; Paul appeals to it as the basis for handling a difficult disciplinary problem. The congregation must now do what it has not yet done. It must become what it is: the unleavened bread.

[7] One Loaf

The most relevant passages that link the idea of the church to bread may be found in the Gospel of John and in Paul, but in neither is bread as a metaphor directly applied to the church. In John, ch. 6, Christ is himself the bread of life, that is, the living bread that came down from heaven to give life to the world. By his sacrificial death he constituted and gathered a new community. This bread symbolized and recalled to consciousness the manna given to Israel in the wilderness, the Torah given to Israel, the fulfillment of the Passover, and the coming of eternal life to men. (II Bar. 29:8.) It is made entirely clear that the church depended upon this bread for its source, sustenance, and solidarity.

In Paul the key statement is I Cor. 10:16-17: " The bread which we break, is it not a participation in the body of Christ? Because there is one loaf, we who are many are one body, for we all partake of the same loaf" (cf. Did. 9:4). The context offers a sharp antithesis: bread also establishes the community of idolaters with demons. To eat from the same loaf makes men partners (*koinōnoi*) in the one body and "partners in the altar" on which that body/loaf is broken. They are bound together in a unity and a community in which they find common dependence and nourishment. Speaking for the whole company of Christians, Paul says quite directly, "We are one loaf"; and he makes that fact the sure basis for drawing important inferences concerning the structure and obligations of the church.

The image thus intimates the depth and thoroughness with which the liturgical idioms of both Jewish and Hellenistic traditions had penetrated the ecclesiological consciousness of Christians. In this complex of concepts, however, the term "bread" appears to be less decisive than the words "body" (cf. [88]) and "partnership," and even than "table" and "altar."

[8] The Table of the Lord

In the case of the table, we do not find a "one-one correspondence" between church and table; nevertheless, there are various snapshots of the church as a world-wide company sitting at this one table. To be partners in the loaf is the same thing as eating at the Lord's table (I Cor. 10:21). Although this image is suggestive of many thoughts, it defines none with precision. Both in the Gospels and in The Acts the tablefellowship of the disciples with the Lord was of great moment. This is indicated by the centrality of the Last Supper in the Gospel narratives, by the description of the disciple's treachery at that table (Luke 22:21), and by the promise of renewed feasting at his table in the Kingdom (v. 30). Any community is distinguished from others by the character of the host at whose table it eats. (Cf. [24]) The table signifies the power of the covenantal bonds, just as in both Israel's tent of meeting and in the temple were to be found a table (altar) and bread. In Christian use the thought of the Lord's table was fused with the thought of his total self-giving. The idea of sharing in his table was not far removed from sharing in the altar and its sacrifice. There the Lord of the table constituted this community as a people bound together in his death. (Cf. [88]) *

[9] The Altar

In Heb. 13:10 the altar is identified with Jesus Christ himself in his sacrifice, which " sanctifies the people through his own blood " (v. 12). Those who have this altar, those who on it offer up their own sacrifice (v. 15), those who are sanctified there by Jesus' self-oblation — these constitute the people of God. In a similar fashion, Paul compares the preaching of the gospel to serving at the altar (I Cor. 9:13), and the prophet John sees under the altar the souls of those who have been slain for their witness (Rev. 6:9; 16:6-7). We shall later see how the Holy City and the temple were to be located where God dwells with his people and how for the apocalyptist this dwelling together reached a point of special intensity at the altar. This symbolism of the altar, dominated by the death of Jesus for men, thus helped to express the self-image, the inner consciousness of the church. We will see this more convincingly, perhaps, when we survey other thought patterns, and in particular those which describe the temple, the priesthood, and the body of Christ. (Cf. [48]–[50], [88])

[10] The Cup of the Lord

In this participation at the table of the Lord, the one cup exerts a meaning that is exactly parallel and corollary to that of the one loaf. What has therefore been said of one applies to the other. (Cf. [7]) Are there, however, additional nuances in the symbolism of the cup? The cup " which we bless " (I Cor. 10:16) is the cup of the Lord (v. 21). This cup signifies partnership in the blood of Christ. Of the sanctity of the cup, as of the loaf, the Lord is himself the strong defender (v. 22). The church is not the cup, but the unity of the church is indicated by its participation in the cup, i.e., the blood of Christ.

The allusions which this thought complex evokes are many and far-reaching. Here we will summarize those which dominate five important passages.

1. In a memorable episode Jesus spoke of the cup both as the test that he required of disciples and the promise that he gave to them. (Mark 10:35-45; Matt. 20:20-28.) To drink his cup was equated with drinking the cup that he drank, with being baptized with his bap-

tism, and with being a slave as he was a slave. (Cf. [78]) The New Testament assumed that this truth applied to all followers.

2. This cup was the Passover and Eucharistic symbol. (Mark 14:23-25; Matt. 26:26-28; Luke 22:17-18.) As such it focused many memories and hopes. The act of drinking linked the community directly to the redemptive giving of thanks, to the blood of the covenant that was poured out for many, and to the feast that will be celebrated in the Kingdom. All disciples drink it; all are commanded to do so.

3. This cup was the subject of the agonized struggle of Jesus in Gethsemane: "Let this cup pass from me" (Mark 14:32-42; John 18:11). It was in response to his Father's will that he drank it on Golgotha. Henceforth, drinking became a symbol of dying with him.

4. The apostle Paul affirmed that the act of participation in the cup is a proclamation of the Lord's death until he comes; that unless the participant "discerns the body," he drinks judgment upon himself (I Cor. 11:25-32) and that all members of the body were made to drink of the one Spirit (ch. 12:13). (Cf. [88], [89])

5. The implications of this identification of the cup with Jesus' death were stated very bluntly in John 6:53 ff. In this narrative, the Lord make the drinking of his blood absolutely necessary to the life of the church. "Unless you [plural] drink his blood, you do not have life among yourselves." To drink is to have eternal life now (cf. [65]) and the assurance of resurrection at the Last Day. In drinking, the church abides in Christ and Christ abides in it. This action makes the existence of the church as church quite inseparable from the life of the Father (v. 57), of the risen Son, and of the life-giving Spirit (v. 63).

In brief, then, we must conclude that throughout the New Testament this symbol stands as an important clue to the church's self-understanding. By itself the cup was not a church image, but undoubtedly the church recognized the symbolic significance of the communal act of drinking from the one cup at the one table/altar. Because of its importance, the cup will recur in connection with our treatment of such terms as "body," "spirit," "temple," "sacrifice," "exodus," and "passover." (Cf. [48]–[52], [67], [88], [89])

[11] Wine

Recognizing the importance of the cup, we are a bit surprised to find no clear or prominent use of wine to suggest the nature of the church's life. Two pericopes invite interpretation by reference to the church, but such interpretation remains at best quite dubious. One is Jesus' warning against pouring new wine into old wineskins: " No one puts new wine into old wineskins; . . . new wine is for fresh skins " (Mark 2:22). The Gospels place this saying in a debate concerning fasting and feasting. It deals with the significance of table-fellowship between Jesus and his followers, but it follows closely the prediction that a time will come when he will no longer be present. Feasting signifies the presence of the Messianic Redeemer; fasting, his absence. As usually interpreted, therefore, the new wine stands for the newness of the gospel and the life that it mediates, while the old skins stand for the inherited institutional forms of Jewish religion.[7] But even this interpretation is far from certain.

The second episode dealing with wine also comes in connection with a symbolic wedding feast. Here we encounter the first sign wrought by Jesus according to the Gospel of John. The needs of the bridegroom and of the wedding guests are met by the turning of six jars of water into wine (John 2:1-11). Does the idea of the church appear at all? If so, only by implication. Do the water pots suggest the Mosaic religion with its provision for bodily purification? Does the wine represent the joyful life of the Spirit, first made available by Jesus? Have we here an anticipation of the Lord's dispensing of redemptive wine through his Passion and resurrection? It is certain that some deep symbolism was imbedded in the story, but sure clues as to what this symbolism was are hard to unearth. The picture as a whole shows us Jesus in his hidden glory providing joy and life for a wedding feast " on the third day." [8] If the church is symbolized at all, it would seem to be represented by the guests of the feast. (Cf. [24])

This series of Passover and Eucharistic symbols (leaven, bread, table, altar, cup, wine) prompts at this point some observations concerning the mode of imagination that they reflect. Each image is used with intense seriousness. None represents the idle play of a clever and ingenious fancy. They appeal variously to different senses (sight, taste, smell, touch), but their analogical value is not derived from exciting the activity of those senses. They have an anchorage even deeper than these senses, within the regular daily and weekly experience of the community, especially its communal worship. This recurrent cultic action is anchored still more deeply and securely in the gospel proclamation of God's saving action in Christ. Although cultic in form, every image points behind church ritual to a non-cultic event. For example, Christians were quite aware that the altar had been in actuality a gibbet, and that the cup of wine was a cup of blood. This essential anchorage in the Passion story forged a link between the ancient Scriptural accounts of Israel's history and the contemporary work of the church. Because all the images referred back to the Lord's death and through it to the ancestral sagas, imagination could pass very quickly and easily from one image to another. Because all the images referred back to the same event, moreover, each image actually needed the others to convey its own full import.

In very few cases was an image equated with the church or used primarily to define what the church is. The apostles apparently were not aware of a need for a fully explicit and inclusive image of the church. Yet they were constantly made aware, by treasons within the church, of the need for more profound self-understanding on the part of particular congregations. The images we have thus far reviewed contribute to that self-understanding by inviting Christians to perceive what happens in what happens. What actually happens when they as a church happen to eat together? What happens when they boastfully approve immorality or humbly accept the inferior place? The image of the cup elicited a comparison between the inner meaning of the cross and their own action, whatever its motives and results. The image thus helped them to perceive the reality of the church in a way most germane to the judgment of their own secret behavior. "You are not able to share the table of the Lord and the table of demons. Or do we drive the Lord to jealousy? We surely are not stronger than he." (I Cor. 10:21-22.) So these images, used to elicit a lively awareness of the church's kinship to Jesus, were used simultaneously to produce an awesome sense of the fearful judgments which that Lord would execute ("Are you able to drink the cup? ") and an equally awesome sense of his fearful promise (" You will drink the cup which I drink ").

[12] Branches of the Vine

The analogy of the grapevine is applied to ecclesiological concerns in one passage only, but this passage is so important and so familiar that we must give it careful scrutiny. I refer to John, ch. 15. The metaphor is a complex one, but the central accent falls upon the total dependence of the branches (the disciples) on the stock (Jesus Christ). " I am the vine, you are the branches." It is characteristic of many images, but never more succinctly expressed than here, that Christological reality is absolutely basic to the ecclesiological reality. It is also characteristic of many images that the decisive " you are " can be said to the church only by the decisive " I am " of the Christ. This elaborate allegory indicates quite clearly several alternate ways of expressing the branch-vine relationship. The author describes this relationship in terms of mutual abiding (he in me, I in him, v. 5). Alternately, the relationship is one that assures, under important conditions, the answers to prayer (v. 7). Still another way of expressing the relationship is to make clear the interdependence of obedience and love (vs. 9-10). Yet another sign of reciprocity is the intimate sharing of Christ's joy (v. 11). It is made unmistakably clear that the continuing purpose of the whole vine, stock and branches, is the bearing of fruit. It is Christ's indwelling word that bears this fruit. Every fruitless branch is purged or pruned away. And in the whole life story of the vine the hand of the husbandman, God, is at work. It is his work that is accomplished through Christ and through his community, the branches and the vine being mutually essential to each other's existence. These basic meanings of the allegory lie on the surface because each is stated clearly in terse, nonfigurative terms. In fact, these explanations appear to prompt the choice of the image. Thus, for example, the relation of branches and vine is described as a mutual abiding (the verb *menein* occurs ten times), a basic category of Johannine thought whose meaning in other passages does not derive from the vine complex. This *abiding* is an image on its own that may be far more determinative of thinking about the church than is the figure of the vine.[9]

The foregoing are meanings that are quite explicitly accented by

John, ch. 15. Other meanings may be implied by this figure. One such grows out of the fact that already in the Old Testament the vine had long been used as a symbol of the people of God.[10] Because of this tradition, it is likely that John intended to stress the conviction that Christ-with-his-disciples was to be understood as the true Israel. In them, in the Messiah-with-his-people God was manifesting to the world his fulfillment of the agelong promise.[11] Moreover, if one considers the frequency with which the vine is used in apocalyptic literature to symbolize the fruitfulness and joy of life in the Kingdom of God, then the declaration that the vine of God is already bearing fruit and producing joy becomes a plain proclamation of the presence in Jesus and in the church of the final eschatological joy and judgment. Still further implications are possible if the background of the vine symbolism is traced to Oriental myths concerning the Tree of Life, or to the Dionysiac or related cults of Hellenism. Because none of these implications is fully explicit and because scholarship is so divided on them, one cannot safely place much weight on any single hypothesis.[12]

[13] Vineyard

This figure is limited to the Synoptics and to Paul. In Paul's writings, the only reference is quite oblique: " Who plants a vineyard without eating any of its fruit? " (I Cor. 9:7). Here the correspondence is not clearly that of vineyard to church, but that of the husbandman to the apostle in terms of their right to support from their respective labors. But it is perhaps noteworthy that in the *argumentum ad hominem,* Paul appeals to three figures: the army, the vinedresser, and the shepherd, all three of which had already become associated with God's people. (Cf. [12], [45], [59]) These associations with the community would make his pleas all the more effective.

All three Synoptic Evangelists recount a parable of Jesus' which to them spoke clearly of the vineyard as an analogy for describing God's dealings with his people. (Matt. 21:28-41; Mark 12:1-9; Luke 20:9-16.) This parable, if it was that originally, soon developed into an allegory that was directed against the priests and scribes. It was to them that God had rented his vineyard. They had persistently refused to yield to the owner his share in the produce and had carried the refusal to the point of killing his son, through desire to usurp the ownership. Such behavior prompted decisive action by the true owner; he must evict the former tenants and install new tenants. To the Evangelists, the allegory clearly presaged the shift of God's Kingdom from the Jews to the Gentiles and thus it had compelling relevance to the church.[13]

But if we would rightly assess this relevance, several notes of caution should be observed. The vineyard should not be too hastily or too completely identified with the church. Matthew identifies it with the Kingdom of God (Matt. 21:31). It could well be viewed as the world, or at least as God's method of dealing with all men. Moreover, it is the tenants, not the vineyard, who stand at the center of the parable. If these tenants represented the faithless leaders of Israel, then the new tenants represent the leaders of the church. Throughout the story the vineyard remains the same entity. And since this is so, the threat under which the former renters stood remains doubly valid for the new renters. In other words, the allegory becomes a two-edged sword, with a message for every generation of tenants.

[14] The Fig Tree

In the Old Testament and in popular rabbinic expositions of Scripture the fig tree had become a vivid symbol of Israel's life. This tradition, varied and colorful, lies behind at least three passages in the Gospels. There is, first of all, the Lucan parable of the owner of the vineyard who comes to gather fruit on the fig tree and finds none (Luke 13:6-9). He decides to cut it down, but the orchard keeper begs him to give the tree another and better chance, although he consents to its destruction if no fruit is produced during the following season. There is probably involved here an identification of God's people with God's tree. Less probable, although still likely, is the figurative understanding of the fig tree which Jesus cursed as the fruitless people of God, represented by their temple officials (Mark 11:12-14). It is also likely that John intended a reference to Israel in the mention of the fig tree under which Nathanael was sitting, " an Israelite indeed, in whom is no guile " (John 1:47).

These passages reflect a common tradition and a common readiness to associate God's people with the fig tree. But they add very little that is certain or significant to the doctrine of the church as

such. One principle seems to apply to all kinds of orchard metaphors, whether dealing with fig tree or grapevine or grain: " Every
plant which my heavenly Father has not planted will be rooted up "
(Matt. 15:13).

[15] The Olive Tree

The figurative use of another tree, the olive, appears only once in
the New Testament (Rom. 11:13-24); we cannot therefore claim a
wide use of it among early Christians. Nevertheless, it undoubtedly
expresses important ecclesiological notions that were developed by
Paul to an extraordinary extent. The occasion that prompted his use
of the figure was a double one: he wanted to explain the mystery of
Israel's apparent rejection of the Messiah and at the same time to
counteract the tendency of Gentile Christians to assert, by their flip-
pant and arrogant scorn of the Jews, their independence of Israel.
Paul wanted not so much to define the nature of the church as to
disclose the mystery of God's saving plan for both Gentiles and Jews
through the church.

'For if you have been cut from what is by nature a wild olive tree, and
grafted, contrary to nature, into a cultivated olive tree, how much more
will these natural branches be grafted back into their own olive tree.
(Rom. 11:24.)

Although Paul's treatment is fully developed and enriched by
many specific inferences, it is not easy to translate the message of
the olive tree into fixed and precise terms. The fluidity of imagination produces a mixing of metaphors which creates ambiguity and
uncertainty. On the one hand, the analogy of the root and the
branches seems to run parallel to the analogy of the first dough and
the whole loaf (v. 16). On the other hand, one notes the contrast
between the wild olive and the cultivated olive, with the corresponding contrast of natural branches to grafted branches. Thinking only
of the second, readers are prompted to identify the cultivated olive
tree with the church as Israel. But if we think of the root-and-the-
branches metaphor alone and of Paul's effort to show the life-giving
dependence of all the branches on the root, then the identification
of the root with Israel, the church, is less convincing.

It is clear that to Paul the root is the embodiment of God's gift
and call (v. 29), his foreknowledge (vs. 2, 7, 28), his grace (vs. 4-6),

and his promise (v. 26), which together have brought Israel into existence as His peculiar people. The holiness of the whole tree derives from this one holy root. Moreover, there is only one such root, a root that includes the life history of the whole tree, in which Paul sees encompassed the history of mankind, both Jew and Gentile. It is from this root that the Messiah comes as a deliverer who will banish ungodliness from Jacob (v. 26). In one sense the covenant between God and his people is the root, for it constitutes the people as both one and holy (v. 27). Here again the existence of the people of God is set forth wholly in qualitative terms, in terms of its living faithful dependence on the root that God planted, and not in quantitative terms that would envisage fixed boundaries between this people and all other peoples. The church is defined, not by its separation from the world (i.e., what is not the church), but wholly by its intrinsic dependence (v. 20) on God's foreknowledge and election. This one root is indeed the source of riches for the world (v. 12). Paul, to be sure, allows no such ultimacy or unity to the root of the wild olive tree. The world (Jews and Gentiles) receives true life only through the one root, the olive tree. Yet the world is promised that it will receive such life. We can therefore think of the tree as connoting the source and instrument and sphere of God's salvation, while salvation means communal existence as branches of the tree, wholly dependent on its root. Faith and grace are words pointing to the means by which this life is communicated. The story of Israel, past and future, includes both stumbling and forgiveness, and both point beyond the " remnant " or the " pruned branches " to an absolutely certain, permanent, and ultimately redemptive power: God's planting of the holy and elect root.

Difficulties appear when we equate the church or Israel as the people of God too precisely with any single item in the allegory. To equate it with the branches alone would make the church too narrow, too occasional, too provisional, too much a subject of historical pruning and grafting. But to equate it with the root alone would blur the distinction between root and branches, between the sources of holiness and its channels, between God's mysterious action of free grace and the historical ambiguities of Israel's story. To draw a line between the church and individual members, which would follow exactly the line between root and branches, would also violate the structure of Paul's thought. It would perhaps be sounder to suggest that the whole story of God's dealings with men is comparable to the story of the olive tree as a whole. Within that story the people of God can be described accurately as " sharers together in the riches of the root " (v. 17). As composed of mutual participants in those riches, the people of God is holy, as the root is holy. But this same people should also be thought of as branches that are ever dependent on the root; the people, therefore, will always stand in fear and awe, impressed alike by both the severity and the mercy of God. The allegory articulates Paul's confidence and fear, along with his intention to evoke fear and confidence among both Gentile and Jewish Christians. Their own self-understanding, their perception of what it means to live as branches of this tree, will be expressed in such confidence and fear. Their confidence is directed to the root, their fear springs from their own self-knowledge as branches.

Parenthetically we may suggest that this tree image of Rom., ch. 11, offers an analogue to the twentieth-century discussion of whether the church is sinless or sinful. As branches in the olive tree, the Israel of God has a long history of stumbling, a stumbling that can hardly be limited to the waywardness of individuals. But as the root of the tree, Israel's existence as the covenant people is holy and is the sure guarantee of holiness for the world.

The discussion of this passage has involved us in the extremely complex question of the New Testament understanding of the church as the Israel of God. We have judged the image of the olive tree to be a minor one and the image of Israel to be major. The later treatment of the church as Israel therefore furnishes a more complete answer to this question. (Cf. [34]–[44])

We have now examined four associated images: the vine and the vineyard, the fig tree and the olive tree. Before drawing other idioms into our survey, we may well pause for a moment to ask what clues these four offer as to the mode and mood of imagination. The use of them all is grounded in well-established idioms of the Old Testament, suggesting that their power depends not upon their novelty but upon the depth and range of associations with Scriptural motifs. Here as elsewhere we are dealing with corporate as well as individual imagination. All these associations are profoundly Christological in orientation, for they make clear how the story of Christ has converted their earlier meanings. All of them express the conviction that the whole history of Israel has been summed up in the person and work of Israel's Messiah and that he is therefore the living link between Israel and the church. None of the metaphorical elements is subject to reduction to quantitative formulas or algebraic equivalents. Moreover, they do not encourage the individual Christian to picture himself as guaranteed a permanent place in the scheme; every image voices a trenchant warning that is as uncompromising as is the confession of Christ's centrality. To the extent that each idiom fosters self-recognition on the part of the individual or the church, to the same extent it fosters both humility and hope. The figures resist translation into speculative doctrines but encourage translation into the more existential attitudes of trust and joy, fear and obedience. Yet these existential components do not become the object of introspective concentration. The readers are not prompted by the images to analyze their own inner dilemmas of decision. Rather, the images assume, and therefore induce the listeners to assume, that private experience and individual destiny are dependent upon the plan of God for the community, and that the communal life, in turn, is everywhere dependent upon the life of Christ; that the whole work of Christ, which involves the whole of history from beginning to end, is finally subordinated to the husbandman to whom alone the vine and the vineyard, the fig tree and the olive tree belong. Thus all the images presuppose a profound concern with the universal and eschatological dimensions of God's purpose, with his plan for all men. This surely is one reason for their elusiveness. The fluidity of meaning is due, not to an inability to develop allegories that could be decoded with mathematical exactness, but rather to a lively sense of the cosmic dimensions in the mystery of God's control of human destiny.

[16] God's Planting

There is still another figure drawn from horticulture. In his dealing with partisanship and rivalry in Corinth, Paul is prompted to say to the congregation, "You are God's planting" (*geōrgion*) (I Cor. 3:9). Because this Greek word appears only this one time in the New Testament the choice of an English equivalent is uncertain. The major options are: field, plantation, planting. The context indicates three meanings of the image. Paul is asserting that the congregation belongs to God, to whom alone all the processes of growth may be attributed. He is asserting that, although he himself and Apollos have accomplished important tasks in sowing and irrigating, they have done this only as servants through whom the Lord has given a harvest. And finally, he is warning the partisans, whether of himself or of Apollos, that this very partisanship contradicts the character of the church as God's plantation or planting. The figure thus expresses the common dependence, not in an external, mechanical way, but in terms of the inner, personal, vocational processes of cohesion and growth. The existence of the community as a whole, including the work of the apostles and the response of the believers, including also the soil, the sowing, the germination, the cultivation, and the harvest, marks it out as God's work and as God's possession.[14]

[17] God's Building

"You are God's planting, God's building." (I Cor. 3:9.) In a characteristic way Paul's mind moves from one image to another in the middle of a sentence. The Corinthian church is not only God's field or planting, it is God's building. Clearly we are dealing with the same thought: the basic message of the two images is the same. The image of the field is more congenial to the sequence of thought (planting, watering, growing) in the previous verses. The image of building, in turn, introduces another series of subimages. Now Paul pictures himself as the foundation layer rather than the sower, and Apollos as the wall builder rather than the irrigator. Each has his appropriate task and must give his own accounting to God. In this case the foundation of the whole process of building is Jesus Christ, and the earlier assertion holds firm: the stonemasons and carpenters are alike fellow workers with God, who alone can establish their work (Ps. 127:1). If we are invited to visualize something here, it is not the entire structure in which each part has a separate allegorical equivalent. (Compare the treatment of the building in Ignatius, *Ephesians,* ch. 9, and in Hermas, *Visions* III, chs. 2-8.) Rather, attention is concentrated on the processes of construction and the crucial relationship between the one essential foundation and what every workman builds upon it. In other words, the image directs our minds to the continuing dramatic action on the part of both God and man, rather than to the contour of the completed house. Paul also invites us to visualize what happens when God tests by fire the results of human building. The "Day" will disclose what kind of construction every man has erected, whether gold, wood, or hay (I Cor. 3:10-15).

We find, therefore, in this Pauline picture of a building, many of the elements of an allegory, an allegory destined to be developed to a fantastic degree: a God who gives a contract, Christ as the foundation, the apostle as the master builder, the varying materials of construction, and the final acceptance or rejection of the structure. All of these are involved in the simple address: " You are God's building."[15] To a more thorough analysis of the idea of the growth of the church through the work of the builders ("edification") we will come back at a later point. (Cf. [82])

[18]　Building on the Rock

In the Gospel of Matthew the picture of a building is explicitly linked to the ecclesia, in a passage that is well known and the meaning of which is extremely problematical:

And I tell you, you are Peter, and on this rock I will build my church, and the powers of death [literally, the gates of Hades] shall not prevail against it. I will give you the keys of the Kingdom of Heaven, and whatever you bind on earth shall be bound in heaven, and whatever you loose on earth shall be loosed in heaven" (Matt. 16:18-19).

Many readers fail to notice the complex interplay of metaphors and allusions. First, the verb for building (*oikodomein*), with Jesus Christ as the builder, evokes the picture of a house (cf. [82], [83]) or a temple of which Jesus remains the owner (*my* church). Second, the verb " prevail " summons up the vision of a war between the Messiah and Satan for supreme power; in this case the gates of Hades are unable to conquer the gates of the Kingdom of Heaven. (Cf. [59]) Third, there is the associated picture of binding and loosing, with its implication of control over Satan and his demons, over sin and sickness. (Cf. Matt. 18:18; John 20:23) Fourth, this power

to bind and loose, as part of the eschatological conflict, is visualized
in terms of the keys, which elsewhere in the New Testament are
considered the prerogative of the Messiah (Rev. 1:18; 3:7; 9:1; 20:1).
Fifth, the picture of the rock accents the indestructibility of the house
that Christ builds (Matt. 7:24-27). Sixth is the word play on the
name Peter.

The verses bristle with riddles and would do so even if so much
partisan Christian debate had not swirled around them. Some of the
issues do not directly bear on our study, for example, the question
whether the saying stems from Jesus without important alteration,
or whether the Matthaean Evangelist added it to the Marcan tradition. (Cf. Mark 8:27-30.) The origins of the saying cannot be recovered with assurance. Some who accept its basic authenticity re-
locate the setting in a postresurrection appearance of Jesus to his
disciples.[16] Assuming that the words were actually addressed to Peter
(and this remains a large assumption), who can now prove with
certainty that they were spoken to him as an individual, or as a representative of the Twelve, or as representing the whole church after
its later emergence? How is the authority of the keys to be interpreted, and how is this authority to be related to the rebuke of Peter:
" Get behind me, Satan "? (Matt. 16:23.) This is no place to venture
new solutions to such puzzles.

We must content ourselves here with three observations. In the
first place, we cannot foresee in the future that any single interpretation of this pericope will be endorsed by the majority of exegetes.
In the second place, we believe that it would be unwise to depend
on this text for a comprehensive and cogent view of the church, because there is little evidence that New Testament thinking as a whole
was derived from it. Few passages in the New Testament can be
proved to support it as it stands, either in its literary form or in its
apparent appointment of Peter to a unique and continuing position
in the church. There is, in fact, some important evidence that the
first-generation church either ignored or rejected such a position for
Peter.[17] Third, and this is the point of greatest relevance for our
study, the pictures of the church (as distinguished from the role of
Peter) are, in fact, paralleled in many other New Testament passages. Building, warfare, gates, keys, Kingdom, binding-loosing—

all these were widely current. Because their use in other contexts provide more adequate evidence of their meaning, we must place greater reliance upon these other contexts than upon this tormented fragment of tradition in Matthew.

[19] Pillar and Buttress

The richness of associations in the use of the various figures for planting and building is radically diminished when a second-century writer uses the image of building in a more rhetorical commendation of the church. He uses two architectural analogies — the pillar and the buttress — as a direct description of the church, but they seem, in contrast to the earlier thought, to be relatively inert and lifeless. The author of I Timothy identifies the church as the house of God, by implication in ch. 3:5 and quite definitely in v. 15. Then he uses for rhetorical effect the phrase " the pillar and the buttress of the truth." The truth that is thus upheld by the church is probably to be understood as the Christological confession that immediately follows (v. 16) and that is understood in turn to require godly behavior on the part of those who confess it. The image of the pillar had appeared earlier in the book of Revelation as a promise given to the church in Philadelphia (Rev. 3:12), and the image of the buttress had been used in Colossians as an appeal to firm faith and unshakable hope (Col. 1:23). The contrasts in mood are instructive: the passage in I Timothy is more explicitly a statement of ecclesiological doctrine, the other passages are more elusive in precise reference, but by the same token they are more evocative and suggestive of the subtle determinants in the authentic life of the church. This contrast may indicate that the emergence of more precise rhetoric is accompanied by less vigorous imagination and by diminished power — a warning to all modern interpreters of ancient imagery.

[20] Virgins

We will now draw into our survey several idioms that had arisen from the realm of betrothal and marriage. The Old Testament discloses that it was a very common practice to think of God's covenant with Israel as a marriage troth and accordingly to speak of Israel as God's betrothed.[18] One term in this vocabulary was " virginity," which connoted that singleness of mind with which the bride (Israel) obeyed her husband (God). By contrast, "harlotry" and "whoredom" were terms connoting duplicity in loyalty and in lords. Wherever formal allegiance to God was used deceptively to hide actual obedience to his rivals, there the prophet detected adultery. Adultery and idolatry became synonymous; both were corporate sins in which the people by their conduct belied their formal profession and official cultic orthodoxy. This vocabulary was widely accepted in the New Testament.

In his vision of heaven (Rev. 14:1-4) the prophet John recognized a choir of saints singing a new song before the throne. Who were they? The singers are persons who have been redeemed from the earth. They are virgins. But parallel ways of describing their chastity also are used. They are those who bear the names of the Lamb and of God (v. 1; cf. [64]); they follow the Lamb wherever he goes (cf. [72]); they give a witness that is lieproof; they are the first fruits of humanity (cf. [54]). All these together describe the church as it is in heaven; the work of the prophet includes the reminding of the churches of Asia of their heavenly origin, ground, and goal, so that God's will shall be done in the church on earth as it is done in Heaven.

It is probable that the preservation of the parable of Jesus concerning the wise and the foolish virgins (Matt. 25:1-13) reflects on the part of the church a readiness to think of itself as a community of virgins whose devotion to the bridegroom was tested at every moment by their alertness or their lethargy. Nor would we ignore the inner congeniality between the stories of Jesus' birth of a virgin mother and the mind of a church that quite normally used the apocalyptic pictures of virginity to express perfect obedience and humility in relation to God. It is significant in this connection that the Apocalypse also attributes the birth of the Messiah to a woman in whom was represented the faithfulness of the Messianic people, although virginity was not explicitly assigned to her.

[21] The Messiah's Mother

And a great portent appeared in heaven, a woman clothed with the sun, with the moon under her feet, and on her head a crown of twelve stars; she was with child and she cried out in her pangs of birth, in anguish for delivery. (Rev. 12:1-2.)

Although this image of the church demands more careful attention than is frequently given it, it also eludes precise definition, partly because the image appears only once and partly because of the general difficulties in translating apocalyptic language into nonapocalyptic categories.[19] This "corporate personality" is described as a woman clothed with the sun (Rev. 12:1). Her introduction quite definitely associates her with Israel (e.g., the crown of twelve stars). Her first-born son is Israel's Messiah, Jesus Christ. Her other sons are identified as "those who keep the commandments of God and bear testimony to Jesus" (v. 17). She lives under the protection of God in the travail of bearing the Messiah, in his victory over all demonic earthly powers, and in her sustenance in the wilderness until the end. She also lives under the continuing treacherous hostility of the devil, a hostility whose intensity stems from his heavenly defeat by the Messiah and by those who have overcome self-love in their love for him (v. 11). It is exactly such traits that elsewhere are characterized as virginity. The opposite traits are assigned to Babylon, the harlot.[20]

[22] The Elect Lady

Akin to the image of the Messianic mother of the book of Revelation is that of the elect lady, a phrase used in II John 1:1 to designate the congregation to which the elder addressed his letter. Associated with this image of the local church as mother is the reference to its members as her children and to another congregation as her sister (v. 13; cf. I Peter 5:13). Blended in this phrase are two common ideas: that of the church as the elect (cf. [44]) and that of the Messianic community as a woman bearing children.[21]

[23] The Bride of Christ

Four New Testament writings apply more explicitly still the image of marital relations to the church as it lives by its covenant with its Lord. But the applications are various and they move in many directions. One ecclesiological use, perhaps the clearest, is found in II Cor. 11:1 f. The apostle writes that he has betrothed the Corinthian community as a chaste virgin to Christ as her one husband. To be a pure bride requires on her part "sincere and pure devotion." But the apostle fears that his bride has committed adultery by her readiness to accept "another Jesus, another Spirit, or another gospel." Such disloyalty to her betrothed is tantamount to the temptation to which Eve succumbed. Behind this pattern of thought is the picture of Jesus, the husband, as Adam, with the church as his Eve. (Cf. [56])

A similar configuration of assumptions lies behind Eph. 5:22-31, where the relation of the church to Christ is compared in various ways to the relation of wife to husband. The image stresses the wife's role of subjection and obedience and the husband's role of self-sacrifice and authority. Their mutual interdependence is so intimate and so permanent that the two become one body. (Cf. [96]) Both share the same goal: that the woman should become "holy and without blemish." It is assumed that the bride represents the whole church and that Christ became husband through his sacrifice of himself as her savior. This sacrifice produces and requires her sanctification and continues to provide care and nourishment for the bride. This whole set of interrelations constitutes, as Paul insists, "a great mystery."

Less fully developed yet echoing the same conception is the testimony of John the Baptist (John 3:29), who identifies the Messiah with the bridegroom to whom the bride (his Messianic community) belongs and who comes to claim that bride. His coming is the occasion for rejoicing on the part of his "friend," a role which according to this Gospel was happily accepted by the Baptist. We should note that just as the bridegroom comes from above, so too his bride is given to him from heaven.

The most highly developed vision of the church as the Messiah's bride appears in the closing chapters of Revelation. Here the bride is virtually synonymous with the Holy City, the New Jerusalem, which comes down from heaven (Rev. 21:2-4). The glory of this city is described in detail, and the concept of the city tends to displace the analogy of marital relations. The prophet describes in turn the foundation of the city, its walls, gates, light, water, and trees. This city as a bride is known by the constancy with which the Spirit enables her to pray: "come" (ch. 22:17). She is also depicted in sharpest contrast to the harlot (the demonic city Babylon) whose idolatries take the vivid forms depicted in chs. 17 and 18. (Cf.[59])

It is typical of both Testaments that this image of bride could coalesce so readily with such disparate pictures as those of nation, city, temple, and body. This fact suggests that the conception of God's people as the Messiah's bride did not by itself form the decisive or determinative pattern. Although important, valid, and illuminating, it was not the controlling concept. For this reason, as well as the fact that the explicit correlation of the church and the bride appears in only four New Testament writings, we have judged that it belongs in the category of minor images, in spite of the increasing use of the image in modern ecclesiological controversies.[22] We have also chosen to separate the image of the bride-bridegroom from the affiliated image of the wedding feast and the guests, to which we now turn.

[24] The Wedding Feast

In the use of this image, thought tends to be focused upon the feast as a promised Messianic event for which men must prepare. The invitation to the Lamb's supper is a supreme expression of blessedness (Rev. 19:9). The presence of the bridegroom with his guests is the signal for feasting and rejoicing (Mark 2:19). The disciples of Jesus are named as such guests, as sons of the bridegroom, in a passage which, however, accents the coming of the bridegroom rather than the character of the disciplic community, although one might infer that the joy produced by the Messiah's presence is constitutive of that community.[23] As Jean Danielou writes, " The theme of the sacred banquet . . . always implies an intimacy with God, the social union of the people, and the enjoyment of heavenly gifts." [24]

In a Lucan parable (Luke 12:36) the disciples are urged to emulate servants who wait patiently for the master to return from the marriage feast. They must remain awake and watchful. If they stay awake, he will invite them to his table and gird himself to serve them, just as they have girded themselves to serve him. This feast, by its emphasis upon a common table, a common loaf and cup, absorbs into itself the symbolism of those figures. (Cf.[7]–[11]) The hope for this feast also dominates the celebration of the Eucharist in the early church.

In the Matthaean parable of the marriage feast the king has invited men to the nuptials for his son (Matt. 22:1-10). But those who had received the invitation made light of it and all made excuses for declining. Here the problem consists of where the king will find enough guests to fill the wedding hall. This parable, like the story of the ten virgins (ch. 25:1-13), is based on the assumption that inclusion in the marriage feast of the son is the greatest conceivable good and that exclusion is final woe. Guests must therefore give serious consideration to the question of preparation, whether those guests are described as sons of the bridegroom, as his servants, or as his attendant virgins. In Rev. 19:8, the preparation consists of securing bright and pure clothing, " the righteous deeds of the saints."

As in the preceding section, we note here the abundance of Old Testament antecedents for thinking of Messianic deliverance in terms of a royal marriage feast. It does not matter that a logical contradiction appears in picturing expectant Israel both as the bride and as the friends of the bridegroom. This and other contradictions simply suggest that the truths being communicated lay at a level deeper than the shifting images. The emphasis falls all the more insistently upon the unique obligations of the community in its unique opportunity of recognizing and receiving the bridegroom. We are probably justified in assuming that this idiom, with its various implications, was present in the minds of the early church whenever it told the stories of Jesus eating with harlots and tax collectors, his feeding the multitude in the wilderness, his suppers with the disciples, and his promises of a rendezvous in the Kingdom.[25]

[25] Wearers of White Robes

In the vision of Revelation (Rev. 19:7) and in the parable of Matthew (Matt. 22:1-14), the picture of the wedding feast brings into play a reference to white and glorious wearing apparel. In one case the bride wears " fine linen," in the other the guests wear " wedding garments," except for one hapless culprit who was ejected for lack of proper clothing. The freedom and casualness with which New Testament authors allude to clothing as a sign of character reveal the currency of this idiom among their readers.

For some writers, notably the prophet John, the whiteness of the costume is an important element. Just as the Heavenly Judge sits on a white throne (Rev. 20:11), so the hair and the robe of the Messianic deliverer are white (Rev. 1:14; cf. Mark 9:3). He is worshiped by twenty-four elders in similar garments (Rev. 4:4). Riding a white horse, he is followed by heavenly armies on similar horses (ch. 19:11, 14). A variety of explanations is given for the wearing of white clothing. The fine linen of the bride "is the righteous deeds of the saints" (v. 7). This linen is bought from the Messiah by watchfulness and by willingness to sacrifice everything for his form of wealth (chs. 3:18; 16:15). The whiteness signifies that men are worthy to walk with Jesus because they have witnessed to his death through their own dying (chs. 6:11; 3:4-5). The opposite alternative is to wear soiled garments, an index of treachery and divided allegiance (v. 4); still another option is nakedness, a sign of ultimate insecurity and nothingness (v. 18; ch. 16:15). The great multitude of men who have been redeemed from every nation, tribe, tongue, and people (i.e., the true church) are clothed in white robes that have been washed "in the blood of the Lamb" (ch. 7:9-11). Those who are faithful to Christ can thus be described alternatively as wearing white clothes, as virgins, as friends of the bridegroom, as his guests at the wedding feast, as his bride, or as children of the same chaste mother.[26] It is the concept of faithfulness as a seal of covenantal solidarity that permeates all these symbols.

[26] The Choice of Clothing

A slight variation in language allows the central accent to fall on the putting on of clothing, rather than on the color or condition of the clothing itself. It is Paul who is especially fond of this idiom and who applies it in sundry fashion. For him the Christian has a single inclusive obligation: to put on the Lord Jesus Christ (Rom. 13:14), and the exhortation to the individual is surely transferable to the community. All who have been baptized have been clothed with Christ (Gal. 3:27), a symbol of their oneness in sonship. The choice of clothing can as well be described as the works of darkness or the armor of light (Rom. 13:12), nakedness or heavenly dwelling (II Cor. 5:2-3), the deeds of the night or the weapons for the day (I Thess. 5:5-8), the old man or the new man (Col. 3:9-11; Eph. 4:22-24). Positively, the clothing to be donned by the faithful is described as the armor of God: truth, righteousness, faith, the spirit (cf. [67]), or less grandiosely, as deeds of compassion, kindness, meekness, and love (Eph. 6:11 f.; Col. 3:12 f.). But the choice of clothing is never viewed as a casual or incidental matter. When one puts on love he puts on the very image of his Creator, and this new nature is tantamount to membership in a new humanity where " Christ is all, and in all." [27] The idiom of robes and of clothing thus has profound and far-reaching implications for the definition of the new community in Christ. Paul does not hesitate to describe the resurrection of the dead, whether of Jesus Christ or of that humanity of which he is the first fruit, as mortal nature being *clothed* with immortality (I Cor. 15:51-54). The minds of both the prophet John and the apostle Paul pass with the greatest ease from the thought of white robes and of "putting on" meekness to the thought of the church as body and as the new humanity. We shall therefore have occasion, when we discuss these more decisive images, to recall the symbolism of the new clothing.

Having surveyed another corridor in the church's gallery of self-portraits, let us pause a moment to observe some common artistic traits in these pictures. In this series the early followers of Jesus visualized themselves as virgins (both wise and foolish), as the bride and the mother of the Messiah, as the sons and friends of the bridegroom and guests at his wedding feast, and as those whose clothing was the index of their chastity and their faithfulness to him. Every allusion — and there are many — belongs to some strand of a tradition of long standing. So traditional have the metaphorical meanings become that the " literal " meanings almost disappear from view. The original context has been forgotten and one might almost say that the traditional metaphorical connotation has become the accepted (i.e., " literal ") denotation. At least the figurative associations have become by all odds the most important. The Messiah's wedding, for example, is far more significant than all other weddings, and virginity vis-à-vis his covenant is far more decisive and determinative than observance of any convention of sexual behavior. So central is the relation of the community to Christ that the development of the imagery does not rely upon novel comparisons with customary marriage practices, but upon new insights into the common life in Christ. If we view the metaphor as only a literary device, its simplicity and integrity may destroy these insights. None of the authors, for example, was troubled by the contradictions involved in speaking of Christ simultaneously as a bridegroom who had died for his bride, as a living husband who cherishes her, and as a lord who will return to celebrate the wedding feast with her. No image bears a single meaning; all convey a medley of nuances that tend to move beyond the normal bounds of the original analogy. The image is made for the message, not the message for the image. It is also clear that the images did not develop by some sort of inner law, e.g., from metaphor to parable, from parable to allegory, and allegory to symbol. Rather, one analogy developed through its association with others, often quite incongruous, and all were transformed by their common reference to the gospel events. Seldom do the developments reflect an intellectual delight in spinning out a fine web of literary allusions. Rather, the basic changes emerge from the multiplex traffic between a living community and its living lord. It was the actualities of their shared life and work that prompted the profusion and confusion of imagistic patterns. The basic impulse for each detail of a complex analogy must be sought in this common life. Efforts to recover the precise meanings of those allusions are not conspicuously advanced by an examination of social customs or by extensive research into the mythological symbolism of the ancient Near East. Much greater help may be found within the New Testament itself — in the explanations of a particular allusion (" the white garments are the righteous deeds of the saints "), in the frequent combination of separate analogies (" the virgins are the sons of light "), in the mode of imagination that operated throughout the entire vocabulary, and, most of all, in the conception of theological and Christological activity that permeated the formulation and appreciation of the various idioms.

[27] Citizens

We turn now to a series of analogies that picture the Christian community in terms drawn from economic and political realms. First is the concept of citizenship. " You are no longer strangers and sojourners, but you are fellow citizens [sumpolitai] with the saints."

A parallel expression is " members of the household of God " (Eph. 2:19; Gal. 6:10). The choice of metaphor seems thus to depend on whether the church is viewed as a city or as a household, although the two are here virtually interchangeable. The commonwealth [*politeia*] from which these Christians had been estranged is explicitly designated as Israel, and Israel is in turn defined by " the covenants of promise " (Eph. 2:12). The metaphor describes how their earlier distance from God's people has been supplanted by present nearness to God and to one another (vs. 13-18). A slightly different nuance is found in Phil. 3:20: "Our commonwealth [*politeuma*] is in heaven, and from it we await a Savior." Here the apostle may have been comparing the church to an encampment of soldiers in a foreign land who retain their citizenship in the capital city. In any event, the community is both a heavenly and an earthly reality which links the present citizenship to the coming city. But because the accent falls upon the city rather than upon the citizen, we shall defer further comment until the following chapter. (Cf. [47])

[28] Exiles

Superficially this metaphor runs counter to its predecessor. It visualizes Christians as exiles, as sojourners, and as strangers (I Peter 1:1; 2:11; Heb. 11:13). How can the same community be composed of those who are no longer strangers and those who are pilgrims and sojourners? The answer is quite simple. The meaning of the term depends on the land from which they are estranged. Gentile Christians are no longer strangers from the commonwealth of Israel (Eph. 2:12-19), but they have become aliens from the kingdom of darkness where fleshly passions are in control (I Peter 2:11) and estranged as well from their former companions (ch. 4:1-6). This estrangement or exile will last as long as they live (chs. 1:17; 4:2). There is yet another nuance, illustrated profusely in Heb., ch. 11. Men of faith testify, by their continuing status as exiles and strangers, to their desire for a better country, a heavenly city, a homeland. By their very pilgrimage they give witness that they are in fact already citizens of that community. Hebrews pictures the Christian community on earth as living like Abraham in tents " in the land of promise, as in a foreign land" (v. 9). The church is by its very nature composed of tent dwellers.

[29] The Dispersion

In two passages the habit of thought just described induces writers to address the church as the Dispersion (James 1:1), an image that I Peter directly co-ordinates with that of exiles (I Peter 1:1). Although it is possible that the authors thought of the *earthly* Jerusalem as the center from which the faithful have been scattered, it is much more probable that they were thinking of the *heavenly* city as the homeland. As Christians, men remain pilgrims throughout their life on earth. The master image behind these specific pictures was furnished not by the Babylonian exile, normally looked upon by Jews as punishment for sin, but by the exodus of Abraham from Haran and the exodus of Israel from Egypt. (Cf. [41]) This kind of exile always followed upon God's election and always sought the fulfillment of his promise (Heb. 11:8-28). It was this kind of pilgrimage which became a normative symbol of the Christian way. To early Christians, exile was a necessary corollary of promise and election (I Peter 1:1). They had been chosen as a company of exiles; their common election made them tent dwellers and created among them a fellowship in the Promised Land as their goal.

Of course, by the first century the Diaspora seems to have become a technical term among the Jews, used to refer to those Jews who were living outside the homeland. Christians made little use of it as such.[28] But the less technical idea that the faithful people would be scattered until the Messiah should come and that his salvation would take the form of a final gathering of the scattered "sheep" was much more congenial, although at the same time more fluid. The best expression of this thought is perhaps John 11:51-52: "He prophesied that Jesus should die . . . to *gather into one* the children of God who are scattered abroad." Other texts also reflected this picture of scattering and gathering: there was the warning that whoever does not gather with Jesus scatters (Matt. 12:30), and there were the stories of the shepherd gathering his scattered flock in order to feed them (e.g., Mark 6:34 ff.). Then, finally, there was the picture telling how the disciples were scattered by Jesus' death and gathered again by his resurrection (Matt. 26:31-33; 28:16-20).

[30] Ambassadors

Now we may mention an image that again seems incongruous with what precedes — the picture of Christians as ambassadors. How can a company of exiles serve as ambassadors? Again the incongruity vanishes when we note the character of the Kingdom of which they are the deputies. They receive power and authority as accredited representatives of Christ's Kingdom, but the power operates through them only as they share in his love for the world; and it is this very activity which makes the world reject them. They live in the world as his embassy, proclaiming his reconciliation, entrusted with the authority of his commission. As such, they are God's ambassadors. (II Cor. 5:18-21.) The Greek text here has no noun, but only the verb (*presbeuein*). The verb appears only twice in the New Testament, in the passage cited and in Eph. 6:20, where the picture of an ambassador who is accredited by his chains exactly corresponds to the paradox of a citizenship that makes a person an alien. This image should not be unduly stressed, for Paul may have had in mind the unique work that had been reserved to the apostles.

This term " apostle " did become, of course, a technical word that referred to a small circle. But that did not prevent the verb (*apostellein*) from being used for the whole community. This idiom bound together the whole history of redemption into a single chain. God sent the Messiah, the Messiah sent his apostles, and all whom they called were also sent. There is but one destination of this fellowship of messengers: the world. " Mission " is a word that spans the total distance between God and the world's salvation. The whole dynamic of the church's life may be conveyed by this single verb.[29]

[31] The Poor

In the Old Testament may be found evidence of the tendency to describe the righteous saints within Israel as " the poor," a term wherein the component of humility tended to displace the component of financial dearth. Later in the second century, a Jewish-Christian group (the Ebionites) may have adopted this designation, " the poor," as a title for the church. It is difficult to state the extent to which New Testament writers had moved in this direction. Decision depends upon the interpretation of several key passages.

One of these is the series of four Beatitudes in Luke, a Gospel in which great interest for the helpless is expressed: "Blessed are you poor" (Luke 6:20). Does this imply that all disciples were called the poor? If so, does this show that the church recognized itself as a whole as the poor? If so, this figure probably parallels the image of exiles and pilgrims. It is quite certain that in adopting Isaiah's prophecies of a messiah who would bring good news to the poor, Christians acknowledged a sense of genuine solidarity with the blind, the deaf, and the captives of Israel,[30] But the more we stress the association of poverty with blindness and captivity, the less does the designation "the poor" become adequate to describe this solidarity.

The Letter of James denounces a meeting for worship where the rich are solicitously honored and the poor are held in open contempt. (James 2:2-6.) If this is a picture of a Jewish synagogue before the rise of a separate Christian congregation, then the reference to the poor being oppressed by the rich may be construed as a reference to all Christian believers. But more probably the author has in mind a single congregation that includes both the poor and the rich. In any case, he uses the occasion to stress the poverty and the wealth of all whom God has chosen. Poverty in the world corresponds to wealth in the Kingdom of God.[31] As such, the Lucan Beatitude preserves a permanent reminder in metaphorical language of a permanent paradox of discipleship. But little is made of this as a significant ecclesiological category.

[32] Hosts and Guests

More strategic than the designation "the poor" is the picture of the church in which all the poor, the naked, the hungry, the prisoners are welcomed as if they were the Lord himself (Matt. 25:31-46). Hospitality became a distinctive and essential mark of this community. God had welcomed them all without making distinctions among them. (Rom. 14:3.) So too, Christ had welcomed them all, to the glory of God. (Ch. 15:7.) Those who had received such hospitality were therefore under an absolute obligation to welcome one another and to serve one another, each accepting as his own the failings and the needs of his neighbor. (Chs. 14:1; 15:1, 7.) Such hospitality was far more than a private virtue; it was an essential ingredient in communal life, which only gradually became institu-

tionalized. Its practice was understood in terms of Jesus' word: whoever welcomes you, welcomes me; whoever welcomes me, welcomes
him who sent me.[32]

Mutuality of welcome within this society was thus a meeting point
for the accent of many images. Here exiles accepted one another as
fellow citizens. Here the scattered were gathered. Here the prisoners
became ambassadors and ambassadors were received by the poor.
Here all were impoverished and all enriched. Those sent were received by others who were also sent. Hospitality was the sign of the
existence of a new kind of community where every image was destined for incarnation.

III

THE PEOPLE OF GOD

W E HAVE now completed a first step in our survey of the whole range of ecclesiological imagery in the New Testament. Some thirty metaphors and pictures have thus far come under scrutiny. Of course, it is hazardous to term any one of them as marginal, and many readers will want to upgrade their favorites. Our classification, we repeat, is both rough and tentative. It would be quite wrong to suggest that the analogies of the bride or cup, for example, carry the same measure of significance as the metaphors of salt or fish net. Surely there are vast differences in the degree of vitality. The classification is based on two factors: the infrequency of appearance in the New Testament and the dearth of evidence that a particular analogy exerted wide power during the New Testament period to stimulate and to dominate the self-image of the church. The power of the figures hitherto treated did not, in our judgment, extend far beyond the specific passages in which they were found. This is not to imply that these figures were in themselves insignificant, but rather that we can, at least for our immediate purpose, concentrate upon more decisive forms of description. In so doing, we will often recall into the discussion the contributions made by images that we have provisionally classified as minor.

We turn, therefore, to configurations of images that should be regarded as major and decisive. We now have to handle large clusters of analogies, none of which can be dealt with in isolation. By the word "major" we express the conviction that each configuration so dominates at least a broad sector of early Christian thought that to ignore it would produce a serious distortion.

Though we will be dealing with whole constellations, there is, of course, grave danger of faulty evaluation in the scheme of selection itself. The fact that more than fifty separate figures are involved makes a classification of some sort imperative. But any particular scheme of classification is bound to be somewhat arbitrary and artificial because it will force specific images into affiliations that may contradict their original connotations. We must, therefore, in the choice of categories, seek to adopt a logic at least not too remote from the logic of the New Testament. Accordingly, we will distinguish three constellations according to their basic function of indicating the context within which the Christian community is viewed.

1. Images that gravitate around the conception of the church as the people of God. (This chapter.) The basic function in this case is to relate the contemporary Christian generation to that historic community whose origin stemmed from God's covenant promises and whose pilgrimage had been sustained by God's call.

2. Images that gravitate around the activity of God in creating a new humanity to which was attributed a genuinely cosmic beginning, vocation, and destiny. (Chapter IV.) The basic function of this galaxy is to set the life of the Christian society within the context of God's eternal glory and life, and therefore within the context of the redemption of the world.

3. Images that gravitate around the conception of the church as a fellowship of saints and slaves whose life together is characterized by a unique kind of mutuality in gift and in vocation. (Chapter V.) The function of these images is to express the interdependence of men within this fellowship.

The separation of these three categories remains provisional and at best imperfect, because many of the specific images serve all three major functions. We will find that it is difficult to restrict any image to a single function. The validity of our classification will be tested most effectively during the very process of analysis. So we turn to the first:

[33] The people of God [1]

In his initial reactions to designation as " the people of God " the modern reader almost inevitably falls prey to two errors. First of all, he is in the habit of using the word " people " in the most casual and vague way to indicate human beings in general. "How many people attended last night's concert? Perhaps about three hundred." People here denotes simply the aggregate number of individuals present at however temporary or fortuitous a gathering. One can find very few occurrences of *laos* in the New Testament that convey this meaning.[2] People in general do not exist; there are only particular peoples. Each people has a separate and cohesive actuality of its own. Every person belongs to a particular people, just as he belongs to a particular tongue or nation or tribe; and this people is not reducible to the mathematical aggregate of its members. The people defines the person; its existence is determinative of who he is. Hence, when an individual shifts from one people to another, a drastic change in his status and selfhood is involved.

A second misconception stems from the habit of applying the term to all men as men. "People are like that!" We do not often use the word in the plural. By contrast, when New Testament writers want to refer to all men either they speak of Adam, the representative man, or they speak of "all the peoples." Humanity is not visualized as a world-wide census of individuals, but as the separate peoples that, taken together, comprise mankind as a whole. Each people retains its own discrete unity. Therefore, to identify a particular society as the people of God is immediately to set it over against all other peoples. This people and it alone has been constituted in a special way by this God's action, by his taking it "for his own possession." Henceforth it can be spoken of as his people. To avoid these two misconceptions, then, it is well to take the phrase as a whole and to accent the article and the prepositional phrase: *the* people *of God*.

When, however, the modern reader hears this phrase he is usually repelled. Isn't this an arbitrary claim to special privilege on the part of one people at the expense of all the others? Isn't it a prime example of chauvinism and group egoism? Although this protest may often be justified, it springs from a misconception of the true force of the phrase "of God." It assumes that first there exists a community of men held together by the same cement — political, economic, cultural — as are other societies, and that this society then claims absolute virtue and power for itself. The assumption on the part of those who understood the covenant action of God was precisely the reverse: first God and his purpose, then the emergence of this people as a manifestation of his purpose. The accent must be allowed to fall on the God who creates this society as his people by his choice of them. So understood, the phrase asserts the priority and power of God's action. A shift of accent (and how easy that is!) replaces the sense of complete dependence with the sense of invidious superiority. That shift took place all too often in both Old Testament and New Testament times. The same shift of accent also leads to the adoption of naturalistic and objectivistic criteria for describing this people, whereas theological categories should remain primary in the process of definition. Time and again in the following chapter we will be obliged to recognize how persistently the New Testament writers sought to preserve the accent upon the mysterious operation of God's grace and thus to retain as primary the theological differentiation between this and all other societies.

Everywhere in the Bible we hear the assertion that the birth and survival of this people are due alone to God's gracious and faithful action in creating, calling, sustaining, judging, and saving it. They are a people only because he dwells within them and moves among them.[3] It is because of this Presence, mysterious and yet absolutely trustworthy, that the New Testament writers affirm the centrality of Jesus Christ. He it is who serves as shepherd, judge, king, and savior.[4] Two passages illustrate with particular force the dependence of this people upon God's action. In both of these the Christian author is tacitly claiming, by citing Old Testament texts, that from its inception this society has been created and sustained in the same way.

You are . . . God's own people, that you may declare the wonderful deeds of him who called you out of darkness into his marvelous light. Once you were no people, but now you are God's people; once you had not received mercy, but now you have received mercy. (I Peter 2:9-10.)

This passage suggests three inferences concerning the life of this people. Its previous existence was one of shadowy nonexistence in darkness. The transition into being coincided with the transforming operation of God's mercy. This transition was, in turn, inseparable from the vocation of declaring God's wonderful deeds. This same triple emphasis marks the confession of another writer:

Those who were not my people, I will call "my people," and her who was not loved, I will call "my beloved." In the very place where it was said to them, "You are not my people," they will be called "sons of the living God" (Rom. 9:25-26).

Apart from God's gracious activity in giving children to this people, it would long ago have become as extinct as Sodom. (Rom. 9:29.) Conversely, from the beginning of his people-creating work, this God had shown himself to men who did not ask for him. He had been found by those who did not seek him. (Rom. 10:20.)

The line between this people and other peoples is thus drawn in a unique manner. God alone draws this boundary, and therefore the boundary remains at least partially intangible, because it is constantly being redrawn by the mysterious movement of grace. A double consequence must be noted: the definition of this people by its Lord permanently prevents it from finalizing or absolutizing its own map of the boundaries that divide it from those who are not his people. Such a definition also prevents us from treating this category "the people of God" in naturalistic terms. Its theological quotient is the primary factor in the complex of meanings. Accordingly, the term "people" must be treated "figuratively," i.e., it cannot be transposed wholly into the "literal" objective categories of the usual sociological or historical research. Or we may say that the term itself was used analogically. In some respects this people is like other peoples. Yet in other respects, and in respects that are intrinsic to its character, it is unlike any other people. Therefore if the reader has begun with the assumption that other images (e.g., the bride of Christ) are less prosaic and more imaginative than the term "God's people," he should be warned that this assumption may well be untenable.

We have suggested, however, that the galaxy of images that oscillate around this conception served in a distinctive way to place the New Testament church in the setting of the long story of God's dealings with his chosen people. To apply this analogy to the Christian community was to assert an enduring solidarity with that Israel of whose story the Law and the Prophets provided the authoritative account. The early Christians did not date the beginnings of God's people from Jesus' birth or ministry, from his Eucharistic feast or resurrection, or even from the descent of the Spirit at Pentecost, but from the covenant-making activity of God in the times of Abraham and Moses. This fact, of course, did not exclude the reality of election in Christ or lessen its eternal significance, as we shall see. The people of God is that people to whom God sent his Son as savior and king. Perhaps the use of cognate terms will illuminate and enrich the New Testament understandings of the church as God's people. With this possibility in mind we turn first to analogies that utilize national, political, and racial idioms.

Political and National Analogies

In beginning a discussion of these analogies, we should perhaps recognize the presence of some exceptions to the close associations of the church with the people of God. In a few texts the Christian church is set over against "both the people and the Gentiles" as if it marked the appearance of a third race (e.g., Acts 26:17). Such cases usually appear in contexts of conflict where the opposition to Christians is so universal that this totality of resistance prompts the writer to separate the emerging church sharply from Israel. There are other texts in which the Christian community is described as including both the people and the Gentiles (e.g., Rom. 15:7-12). In most of these, however, the newly enlarged community is also called the people of God, now seen to include Gentiles. All this illustrates the flexibility with which Christians used such terms as "the people of God," "the Gentiles," and "Israel." These terms do not bear fixed weights in the New Testament lexicon. Each may bear meanings in different contexts that seem quite contradictory, and no amount of exegetical juggling will wholly eliminate this ambivalence.

Among those names which belonged to the people of God and which were adopted by the church, one of the most significant surely was the name [34] Israel. This designation was given most directly in a letter of Paul to the churches of Galatia. These churches were composed largely of Gentiles who had been suffering from the inroads of Judaizers. Yet Paul closed his sharpest polemic against the Judaizers by the surprising benediction: "Peace and mercy be upon . . . the Israel of God." Those waging bitter battles against the Jews were thus reminded that they themselves were God's Israel. This Israel included all who walked according to the rule that circumcision "counts for nothing" (Gal. 6:15-16). Even though two groups

were thus contesting the name, Paul did not fall back upon a concept of two Israels, the old and the new, or the false and the true.
He defined God's Israel as one people, as measured qualitatively by
God's mercy in the cross of Christ. This same qualification appears
in other writings that speak variously of the church as the commonwealth of Israel (Eph. 2:12), as the house of Israel (Heb. 8:8-10;
11:25), as the sons of Israel (Rev. 2:14), or simply as my people
Israel. It is in relation to this people that the mission of the Messiah
is understood. He is sent to Israel (Matt. 15:24) as its shepherd,
ruler, and judge, to bring repentance and forgiveness (Acts 5:31).
His advent is designed for Israel's glory (Luke 2:32), and for the
rising and falling of many in Israel (v. 34). Though many in Israel
do fall, nowhere in the New Testament is it conceded that God had
rejected or could reject "his people whom he foreknew" (Rom.
11:2). In its liturgy and life the church knows itself to be addressed
by the familiar words: "Hear, O Israel" (Mark 12:29). Its God is
none other than the God of Israel, and the fulfillment of all his purposes is shaped by the terms of his steadfast love for Israel. To be
sure, some Christian writers appealed to the fact that a new covenant
had been promised by the old, but they continued to insist that this
new covenant was one that God established with the house of Israel.
(Heb. 8:8-13.) So strong is this sense of solidarity that one must conclude that the continuity between the two Testaments is grounded
in the fact that both tell the story of how the same God fulfills his
covenant promises to the same people. It is significant that no change
of name was considered necessary to make room for the new community. The Israel to whom the gospel comes and through whom
the mission to the world is accomplished is the same Israel to whom
the promise had been given.[5]

There were, of course, many different methods of referring to this
one people. "You are [35] a chosen race." (*Genos eklekton,* I Peter
2:9.) Usually, to be sure, the term "race" refers in the New Testament to biological continuity (e.g., Acts 13:26; Phil. 3:5). But that
cannot be its reference in I Peter, the only ecclesiological use. In this
letter the author is quite obviously addressing a congregation composed largely of Gentiles who through divine mercy have been called
out of darkness into light. Their racial identity is here determined
by the fact of their election.

"You are . . . [36] a holy nation." (*Ethnos hagion,* I Peter 2:9.) Again we observe the ease with which Gentile Christians adopted the traditional idiom along with the consciousness of being God's people. Again, the adjective "holy" is more than a secondary characteristic of the community; rather, it defines the nation as set apart by this holiness (cf. [69]). This application to the church is rare in the New Testament (Matt. 21:43); ordinarily, the term *ethnos* preserved its traditional objective meanings.

More frequently the consciousness of the church's existence as Israel is expressed by reference to [37] the twelve tribes.[6] The identity of these tribes was of course inseparable from [38] the patriarchs who were their living representatives. (I Cor. 10:1-10; Rom. 15:8-10.) This range of pictures then as now appeared to stress the fact of racial descent. When, therefore, early Christians, including many who were Gentile by race, identified themselves so fully with these tribes and with their fathers, we must ask how they could do so. It is clear that they could not do so without a radically new understanding of all the items in this extensive vocabulary, such as tribe, father, and descendant. (Cf. [83], [84])

Do their discussions help us to uncover the roots of this fundamental difference? One root may be discerned in the tendency to think not so much of sociological entities as of the theological ground. On this ground the fundamental presupposition is this: the God of the apostolic community is identical with the God of the fathers. (Acts 3:13; 5:30; 7:32; 22:14.) Moreover, the reference to the twelve tribes asserts the oneness, the fullness, and the wholeness of the people of God. (James 1:1; Acts 26:7.) This wholeness is frequently conceived in terms of a single inclusive promise and the equally inclusive hope. It was this conviction which enabled Luke to comprehend the whole span of time under the rubric "Abraham and his posterity forever" (Luke 1:55). The prophet John gave picturesque form to this rubric when he visualized the Holy City as bounded by a wall through which are twelve gates, each gate representing one of the twelve tribes. (Rev. 21:12-14.) These gates into God's city would never be shut. (V. 25.) All nations would have access through them; accordingly, there would be no need for additional ones. The same prophet numbered the population by speaking of twelve thousand from each of the twelve tribes, but he destroyed the mathematical exactness by speaking of multitudes whom no one can number. (Ch. 7:4-9.) The symbolic force of the number twelve was made obvious by the symbolism of twelve disciples to whom the Messiah had promised a place at the wedding feast (cf. [24]) and by the thrones from which they would judge the twelve tribes (Matt. 19:28; Luke 22:30). These twelve provided the foundation of the wall of the Holy City. (Rev. 21:12-14.) Permeating this whole welter of images was a common conviction that the eschatological fulfillment, in which the church already shared, would be a genuine consummation of the life of God's people, which from the beginning to the end had been one nation, one patrimony, grounded in the actualized power of the covenant promise.

There are other passages, however, that attempt to distinguish between those who do and those who do not belong to the "fathers" and the "twelve tribes." This was, of course, a very complex problem for early Christians who at most points were in bitter conflict with Jews who denied them the right to such patrimony and who claimed that patrimony exclusively for themselves. It is more than a little amazing that the Gentile churches did not react to this polemic by surrendering "the fathers" entirely to their antagonists. Instead of this, they reaffirmed their own identity with the patriarchs and rejected, at least in part, the claim of their adversaries. The critical principle to which they appealed was this: a person or a group manifests paternity and heritage by present decisions of faith and obedience. (Cf. [83], [84]) So, for example, scribes and Pharisees, who verbally revered the ancient prophets but had rejected Jesus, were only demonstrating the fact that their fathers had been those who had always murdered the prophets. (Matt. 23:29-32.) The mental complacency and the verbal arrogance involved in claiming *the fathers* for oneself proved the emptiness of the claim. Whether or not they were actually sons was determined by factors other than genetic lineage or pious claims. In John, for example, posterity is determined by whether men rely on bread from heaven or reject that bread in their preference for the ancient manna. Those who reject the present life and its food actually disclose their sonship to the devil, not their heritage from the twelve patriarchs. (John 6:31 f.) Thus the story of Israel reminded Christians of how men could deceive themselves in this matter of paternity. (Heb. 3:7-19.) Participation in the living covenant alone became definitive of membership in the twelve tribes. (Ch. 8:8-9.) Moreover, the apostles did not restrict the use of this criterion to polemic with Hebrew antagonists; they also used it to support their warnings to Christians. (I Cor. 10:1-10.)

In Christian as in Jewish thought, membership in the holy nation was indicated by [39] circumcision. "Circumcision" as a term could be used as general equivalent to the "nation." (Rom. 15:8-10; John 7:22.) Circumcision was the seal of being a son of the fathers. To those who valued this sonship, circumcision was obviously necessary as qualifying a person for citizenship in Israel. In fact, the term "circumcision" normally referred not to the rite but to the people. (Acts 10:45; 11:2; Rom. 3:1, 30.) Circumcision thus became a symbol of community both in the Jewish synagogue and in the Christian congregation. And the struggle occasioned by the power of this symbol tormented the Christian congregations and precipitated the sharpest conflicts within the church. Such conflicts are most directly reflected in Paul's letters, which show how difficult it was for the church to arrive at a common understanding of circumcision. We should not, therefore, expect perfect unanimity on this issue in writings that stem from this conflict. It would distort the ancient conflict to suppose that Paul's thought in fact represented the whole Christian outlook. But the conflict would not have been so difficult to solve had the early church not identified itself so fully with the Israel of the promise. It was that solidarity which made the issue so decisive. And although Paul did not represent all the apostles, it was he who saw and stated the issues most clearly. What is meant by circumcision? How essential is it to the community in Christ? Only when these questions are answered do we have an adequate conception of what Christians thought when they said "Israel."

Here we may segregate several answers to the question of what circumcision meant. Answer 1: In the period since the cross of Jesus it no longer "counted for anything." That is, it no longer served to establish the question of membership in Israel. (Gal. 6:15.) The need for circumcision, as upheld by Paul's opponents, had been abolished by the cross. Answer 2: "We are the true circumcision." (Phil. 3:3-11.) This could be affirmed, however, only if the definition of his opponents was wrong. In his own definition, Paul identified circumcision with that community which worships God in spirit, which glories in Christ Jesus, and which puts no confidence in the flesh. From this standpoint Paul viewed the privileges that his opponents attributed to circumcision as " loss for the sake of Christ." Answer 3: Circumcision is of value only if it is accompanied by full obedience to God. Through disobedience circumcision is actually transformed into uncircumcision. Circumcision is therefore nothing external, physical, literal, but something inward and spiritual, a matter of the heart, which only God can see. (Rom. 2:25-29; cf. also Acts 7:51-52.) Answer 4: Circumcision could be rightly affirmed as the bond of Christian community because Christ's death and resurrection consti- tuted a circumcision in which all members of his body participated. In being buried and raised with him " you were circumcised with a circumcision made without hands." (Col. 2:11-12.) In this sense, cir- cumcision, made virtually synonymous with baptism in Christ's death, was viewed as essential. There was ample reason, then, for the term " circumcision," thus understood, to be accepted as a clear-cut ecclesiological designation. The church is the circumcision, and therefore it is the Israel of God.

With similar bluntness Christians were called [40] Abraham's sons. (Gal. 3:29; Rom. 4:16.) On what did this sonship to Abraham depend? Here we may find much the same range of answers. An- swer 1: Sonship means doing the same works and deeds that Abra- ham did, e.g., sacrificing Isaac.[7] Answer 2: Sonship means sharing the faith of Abraham, which included readiness to rest every hope on God's promise and on that promise alone. Abraham's new children exemplified the power of this promise to produce sons.[8] Answer 3: Sonship means sharing in Abraham's posterity by being granted the inheritance that God had promised to Abraham. " In your posterity shall all the families of the earth be blessed." (Cf. [83], [84])

In this last point we touch upon a factor essential to the self-con- sciousness of the community. The original promise of God to Abra- ham had assured a blessing for all the families of the earth. God had sworn to bring many nations into this one patrimony. (Acts 2:25; Gal. 3:9-14.) In Jesus Christ this oath had been fulfilled. A new age had dawned in which the inclusion of the Gentiles as sons of Abra- ham was the key event. Gentile believers were now Abraham's chil- dren; they were heirs according to this promise (Gal. 3:29). When men denied it, they denied Abraham's faith in this promise, i.e., they were no longer his sons even though their formal genealogy was undisputed. Just as Christ's death and resurrection constituted a radical redefinition of circumcision, so those same events constituted a radically new creation of Abraham's posterity. God had demonstrated power to raise up children for Abraham "from these stones" (Matt. 3:9; Luke 3:8). The Day of the Son of Man was something that Abraham had rejoiced to see. (John 8:56.) Those Jews who hated this Day and who sought to kill its Man could succeed only in destroying the claim that they were Abraham's sons. (Vs. 39 f.) For Jesus Christ antedated Abraham (v. 58), or, in the allegory of Hebrews, he was the eternal "king of peace," to whom as his superior Abraham had given allegiance (Heb. 7:1-9). The Messianic feast in the Kingdom of God would bring to the same table with Abraham those whom the Messiah made sons of Abraham. (Matt. 8:11-12; Luke 13:28-29.)

This sense of identification with Abraham was, of course, only possible in a community that had a time sense in which Abraham could be genuinely present in his descendants and in which they could be genuinely represented in their forefathers. As sons of the Day or as sons of God's Kingdom (cf. [58], [63]) they belonged to a society that had its true being "not simply within any moment or segment of time, yet not apart from time, since the grace of God, the decisive redemption in Jesus Christ, and the power of the Holy Spirit work within time and space and history, yet from beyond all these." [9]

The analogy between the church and Israel therefore became a method of co-ordinating two stories, not two entities. One story was the long epic of God's dealings with Abraham, a tradition in which the events of promise and faith were considered the essential key; the other was the gospel of God's dealings in Christ with his people, the children of Abraham, the church. The points of greatest relevance in these parallel stories were found in such acts as Abraham's sacrifice of Isaac and God's sacrifice of his son. The memories of these acts became stories that, as paradigms of communal history, conveyed the inner dynamic of the life of God's people.

This observation is well worth underscoring if we would understand the living tradition that comprised the corporate memory. The images that most powerfully activated their imagination were analogies, to be sure, but the major terms of comparison linked together the past and the present, relating the Scriptural sagas to contemporary events. Israel was more than a name for a people; it was the name for a story that, when held in the mind, recalled the inner dynamics of this peculiar society. What was at stake in the struggle between synagogue and church was the validity of this memory.

Which community, the synagogue or the church, exhibited the closest inner solidarity with that Israel which had been redeemed from bondage in Egypt? The New Testament defended vigorously and variously the validity of the church's memory. Point by point, it sketched the coincidence of the two stories. Christians were repeating the communal experience of the exiles from Egypt, slowly making their [41] **exodus** through the wilderness to the Promised Land, under the leadership of Moses. (Cf. [28]) Moses, the great prophet, had promised his people that God would raise up another prophet like himself to deliver them from bondage. (John 3:14; Acts 3:22; 7:34.) As the Messiah was this prophet, so too were his followers a new community of pilgrims making their way out of bondage into freedom. The faithfulness of Moses became the epitome of the faith required of them. (Heb. 11:23-29.) The treacheries of Israel at Sinai and in the desert became warnings that they must heed the more carefully because now they were a company on whom " the end of the ages has come." (I Cor. 10:1-12.) Many episodes and many symbols from the earlier exodus were adopted by these exiles of the last days: the clouds, the baptism in the sea, the " supernatural food and drink," the serpent, the Rock, the Destroyer, the wonders and signs, the Rod. To deal adequately with the church's self-recognition in the story of the exodus would in itself require a book. This recognition did not crystallize into one image but proliferated into many, all of which articulated the analogical congruity of the two exoduses, which in a sense were but one and the same. Because these separate analogies are so diverse we must deal with them in many different paragraphs (e.g., the tent of meeting, the festival, the flock, the Passover). But if we were fully to grasp this mode of imagination, we would need to reconstruct the whole complex pattern of exodus typology.[10]

We move on to a survey, again all too brief, of patterns of thought that focus upon the story of King David and which by speaking of the church as [42] **his house** or **kingdom** suggest strong political overtones. And in this we are surprised that the positive findings are less abundant. In the other instances we have found early Christians eager to establish the solidarity of their community with all the earlier patterns of Scriptural thought. In the realm of this new group of images they are more hesitant to do so, a fact suggesting that their selection in other cases as well was not entirely without discrimination.

In the New Testament the great majority of references to David center in the picture of Jesus rather than in that of the church. And a large proportion of the references to Jesus are content simply to affirm his Davidic origins.[11] In the Synoptic reports of the ministry of Jesus the shouts to him as son of David emanate, not from the disciplic band, but from those sick whom Jesus healed (Matt. 9:27; 15:22; 20:30-31) and from the crowds, as an expression of their amazement or adulation (chs. 12:23; 21:9, 15). On at least one occasion Jesus appealed to David's precedent (Mark 2:25), but on another, his appeal to David's authority is far from unequivocal (ch. 12:35-37). It is quite clear that the Davidic lineage was not in itself sufficient to explain Jesus' authority and power. (Rom. 1:3; John 7:42.) It is significant that both genealogies of Jesus in the Gospels carry his ancestry beyond David to Moses and Abraham, and in Luke's case, to Adam. (Luke 3:23-31; Matt. 1:1-40.) David is cited as giving his witness to Jesus, but always in terms that qualify David's greatness. (Acts 2:25-34; 13:36-37.) Nevertheless, it may be said that the prevailing tendency is to picture Jesus as the legitimate heir of David's throne and key, his tent and city, his house and kingdom. Even where this is true, however, we may observe two things: (1) In passages where both Jesus and his people are mentioned and where Jesus is visualized as son of David, his people are described as "the house of Jacob," the patriarchal covenant people, or "the family of Abraham."[12] That is, the church identified itself not directly with the kingdom of David but with the Kingdom that has no end. (2) Moreover, in the one case where the church is pictured as the rebuilt ruins of the dwelling of David (an Old Testament citation by James at the Jerusalem Council, Acts 15:16-18), the rebuilding of David's house is accomplished for the sake of "the rest of men," i.e., "all the Gentiles who are called by my name." When Christians used the image *Kingdom* they normally spoke of the Kingdom of God rather than the kingdom of David. (Cf. [58]) Jesus, to be sure, ful-filled the promises that God had made to and through David, but the Kingdom inaugurated by Christ required categories of thought broader than the concept of David's kingdom. Some sections of the church were ready to think of themselves as David's dwelling, but for this picture there was little enthusiasm elsewhere. We cannot be entirely certain of this judgment and hence not dogmatic in defend-ing it. It is quite possible that the choice of images may have been more closely dependent upon Davidic loyalties in the first century than we have suggested: e.g., the City of David (Jerusalem), the tabernacle of David (the temple), the flock of the shepherd. (Cf. [47], [48], [45])

Among the events that were crucial in the history of the people of God under the Old Covenant was, of course, the captivity of Israel and Judah in Babylon. This was a period of great testing for Israel and a period when great prophecy flourished. Many books in the Old Testament library reflect the influence of these events. We cannot doubt that influence of this epoch on early Christian thought is, of course, extensive and pervasive. Nevertheless, the epoch provided few additions to the repertoire of church pictures. We have already noted that the self-image as a band of exiles and as the Diaspora is of minor importance, and that this image was rooted not so clearly in the Babylonian exile as in the Egyptian. (Cf. [28], [29]) But there is one other pattern of thought in the Old Testament that stems from the Babylonian captivity and that is often supposed to condi-tion the community consciousness of the early church. We have in mind the idea of the [43] remnant (*hypoleimma*). Here the closest link stands between Paul and I Isaiah. (Rom. 9:27; 11:5-7.) In his description of God's dealings with Israel, Paul repudiates the sugges-tion that God has rejected his people. Other peoples, of course, have disappeared without survivors, i.e., without a remnant: Sodom, Gomorrah, Damascus, Philistia, Babylon. (Rom. 9:29; Isa. 1:9; 14:17.) To reject his own people would be to leave it without chil-dren, and this is something that God has not done and will not do. To be sure, he judges Israel with rigor and with dispatch, but he does not revoke his calling or his gifts. (Rom. 11:29.) The existence of the Christian church stands as a fulfillment of God's promise: here is " a remnant, chosen by grace " (v. 5).

Certain reservations, however, must be made concerning the use of this analogy. It appears explicitly in only this one section of Romans. Moreover, as the historical analogy for the present remnant, Paul does not stress the deliverance from Babylon but the earlier deliverances at the times of Elijah and of Moses. Finally, it is not clear that Paul applied this analogy to the whole of the church; the context seems to limit it to the Jewish segment of the community. When the apostle desires to indicate the unity of Jew and Gentile within the people of God he turns rather to the Isaian figure of the tree's root and stump.[13] And in Paul's thought the assurance of the redemption of all Israel is stronger than in Isaiah. (Compare Rom. 11:26 with Isa. 4:12.) We conclude, then, that although the traditional idea of a remnant left some noticeable traces in those passages where the fulfillment of the Scriptural prophecies was affirmed, the awareness of itself as being this remnant did not strongly condition the consciousness of the early church.[14]

There is another term that was more widely adopted by New Testament writers. This term appears with clear ecclesiological import in the words of Paul already cited: " At the present time there is a remnant, *chosen* by grace " (Rom. 11:5). A similar qualification appears when in I Peter we note a description of the Christian society as a chosen race. The idea of election, of course, pervades both Testaments, and in both it accents the prior act of God in constituting a people as his people. The correlation in the Old Testament between Israel and [44] the elect is so prominent that we should on a priori grounds expect the same correlation in the New Testament. Nor are we disappointed. Certainly the accent falls more heavily on the elect than on the remnant. This pattern of thinking may be found, with differing degrees of intensity, in at least a dozen writings: in all four Gospels, The Acts, Paul's letters, the Pastorals, I Peter, and Revelation — certainly a representative list. Some of the passages speak of Christ as God's Elect, with a strong implication that as such he is the representative of the eschatological community. (Luke 9:35; 23:35; John 1:34.) It is *in him* as the Elect that men become the elect. (Eph. 1:4.) Other passages focus attention upon the disciples and apostles as God's chosen emissaries into the world.[15] Here again these servants of Jesus Christ are viewed in their capacity to represent and to embody, at least in a proleptic way, the entire Messianic community. In yet other passages individual Christians are called "elect" in a matter-of-fact way, which suggests an application to all members of the community.[16] Finally, in many contexts the term "the elect" appears as a naturally intelligible way of referring to the whole company of God's people.[17] In many of these contexts it is clear that both Gentiles and Jews are covered by this designation. In most cases the Old Testament identification of the elect with the covenant community of Israel was presupposed, although the dominant corollaries, in the New Testament as in the Old, were to be seen in God's foreknowledge and call, his mercy and power, and his intention to redeem the world. The continuity between this calling of the church and the calling of the fathers was everywhere accepted as basic to the thought. (Acts 13:16-33; Rom. 9:1-11; 11:1-12.) In fact, Paul went so far as to say of those Jews who were the greatest enemies of the church: "As regards election they are beloved for the sake of their forefathers" (Rom. 11:28). This statement would justify the inference that this apostle refused to admit the possibility that God could ever elect two communities. Abrogation of God's love for the fathers and for their descendants was quite impossible. Ultimately election produces one people and only one. To sum up, then, the idea of the church as the remnant was nonessential; the conception of it as the elect was quite essential, because it was inseparable from God's faithfulness to his covenant people Israel.[18]

We have now completed our survey of figures that oscillate around the conception of the people of God as a national, racial, and political entity. In the process we have touched upon many key terms:

Israel	sons of Abraham
a holy nation	the exodus pilgrims
the twelve tribes	the house of David
the circumcision	the remnant
the fathers and their descendants	the elect

In every case we have found that the existence of this community is qualified from its creation by God's call and promise. This means that no image is primarily political or racial. The community is not to be visualized basically in terms of "natural" bonds of gregariousness but in terms of God's act. Before we say any of these terms we should first think: God's purpose, his promise, his calling. Before any person could belong to this community he must have been included through new, contemporaneous election and circumcision. "Where is his heart?" This is a question that determined his status vis-à-vis Israel. It is not therefore to be assumed that these images are more "literal" than others. Yet they all serve a double function: first, of linking the New Testament community intimately and strongly to the whole course of Israel's history, and second, of emphasizing the awesome significance of being inside rather than outside this nation. So tenacious was the link with the twelve tribes that hope for the future could not jettison their full inclusion. So awesome was the distinction between this people and all other peoples that salvation for the world could be visualized only through the completion of God's covenant with this one people. The images held a built-in flexibility, through faith's readiness to recognize God's power to create those who are-not-his-people as his people. But this flexibility did not serve as a promiscuous occasionalism that dissolved the cohesiveness and continuity of the story of Creation; rather, it served to disclose the steadfastness of this one God in fulfilling the destiny of the one people whom he had chosen "before the foundation of the world." (Eph. 1:3-10.)

It is this steadfastness of God which preserved the bond between the church and Israel and simultaneously established the radical breach between Israel during the days of the promise and the same Israel during the Day in which the promise was being fulfilled. It may be that we have unduly stressed the degree to which theological components supersede and replace sociological or biological components in defining the continuity in the life of Israel. Can we maintain a "tenacious link" between church and the twelve tribes if promise and faith are made the *sole* bearers of continuity? Did not Paul himself insist that the gospel and salvation must come first to the Jew and only then to the Gentile? Did he not recognize the continued importance of biological descent when he spoke of unbelieving Jews as beloved "for the sake of their forefathers" (Rom. 11:28)? Does not this awareness of biological fact lie behind his own sense of kinship with Israel and his own confidence that in the end "all Israel will be saved" (v. 26)? To all these questions an affirmative answer must be given. Yet the theological perspectives need not thereby be repudiated. Biological continuity is not excluded from God's activity in history. Paul found the truth of this biological continuity assured by God's creation, God's covenant, God's election, God's unfailing faithfulness to the fathers and his redemptive power in Jesus Christ as the Messiah of *Israel*. Paul did not evaporate the social structures into pure " Spirit," but he perceived them all as modes of operation of God's sovereign grace, all subject to the power of God to fulfill his promise *in spite of* social intransigence and even *by means of* it.[19]

If we thus interpret the intrinsic burden of these " political " images, we should be ready to recognize that precisely the same burden was communicated in " nonpolitical " images. To a cluster of these nonpolitical images we now turn, knowing in advance that insistence on drawing a boundary between these and the former cluster is quite arbitrary, a concession more to the modern mentality than to the ancient.

Metaphors Drawn from the Pastoral Economy

Let us first establish the range and frequency of appearance of the picture of the flock (*poimnē, poimnion*). It appears nine times in six different writers.[20] In all but one the texts point to the human community. Of these references two may be cited here: " Fear not, [45] little flock, for it is your Father's good pleasure to give you the kingdom." (Luke 12:32.) " So there shall be one *flock*, one shepherd." (John 10:16.) In addition to these passages one should include others in which the words for sheep (*arnion, arēn, probata*) refer to the band of disciples. Of these there are ten, scattered in at least seven writings.[21] The evidence thus suggests the presence of a widely used idiom. This is doubtless why the analogy is always used at if it would be readily understood.

This material demonstrates clearly that the picture of the flock belongs inseparably to the picture of the shepherd (*poimēn*). The master image, rightly seen, is that of shepherd-and-flock. Never does either shepherd or flock appear without implying the other. In almost every instance the flock is assumed to be the possession of God. (Acts 20:28; I Peter 5:2.) It is God's flock over which Jesus Christ has been appointed shepherd. This is clearly stated in Heb. 13:20 and is clearly implied in the Gospel assurance " Fear not, little flock, for it is your Father's good pleasure," as also in the command " Feed *my* lambs "

(John 21:15). God is ultimately the shepherd-ruler of this flock; Jesus is the chief shepherd; Jesus appoints undershepherds, but the flock throughout remains God's possession. (I Peter 5:2-4.)

This concern for the interdependence of the flock-and-shepherd is reflected in the concern to distinguish the true shepherds from the false or, alternately, from hirelings, the thieves or strangers.[22] The fortunes of the sheep are dependent on the character and fate of the shepherd. (Matt. 26:31.) It is the inescapable task of the good shepherd to bring other sheep into the same fold (John 10:16), to feed sheep who have no shepherd (Mark 6:34; Matt. 9:36), and to gather the lost sheep (Matt. 10:6; 15:24).

It is significant that there are direct and explicit links between the image of the flock and the covenant community of Israel. The concern is with the lost sheep of the *house of Israel*. (Matt. 10:6; 15:24.) *The kingdom* is given to them. (Luke 12:32.) Sheep and shepherd are bound together by "the blood of an eternal covenant" (Heb. 13:20). Behind these conceptions lie multiple associations with Old Testament and intertestamental traditions that must be explored for a full comprehension.[23]

It is also worth noting that the master image invites contrasts not only between sheep that are lost and those which are found, but also between sheep and goats (Matt. 25:32-33), and between sheep and wolves.[24] This latter contrast is applied both to the external enemies of the flock who persecute the sheep and to internal enemies who deceive the sheep, "wolves in sheep's clothing."

When one looks for the most frequent emphasis in the New Testament treatment of this thought complex, he discovers it in the multiple associations between Jesus Christ and his people. The largest single concentration of nuances may be observed in the extensive allegory of John, ch. 10, with its double picture of Jesus as the door and the shepherd. His voice and the sheep's response suggest their daily interdependence. (John 10:4.) In him they find daily access to the fold and to the pasture. (V. 9.) He fulfills his purposes of giving them abundant life by laying down his life for them. This act creates mutual knowledge (v. 14) and this knowledge, inseparable from the life-giving, binds together in turn the Father and the shepherd, the shepherd and the flock.

This Johannine allegory weaves together implications that in the

Synoptic stories had been left scattered. In one story God's work was described in Jesus' parable of joy over the hundredth sheep. (Luke 15:4-6.) In others, Jesus' own concern for the lost sheep was made clear by his own vocation (Matt. 10:6), by his feeding of the multitude (Mark 6:34), by his eating with publicans and sinners (ch. 2:15-17), by his commissioning of the apostles (John 21:15), and climactically by his offering of his life for them (Matt. 26:31). His death for the flock was the climax of all his work as shepherd.[25] Small wonder that the flock image became so closely bound up with the Eucharistic life of the church and that the picture of Jesus as the shepherd became so dominant in Christian art.

The power exercised by the Shepherd's dying is even more strongly underscored by the use of the verb (*poimainein*), which the Revised Standard Version sometimes translates by " to shepherd " and sometimes by " to govern." For the purpose of showing the unities that were preserved in Greek but that are lost sight of in English, we may translate *poimainein* always as " to shepherd." Matthew 2:6, for example, becomes, " From you [Bethlehem] shall come a ruler who will *shepherd* [RSV: govern] my people Israel." In the Apocalypse is the exalted picture of the Lamb shepherding his flock and guiding them to the springs of living water.[26] But this idyllic scene is the counterpart of a more bloody one. Here the picture presupposes " the blood of the Lamb " on the shepherd's part and robes washed in that blood, on the flock's part. Moreover, the shepherd, through the same power, shepherds all the nations with a rod of iron. He is the judge of all the nations. (Rev. 19:15; cf. Matt. 25:32-34.) His cross is his crown. This power to rule is shared with those who share in the power of his death. They become **[46] lambs who rule.** So Rev. 2:26-27 give the amazing assurance to the Christian (or church) who conquers in his own battle: " I will give him power over the nations, and he shall *shepherd* them with a rod of iron, . . . even as I myself have received power from my Father." It may be wise to preserve the translation of " to govern " rather than " to shepherd," but such verses as these remind us again that, throughout the Old and New Testaments, the shepherd image coalesces with the king image, just as the flock image coalesces with that of the Kingdom. In any case, we should remember that the kingly power of Jesus is always congruous with his function as shepherd, and that the kingdom status of the community is always congruous with its life as the one flock of this shepherd. The same congruity applies to the individual Christian. When his own life is seen as a sharing in the life of a shepherd-king, it is because the sacrifice of that dying-rising Shepherd has become binding upon him; when his life is seen as the life of a lamb in the flock, the norm provided by the slain Lamb becomes applicable without reservation. (Rom. 8:36.)

Here we find another instance of the combined elasticity and toughness of this imagistic thinking. The elasticity can be described in various ways. In this flock every shepherd is himself a lamb and every lamb a shepherd. Moreover, the thought about the flock can be translated without difficulty into the ideas of the house of Israel, the kingdom, or the church. Thus it seems that no one item in the complex of images has an unchanging content. There is, nevertheless, a tough core of meaning that resists distortion. This core is the constant reference to the story of Jesus, culminating in his death for men. When a writer mentioned the leaders of the church as shepherds, the norm of their office was the behavior of the Good Shepherd. When a writer wished to warn against false leaders, it was the example of Jesus that made their treachery apparent. When the writer was concerned with the waywardness of individual sheep, he applied the same law to them as to their leaders. The presence of wolves in the flock was detected by the same standard. The idiom as a whole preserves a distinction between shepherd and flock, but it also, somewhat illogically, subordinates both leaders and followers to the same law of self-giving love and divinely shared life.

Our discussion may cast light upon several New Testament passages in which ecclesiological interest seems to be lacking from the flock symbolism. It is true that these passages may be interpreted quite independently, but when we become aware of how deeply this imagery was imbedded in the subconscious mind of Christians, it is difficult not to discern in each passage at least some ecclesiological overtones. Here I have in mind three passages in particular. (1) As Matthew tells the parable of the lost sheep (Matt. 18:10-14) he makes the concern of the shepherd for recovering the hundredth sheep an analogy of the concern of God for the "little ones." "It is not the will of my Father . . . that one of these little ones should perish." Presumably these little ones are members of the church (not children in the literal sense); accordingly, the parable warns Christian leaders against despising any member of the church. (2) The familiar Matthaean allegory of the Final Judgment (ch. 25:31-46) compares the work of the Messiah to the shepherd's separation of sheep from goats. As recounted to a Christian audience, the standards of judgment would be interpreted as applying directly to the treatment by the church of " one of the least of these my brothers." (3) In the Lucan Nativity story the glory of the Lord first shone on shepherds who were " keeping watch over their flocks by night." They became the first witnesses to the Savior's birth, then these witnesses returned to their flocks, glorifying God. (Luke 2:8-20.) This is precisely the task elsewhere assigned to the shepherds of Christ's flock.

There are still other passages in which the church associations are more nebulous and problematic. For example, when Jesus appointed the Seventy and sent them out " as lambs," was he also commissioning them as shepherds of the seventy nations (all the Gentiles, according to the contemporary thought)? Or again, when Jesus commanded Peter to feed his sheep, to what extent was he in effect appointing him to serve in a unique capacity as shepherd and therefore ruler over the whole church (John 21:15-19), charged with the responsibility of appointing successors? (I Peter 5:1-5.) Was the promise of one flock in John 10:16 intended to include all subsequent generations or was it limited in meaning to the inclusion of Jews and Gentiles in the New Testament period alone? Should the " door " of this same passage be construed to signify that only by sharing in the Passion of Jesus does a lamb have access to the one Lord and his one pasture? [27]

It is clear that New Testament writers patterned their thought of the flock along the lines of strategic Old Testament passages. These latter passages must therefore be considered in recovering the full import of their conception of the church. (Compare Matt. 26:31 with Zech. 13:7.)

We have noted how the fact of Jesus' death as lamb/shepherd pervaded completely the inner structure of communal life as God's flock. He had purchased this flock with his own blood (Acts 20:28); he thus established for both sheep and shepherds the final norm of their behavior and of their union with him. This thought of Jesus as the slain lamb was often linked to the prophecy of Isaiah.[28] Moreover, it echoed the ritual of the temple, in particular the liturgy for the Passover and the Day of Atonement and the entire annual sequence of sin offerings and cultic sacrifices. In many ways, therefore, the Scriptural and liturgical traditions shaped the early Christian understanding of their life as God's flock. A fuller treatment of these allusions, however, appears more appropriately in the discussion of the temple and priesthood. (Cf.[48])

We will do well to remember that the development of the image of the slain lamb discloses many meanings in the church's existence as God's flock. Moreover, these meanings permeate other images that may seem to us to be more thoroughly political or universal in tone. For example, the role of Jesus as lamb links the flock-church to Israel in Egypt, delivered from bondage by the Passover Lamb (I Cor. 5:7); this fact binds what we have said about the exodus to what we will say about the temple. (Cf. [48]) It also links together Jesus' service to the lost sheep of the house of Israel with him who as a dying lamb " takes away the sins of the world." (John 1:29, 36; I Peter 1:19.) Finally, it offers the prophet John a key by which he may expound the mystery of the cosmic struggle between the Lamb and the Beast, a struggle that provides the context for understanding the historical travail of all nations and kingdoms. (Cf. [58],[59]) To the relevance of the image in these other contexts we will return.

Metaphors Drawn from Cultic Traditions

In our survey of images that depict certain basic characteristics of God's people, an underlying contrast between the Biblical and the modern employment of these images emerges. Perhaps we will best see this contrast if we note certain traits in modern usage. It is true that our habitual appeal to a particular image comes by way of a polemic by which one communion defends its own distinctive heritage as vindicated by Scripture. For example, some communions accent the image of the covenant people, and others accent the image of the temple. Thereby the former communions justify the priority of the preaching while the latter justify the priority of the sacrificing priesthood.[29] Inasmuch as the historical estrangements of the two traditions tend to condition their reading of the New Testament, one image comes to be claimed as the first line of defense for one ecclesiology while the other comes under attack as the stronghold of its opponents. Over the generations a subtly pervasive cloud of sentiments has thus conditioned personal and group reactions to each Biblical image. This cloud of sentiments has blurred the initial meanings; each image has become the partisan slogan for a particular tradition.

In striking contrast, the New Testament seldom exhibits this same polemic. The image of the temple was not the weapon of a high-church wing, nor was the idea of the covenant the slogan of any other faction. The polemic element was not absent, to be sure, but it did not seek to vindicate the priority of one image so much as to advance the understanding of all the images. Just as in Christ, God had disclosed the true meanings of Abrahamic sonship, so too he had transformed the meanings of temple worship. Behind the choice of radically different images precisely the same basic motivation may be discerned. Apostles and prophets wanted to move their readers from an unconverted imagination to a mind that detected in all the images the outlines of the gospel itself.

As we conduct our review of the cultic analogies, therefore, we will need to observe both their function of relating the Christian community to its heritage in the history of God's temple and their function of indicating the radical revision that the gospel required in all concepts of priesthood and sacrifice. We are dealing, of course, not with a single image but with a cluster of images, a very complex and fluid galaxy indeed. They seem to move in orbit around at least five focuses of thought.

1. The analogies of the City, diversely identified as Jerusalem, the Holy City, and the City of David.

2. The analogies of the mountain, Mt. Zion, and the temple conclave located there, with its cornerstone, foundations, walls, and building stones.

3. The analogies that point to the priesthood and its work of mediation.

4. The analogies that orient thought around the sacrifices that are presented by the worshipers.

5. The analogies suggested by the calendar of festivals and holy days.

Throughout the whole range we may observe the operation of the principle that we have already noted — the tendency to conceive the analogies as dramatic stories enacted in time, rather than as visual objects constructed in space. Moreover, we will notice here, as elsewhere, that this visualization of a community's story simultaneously stressed the continuity of God's people throughout history and the grounding of this continuity in the constancy of God's activity vis-à-vis his people rather than in institutional inertia. For here as elsewhere every image is itself qualified by its reference to God: it is God's city, God's temple, God's priesthood, and God's sacrifices. The correlation of [47] the Holy City (Jerusalem, the City of David) and the Christian community appears in developed form in three New Testament writings: Revelation, Hebrews, and Galatians. All three writers assume that this analogy was commonly understood among the churches, both Jewish and Gentile. This common acceptance of the analogy was grounded in a habit of mind that had been deeply imbedded in the ancient mentality. In every Near Eastern culture each city had its sacred significance, its god, and its altar. Especially in the Bible may be detected a " sacred geography." " Certain geographical terms and places are governed by a theological coefficient apart from which it is impossible to understand their significance." [30] Among all these places, Jerusalem " is at the heart of the history of the old covenant . . . is supremely the place where the history of salvation is enacted." [31] Because this is true the name of Jerusalem carried an inexhaustible wealth of associations. Whenever a writer used this name, countless nuances and allusions may have been in his mind, and it is therefore difficult to be confident that a particular interpreter has caught precisely the exact and full circle of references. One interpreter will differ widely from another, and there may well be justification for both interpretations. No interpreter can be entirely confident that he has drawn the circumference at the right radius from the center.

Our first effort, then, must be to notice the radius that the writers explicitly indicated. For example, all three conceived of Jerusalem as " governed by a theological coefficient," that is, it can be said that this city was above all to be understood as a holy city, a heavenly city, a city of the living God, where God himself has chosen to dwell. In their minds the church corresponded to Jerusalem primarily in the ontological and eschatological sense and only secondarily in the objectively topographical and historical sense. The earthly community was linked first of all to that city which is above. The city that existed in heaven was the ground of reality for the earthly society. Moreover, this heavenly city was one that is to come, to come down from heaven to earth; it therefore signifies the eternal ground and destiny of the earthly society. This heavenly city was, however, not considered something intrinsically foreign to the earthly, but was embodied within it in a form that was hidden and at the same time manifest. Its citizens and heirs were living men and women. That which marked them as its citizens, e.g., the name of God on their foreheads (Rev. 3:12; cf. [64]), also marked them as bound together in a sacred fellowship. It was among them as a society that God had chosen to dwell. Their solidarity on earth was the realm where God's rule was being honored and exemplified. Existing on earth, in however precarious and contested a situation, they looked toward the Jerusalem that is above and that is coming. In and through their faithful decisions the trumpets could be heard announcing the triumphant descent of God's final grace. There was and could be but one such city, and citizenship therein bound together men and women who had on earth lived in many different epochs. In this sense the theological definition of Jerusalem transcended the centuries without annulling them, because each citizen was a pilgrim of his particular generation. This city, theologically conceived, also transcended geographical boundaries, since its walls enclosed men from many different places. But space was not annulled, because the power and glory of this kingdom could be manifested only in such various places.

There was another common mark of this Jerusalem as viewed in Hebrews and Revelation, i.e., it is from beginning to end the Messiah's city. It is the people to whom he comes as savior and judge; and simultaneously his coming is inseparable from the coming of the heavenly city. He bears the meaning and power and love that makes this city the dwelling of God. In the promise of his coming is embodied the promise of its redemption. It is in and through him that Christians enter the Holy City. By this entrance they are brought into solidarity with the city of the prophets, priests, and kings.

As we try to recapture their sense of solidarity with that Jerusalem of which the Old Testament had spoken, we must do justice both to the prior theological definition and to the resultant historical con-notation. We have noted the prior theological definition: their mem-bership in Jerusalem was initiated and accomplished through their citizenship in the heavenly and eschatological city. In their creation as a society by the same God for the same destiny they had become heirs of the historically embodied city, Jerusalem.

What precise historical connotations result from this definition? It may be quite inappropriate to speak of precision in a context of thought where imagination is so dominant, but it is not inappropriate to seek the more concrete filiations of this imagination. For after all, Christian imagination never emptied the picture of Jerusalem of its reference to a specific earthly society. Christian writers readily used the stories of the older city to illuminate the life of the newer city. The inner history [32] of the two cities was continuous and of this inner continuity the centrality of Jerusalem in sagas and legends was a sig-nificant token. Essential to the inner history was the fact that the divine vocation of the kings had centered in Jerusalem. As the Mes-siah had been given the key of David, so he made his followers kings and gave to them that key. Equally central had been the role of this city in the mission of the prophets, from the beginning to the end. The priestly work of mediation between God and men had also been exercised in Jerusalem. These ministries had been continuous within the inner history of God's dwelling among men; they had given to this city a permanent significance. So when the Christian prophet visualized the coming city he described its walls and foundations in terms inclusive of earthly topography. When the writer of Hebrews described the Holy City he saw it as including all the pilgrims of faith.

The story of the Messiah's coming to Jerusalem was so told in all the Gospels as to demonstrate his continuing election of this city and his exercise therein of the final prophetic, priestly, and kingly work. He was born as its king and therefore at his birth all Jerusalem was troubled. (Matt. 2:3.) He died as its king and therefore at his death many saints were raised from their tombs to go " into the holy city " (ch. 27:53). The whole of the Lucan narrative was oriented toward Jerusalem and the time for the Messiah to appear there. The Messiah recognized that as a prophet he could not perish outside Jerusalem. As a king he could not be anointed elsewhere. As a priest the sacrifice must be offered there. He must take his peace to this city even though her daughters mistook the signs of this peace. In advance of his "going up to Jerusalem" he spoke of the exodus that he would accomplish there. When he got there he wept for the city. His father's vineyard must be cleansed, his father's fig tree must be judged, the fruit of his father's trees must be gathered. (Cf. [13], [14]) It was to this Jerusalem that he bade his twelve apostles accompany him. This was to be "the theater where the fortunes of the people of God, and, accordingly, the fortunes of the world are enacted."[33] The Messiah and his apostles, representatives and rulers of the heavenly city, in this Passion story enacted in a fashion then secret but destined to become transparent, the Messianic judgment and redemption of this earthly city. Its character was such that its final redemption could become operative only through Final Judgment. Yet not even the necessity of the most dreadful judgment could frustrate God's intention to dwell there.

The character of the church was thus defined first by reference to God's unfolding redemptive activity in history and consequently by reference to the memories of the historical city that had remained central to stories of Israel and of its Messiah. But there is still another form of definition that may help us recapture their thought, that form of definition that sets the holy city over against its opposite. What this community is may be known by what it is not.

In Gal. 4:21-31 the apostle set the city that is from above over and against the present city. One is the realm of freedom, the other the realm of bondage. One is composed of children born through the promise, the other of children born according to the flesh. Between the two, the conflict of spirit and flesh proceeds. It is well to note that the apostle did not place the boundary between the two cities at a date on the calendar, i.e., before or after the death of Christ. For him the boundary had been in existence as far back as Abraham and Mt. Sinai. Nor did he fix the boundary in spatial terms between the earth and sky or between nature and supernature. For him the boundary ran along the line that separates freedom from slavery within earthly communities. The boundary was ambiguous by its very nature. It did not coincide with obvious sociological opposites, e.g., Jews and Gentiles, but with opposites that could be concealed from every yardstick that measures "according to the flesh." The boundary ran through the Christian community in Galatia itself. In fact, Paul was opposing the effort being made within that community to bound the city of God by such worldly measurements.

In Revelation, the Holy City was engaged in warfare with its demonic challenger Babylon, a warfare, we note, that took place both on earth and in heaven. But here is a point that must be stressed: both foes were represented within the city of Jerusalem, which as the place of crucifixion was the site of the greatest blasphemy and idolatry as well as of redemption (Rev. 11:8), the Lord having redeemed his city from every tribe and tongue and nation. In John's day the visible battleground was neither the topographical Rome nor the topographical Judea. The battleground was the churches of Asia. Nevertheless, even in Asia the ultimate conflict was between Jerusalem and Babylon. By their faithful witness Christians revealed the presence of the messianic city that comes down out of heaven from God. The two opposing cities met in the heart of every Christian and in the inner struggle of every church. For them the problem of choosing the holy city over its satanic enemy was simply the dilemma of obedient loyalty or treacherous idolatry. That is to say, the gospel story of Jesus in Jerusalem had become a powerful paradigm that included the gospel witness of the Christian prophet in Pergamum. There prophets continued to be killed and to be raised from the dead, just as in the Jerusalem of A.D. 30 or in all past and future epochs. Their work served to mark the ingress of God's city and to herald its ontological and eschatological reality.

The writer of Hebrews chose a different foil for this definition by contrast. In ch. 12 he set the city of the living God over against the earlier mountain and over against the community created by the earlier covenant. But why did the author stress this contrast? He did not declare invalid the earlier covenant with its mountain and city. Rather, he was concerned with the anxiety, the apathy, and "the root of bitterness" that had sprung up within the Christian community itself. He said in effect: "If the people of God responded to the covenant of Mt. Sinai with such faith, looking forward as they did to the eternal city whose builder is God, how much more should you, their successors, live and walk by the same faith, since you have received in Jesus and in his new covenant a more immediate access to the same city." He discerned the boundary between the holy city and the city of aliens at the point where Christians were tempted to reject " him who warns from heaven " (Heb. 12:25).

In all these contexts, therefore, we may note the insistence that ultimately there can be but one city of God, one holy community. But this conviction could be maintained only by a form of historical realism that located the enemy of this city within the very confines of a community that bore its name. The line separating the one city from its deceptive competitors could not be drawn by empirical means, whether geographical (Rev., ch. 11), genealogical (Gal., ch. 3), or liturgical (Heb., ch. 12). Yet the irrelevance of such tests did not elevate the one city to a realm distant from the earthly and the historical; the life of the city continued to be embodied within the forms of earthly, historical, communal existence; it continued to establish solidarity among all generations and races of men.

[48] Mt. Zion, **the Holy Temple.** In most New Testament passages the thought of the city merged with the thought of the temple; nor is this surprising, since in imagination the destiny of these two institutions had been inseparable for many centuries. The ecclesiological significance of the two images may at certain points be considered the same. For example, what made either the city or the temple holy was the presence in it of the living God. " The requirement of one Temple depends on the unity of God. . . . Here was the ark, here was JHWH enthroned, here lived His Name, His Glory. From the Temple emanated revelation to the people, and from the Temple they received their blessing and salvation." [34]

Only in certain accents, integral to particular contexts, did the thought of the community as temple (*naos*) diverge from the thought of it as *polis*. We may therefore concentrate on these accents. Of the two Greek words for " temple," early Christian writers commonly chose to use *naos* rather than *hieron,* probably because they wanted to safeguard their conviction that God's temple is something not made with hands (Acts 17:24). *Hieron* referred primarily to the visible structure on Mt. Zion. *Naos* also made easier the typological reference to the tabernacle in the wilderness (*skēnē*) as well as to Solomon's masonry. Similarly, the use of the verb for tabernacling (*skēnein*) stressed the definitive act of God in creating a temple: he created a temple by tabernacling with men, by dwelling in them and moving among them.

Perhaps because of long associations between the temple and the Spirit, the New Testament pictured the temple as a dwelling place of the Spirit. Where God's spirit is, there is the temple. It may also have been this nuance which enabled Paul to speak of the body of each believer as a temple (I Cor. 6:19) without excluding the idea that every congregation is also a temple (ch. 3:16-17) and without excluding the vision of the whole church as a temple (Eph. 2:21). The applicability of the image to all three areas derives from the presence of the Holy Spirit.

This same association of Spirit, Lord, and temple was congruous, too, with the identification of temple with the body of Jesus Christ, which in the Gospels was recognized as a definite replacement for the Jewish institution.[35] Certainly the death of Jesus constituted a radical challenge to all external and visible temple structures (Heb., chs. 8; 9; Mark 15:38), inasmuch as it provided a radically new kind of mediation between God and man. Thus the contrast between the old temple and the new appears far greater than the contrast between the former city and the new one.[36] At least, the Synoptists report Jesus as predicting the demolition of the visible temple. (Mark 13:2.) They report the accusation that Jesus had pledged himself to destroy that temple. (Mark 14:58; 15:29.) The Fourth Evangelist announces the coming of the hour when the worship of the Father in Spirit and truth (i.e., in the Messiah) will replace the worship both on Mt. Gerizim and in Jerusalem. (John 4:16-26.)

The picture of the church as temple encouraged writers to include an emphasis on the temple's growth. The author of Ephesians indicates how the "household of God" "grows into" a holy temple in the Lord. (Eph. 2:18-22; cf. [95]) We are impelled to visualize a story of the process of construction rather than a completed edifice. This element of growth prompted Peter to speak of individual Christians as "living stones" being built into a spiritual house. (I Peter 2:5.) Cognate to this image was one of Jesus Christ as the living stone that served as the corner "in whom the whole structure is joined together."[37] The image also permitted the distinction between the work of the apostles and prophets in laying the foundations and the work of other Christians as stones. (Eph. 2:20; cf. Rev. 21:12.) At these points the image of the temple was utilized in ways not encouraged by the image of the city, although the identity of the two in Rev., chs. 21;22, and in Heb. ch. 12, should warn us against too sharp a contrast. In the basic orientation of both images simultaneously toward the past life of Israel and toward the coming consummation, we detect no great difference. Nor was there any difference in the constant reference to their heavenly ground and goal. The community of men on earth existed in close interdependence with the heavenly temple. They moved toward it and grew into it. It moved toward them as the place where God "shelters them with his presence" (Rev. 7:15). The temple was a heavenly-earthly reality through which human community received its ultimate context in the glorification of God and God's glorification of men. (Cf. [62])

Because one function of the temple was to serve God day and night, the picture of the church as temple merged into the picture of [49] priesthood. Both these pictures remained consonant with the political images. Twice the prophet John combined the status of Christians as priests with that as kings. (Rev. 1:6; 5:10.) When in I Peter the church was called "nation," the adjective "holy" was included; when it was called "priesthood," the adjective "royal" was appended. (I Peter 2:9.)

In dealing with the picture of this royal priesthood, we must observe at the outset that the New Testament did not use the term (whether *hiereus* or *hierateuma*) to refer to a special form of ministry within the church. The community as a whole was a priesthood, and even this explicit terminology appears to be limited to five verses in two books.[38] Furthermore, it should be noted that these passages did not develop at length the distinctively priestly work of this community. Their function is described rather generally: to offer spiritual sacrifices acceptable to God through Jesus Christ, to declare the wonderful deeds of him who had called them, to be priests of God, and to reign with Christ on earth. It is clear that this people of priests was oriented, along with the priesthood of Christ, toward God. Their work was to offer spiritual sacrifices; what precisely these sacrifices were is indicated only obliquely in other passages. Yet the character of the priesthood depends on the character of these sacrifices. We must therefore examine the image of sacrifice, after looking more closely at the picture of priesthood as found in The Letter to the Hebrews.

This image was absolutely central to the mind of the writer, so much so that one can say that in no other instance in the New Testament was an image developed in so sustained a fashion and with so many comparisons and contrasts woven so tightly together. For our purpose, however, it should be noted that this author did not use the priesthood as an analogy for the church. To him the eternal high priesthood was finally and wholly vested in Jesus Christ. The church was involved, of course, but the accent fell upon its position as the company of those who were saved by his mediatorial work. He was the surety of a better covenant by which this people lived, the access into the divine presence which opened to them the Holy of Holies.

From this angle of approach we should ask as we read Heb., chs. 5 to 8, where the functions of the high priest are examined in great detail, in what terms the author visualized the company of those for whom he uses the first person plural, " we " being the church. " We " are the house of Israel, the people of God, the heirs of the promise, the worshipers whose " conscience is purified from dead works to serve the living God." We are those who are sanctified through the blood of our high priest and who therefore eagerly await him. In other words, where the image of the priesthood was the central figure for expounding the work of Jesus, other images were adopted for describing the position of those on whose behalf Christ entered the presence of God. If we enter the sanctuary through him, it is not as priests but as worshipers rejoicing in a hope and confidence, which he as our forerunner has made possible. The church is not the temple, but it is those who enter that sanctuary. The church is not the priesthood, but those for whom the high priest intercedes. He is " separated from sinners " (Heb. 7:26), yet this separation opens the way for their sanctification (ch. 10:10). Thus the way seems barred for them to think of themselves as priests analogous to his priesthood, although the way to God is forever opened to them through his ministry on their behalf.

We do not wish to imply that there was no unity of the church with its high priest, but only that this unity was accomplished by the character of the sacrifice that the high priest offered. In many senses, of course, the [50] sacrifice of this priest is utterly unique; the letter uses every device to underscore that uniqueness, its perfection, its once-for-all character, and its universal power. But this uniqueness includes as an essential element his perfect solidarity with men: " the

children God has given me " (ch. 2:13 ff.). Also this element is inseparable from another equally unique thing: his sacrifice is defined
as the doing of God's will. It was his body that God desired, not
sacrifices and offerings. (Ch. 10:5-9.) By his act of obedience, of
total, voluntary, redemptive self-giving, he abolished the law that
required " sacrifices and offerings and burnt offerings and sin offerings." (Vs. 8-10.) " He offered no victim other than himself; in him
office and offering, priesthood and sacrifice, perfectly coincide." [39]
It was in this one sacrifice for their sakes that the Christian community was rightly expected to participate. They had an altar, but
its nature was such as to forbid their eating from it. To worship at
this altar required sacrifices similarly defined: praise to God, doing
good, sharing " what you have," and bearing abuse for him. (Ch.
13:10-16.) The uniqueness of his sacrifice rested in the opportunity
and the demand for them to share in it with him, since he had so
perfected their conscience that their sacrifice would be self-giving
and not self-securing.

In this whole complex of liturgical images, then, whether the
temple or the priesthood, the central norm that determined the import of all was that of the particular, unique, and inclusive sacrifice.
This was the image that most exactly fitted both the Passion story
of Jesus and the story of the church. This was the image that in the
New Testament appears most frequently, in the widest variety of
contexts and in a manner so commonplace as to indicate ready comprehension by the readers. Let us note a few examples.

Paul viewed his ministry of God's grace as a priestly service (*lei-
tourgos*) of Christ Jesus to the Gentiles. Paul offered it to Christ, but
it was also the channel of Christ's liturgical service for the Gentiles.
The sacrifice of the Messiah and his apostle thus became one sacrifice for others. The proclamation of the gospel represented a temple
act on the part of this common priesthood, and the obedience of
the Gentiles to the gospel was their acceptable offering (*prosphora*)
sanctified by the Holy Spirit (Rom. 15:16). Not only did Paul's
words require a radical transmutation of the concept of sacrifice, but
what is more important, he assumed that his readers had already accepted that transmutation.

Another example is offered by Paul's conception of the fund that
he delivered from Gentile churches to the church in Jerusalem. To

him this act of self-giving was a signal of Jewish-Gentile fellowship in spiritual things; as such it was a liturgical and priestly deed. (Rom. 15:27; I Cor. 9:12.) Still another example may be offered. Paul did not hesitate, in view of Christ's sacrifice, to speak of shedding " his own blood as a libation " in order to sanctify " the faith of the believers." [40] Likewise their helpfulness to the apostle was described as priestly service (*leitourgia*). (Phil. 2:25-30.) Such priestly acts were by no means limited to specific emergencies or to incidents of unusual bravery.

Congruent with this conception of liturgical sacrifice was the association of Christians with the [51] aroma. In Jewish liturgy the altar was a place from which God could smell the sacrifice; it was a place for offering fragrant incense. The imagery of the altar was therefore closely linked to the imagery of incense. This association lies behind the Pauline thought of the aroma. Paul used this metaphor in three ways: (1) Christ's loving gift of himself was a fragrant offering and sacrifice. (Eph. 5:2.) (2) A gift from the Philippian congregation to Paul was described in similar terms. (Phil. 4:18.) (3) By manifesting the knowledge of Christ the apostles spread abroad a fragrance either from life to life or from death to death, so that they could say " we are the aroma of Christ to God " (II Cor. 2:15). Paul did not apply the metaphor to the whole church, although the underlying principle might well be so extended. Just as the whole scope of the Christian's life is a sacrifice, so too their mission in the world releases a fragrance (*osmē*) that carries the knowledge of Christ everywhere. A similar thought was perhaps expressed in Rev. 5:8 and 8:3 where the incense in the heavenly temple consisted of the prayers and songs of the saints. Every believer was enjoined to obey, in connection with his normal routines, Christ's teaching that mercy and love are greater than all burnt offerings. (Matt. 9:13; 12:6; Mark 12:33.) Or in Pauline terms, he was under obligation to present his body as a living sacrifice (Rom. 12:1) by that renewal of the mind which enabled him to overcome evil with good (vs. 2-21). Such a sacrifice of their bodies was fully dependent upon the Lord's sacrifice of his body. (Heb. 10:5.)

Throughout this imagery we can see, therefore, that just as Jesus' definition of power by service revolutionized all images of Messianic kingship, so too did his definition of sacrifice revolutionize all notions of the temple and its priesthood.[41] This revolution could be forgotten only with great difficulty in a "temple" and by a "priesthood" for whom the Passion story constituted the fusion point for daily memories and hopes.

In our earlier analysis of the flock pattern we observed a similar revolution: Jesus Christ had proved himself the Good Shepherd by laying down his life for the flock, yet this act of laying down his life could be seen also as the act of a Lamb. Accordingly, the picture of Jesus as Lamb thoroughly dominated all the analogies of shepherds, folds, and flocks. Now we note that the image of Jesus' self-sacrifice as a Lamb controlled the church's understanding of itself as priesthood and sacrifice. As a sacrificed Lamb he had taken away the sins of the world. (John 1:29, 36.) Those who receive life in him share in this sacrifice by eating his flesh and drinking his blood. (Ch. 6:54.) He was a lamb without blemish or spot. (I Peter 1:19.) Of his slaughter Isaiah had spoken (Acts 8:32; Isa. 53:7-8), and in the sufferings of his body our sins are healed (I Peter 2:22-25; Isa. 53:5-9.)

The prophet John developed this image more fully than any other writer. It was the slain Lamb whose death made his people a company of kings and priests (Rev. 5:9-10), whose prayers and hymns became "bowls full of incense" (v. 8). When a reader focuses his attention in the book of Revelation upon the constitutive relation between the Lamb and the sheep whom he shepherds, he uncovers much that is relevant to the picture of the church as a community of priests. The Lamb, of course, is the temple (ch. 21:22), but in him and with him are all those who bear his name (ch. 14:1-4). He is both the object of their doxologies (ch. 5:9-10) and the one whose song they sing (ch. 15:4). He stands as one slain, in the center of their worship. (Ch. 5.) They join him in his warfare and his triumph (ch. 17:14); they follow wherever he leads. His blood becomes the cohesive element in their word of testimony and in their victory over a common accuser. (Ch. 12:10-12.) His sacrifice provides the unity and power that create this family of brothers, since they, like him, "loved not their lives even unto death." This principle of sacrificial love which makes them his community sets them in sharpest contrast with that community which bears the name of the beast. (Ch. 13.) Their purification by his sacrifice qualifies them to be his bride, his city, to share in his wedding feast. (Ch. 19:7-9.) The images shift across the screen — temple, sacrifice, bride, city, Kingdom, family — but the key element in them all is the death of the lamb as the sacrifice that takes away sin. This key is the key of both Christology and ecclesiology. Apart from it, none of the church images can be rightly comprehended. This key explains the church's adoption of the [52] festivals of the temple calendar as analogies of their own experience, explains also their adaptation of them. As the slain lamb, Jesus was the Passover sacrifice. The fabric of community was therefore seen as a form of celebrating the Festival of Unleavened Bread (I Cor. 5:7-8), a form in which sincerity and truth in all communal affairs becomes the appropriate celebration. (Cf. [6], [7]) Herein lies the reason why the Gospels stressed so much the links between the Passover season and the death of Jesus and why the Lord's Supper became the institution of a new Passover covenant. With the celebration of this Passover the far-reaching conception of the church's story as a new exodus received its anchorage in ecclesiology. (Cf. [6], [10], [28], [41]) So too the celebration of the Feast of Pentecost, as told in The Acts, displayed many ecclesiological overtones. It was " the day of the recreation of the people of God by the outpouring of the Spirit" and a celebration as well as the "unity and universality of the church." [42]

Other days in the temple calendar left their mark on Christian thinking, notably the Sabbath. As a particular day of the week, the seventh day quickly lost its sacredness, at least in large segments of the Christian society. (Rom. 14:1-5.) But as an image of the new age, of the eschatological Rest, the Day of the Lord profoundly conditioned and expressed that society's sense of its own distinctiveness. This is the Day on which the Father and the Son continue their saving work (John 5:17), a work that makes men sons of this Day. (Cf. [63]) To them is opened a Sabbath Rest that they must strive to enter " today." (Heb. 3:7 to 4:11.) They are related to this Sabbath in the same way as to the Kingdom of God. It has come to them and they come toward it. The double coming of this Rest qualifies their existence now as heirs of the promise. [43] (Cf. [60])

We must omit some of the festivals because of lack of space (e.g., the sacrifice of Jesus as the Day of Atonement and the New Year), [44] but we may well omit such data because their meaning as images of communal worship has already been described in the examples above. At no point can one easily and fully identify the church with any one of these images: city, temple, priesthood, sacrifice, festival. Yet all the images throw light upon the community consciousness. They are particularly evocative of those constitutive relations between this community and its God and its Lord. They suggest somewhat less fully the connections between this community and the people of God under the Old Covenant. They provide even less analogical help for describing the interior fabric of community relations or for defining the position of the church vis-à-vis the world. There is, however, one motif that recurs constantly in the vocabulary of temple and priesthood to which we have not given sufficient attention. It is a motif whose presence we have not found in the treatments of the church as Israel or as the flock. This is the motif of the work of the Holy Spirit. The accent of I Peter is characteristic: the temple is a spiritual house, the priesthood and its sacrifices are spiritual, the stones in the building live because of the Spirit. The priestly character of the church's worship, its hymns and prayers, are produced by their spiritual aliveness. In all the work of the temple the operation of the one Spirit may be observed. (I Cor. 12:3.) This motif and its companion, the centrality of Jesus' sacrifice, together carry us a major step forward in our exploration of ecclesiology.

IV

THE NEW CREATION

The Cosmic Reference of Particularistic Images

IN THE PRECEDING CHAPTER we surveyed the New Testament use of those images which relate the church to its background in the covenant history of Israel. We begin now a search for those images which most clearly set the church in a universal and cosmic context. It may at first seem that these two sets of images will be either antithetical to each other (how can a new Israel be harmonized with a new humanity?) or at least in sharp contrast to each other. But to adopt either of these views would be quite wrong. The same community is described by the same writer as sons of Abraham and as sons of God.

We may therefore begin by exploring the universalistic components in those patterns of thought which may have seemed to reflect a narrower parochialism. How can a community think of itself simultaneously as the house of Israel and as the heirs of a Kingdom that never ends? We take up this matter here because to many readers we will thus far have given too strong an emphasis to the bonds linking the church to Israel. It may well seem that we have unduly neglected the evidence for a sharp contrast between those "two" peoples. One motive why we have stressed the bonds of solidarity is this: to counteract the deep distaste among many modern Christians for any such solidarity. So deeply ingrained is the desire to maintain Christian superiority over all competitors that we shy away from these images which are so obviously Hebraic. "Did not the early church repudiate all such particularism for the sake of true universalism? If so, then we can and must play down the vestigial remnants of their outmoded vocabulary." Much can be said in defense of this protest, so much, in fact, that its exponents can find impressive historical and theological support. But often the vigor of the protest stems from psychological roots. For example, we assume that the ultimacy of the Christian way requires its complete separation from the Jewish way. An anti-Semitism can readily don the mask of pro-Christianism. This psychological factor, however potent, need not detain us now. We are more concerned with historical and theological factors. If it is essential to the uniqueness of Christianity for us to maintain a sharp chasm between Israel and the church, why did not the apostles break away more sharply from the distinctively Israelite images? Do we not place ourselves on sounder historical grounds if we first seek to understand their convictions concerning the status of the Christian community as the Israel of God? Or, to shift to the theological argument, is it essential to reject all forms of particularism if we are to make a strong case for the universalism of the gospel? Such rejection may mean that our brand of universalism is vastly different from the universalism of the New Testament. Our brand may be Gentilism rather than universalism. It may be that when we rightly understand Christian universalism we will find it more directly dependent upon particularism than we had supposed.

However that may be, let us review a few of the so-called particularistic images and notice how, to early Christians who shared the communal life in Christ and in the Holy Spirit, all those images tended to become genuinely universal in meaning. One way of proceeding is to classify those images in terms of their increasing age, according to their origins in Israelite traditions. It is noteworthy that among the images we have listed thus far, the origin of none can be assigned to a period later than the Babylonian exile. The sense of continuity for the church did not require the choice of analogues from *each* successive century. None is drawn from the Maccabean period and none from the period of Ezra-Nehemiah. Moreover, the images associated with the captivity of Israel in Babylon are weak in power (e.g., exiles, the remnant, cf. [28], [43]) and few in number.

Corresponding to a dearth of images from this long span of centuries is the fact that in the New Testament the apostolic sermons and historical summaries gave little space to events after the Babylonian captivity. Stephen's speech jumps from Solomon to Jesus, and Peter's from David to Jesus. (Acts, chs. 7; 10.) Why should this be so? The answer, I think, lies here: the sense of community was grounded in the covenants between God and Israel and no new covenant had been sealed during this period. Christian thinkers therefore felt little impulse to relate the church typologically to Israel's experience since the Davidic period. The faithfulness of God to his covenants was the decisive element, and that faithfulness did not require empirical proofs of an unbroken succession of institutional embodiments. The covenant created the people, and the people was the bearer of the covenant. The existence of the covenant-bearing people was assured by the covenant itself; therefore, although the covenant remained alive through the successive generations, its validity was not to be measured by the persistence of institutional forms, whether those of kingship, of priesthood, or of prophecy. That is to say, the consciousness of being members of the covenant people was not for them dependent upon the survival of earthly institutions.

This may be illustrated by examining the place of the Davidic epoch in the ecclesiological imagination. The variety and power of images drawn from traditions that dealt with this epoch are quite obvious. We may recall the images that center in the temple and in the City of David, in the kingship and kingdom of the son of David, in the flock of this shepherd-king. Undoubtedly the Scriptural sagas that centered in the rise of the Davidic monarchy conditioned the "apperceptive mass" of the early Christian community. Undoubtedly the reservoir of imaginative thought patterns had been stocked by the communal memories of David's city and kingdom. (Cf. [42]) But the basic images were not restricted to the repetition of the Davidic epoch, with its communal achievements. This generalization needs, of course, detailed illustrations; there is space, perhaps, to suggest a few. Jesus was hailed as the son of David who would introduce the kingdom of David. But there are evidences in both Gospels and letters that the identification of the Christ with the son of David was affirmed with considerable hesitation and that more inclusive categories (e.g., Son of Man) were adopted with greater enthusiasm. Correspondingly, the conception of the new community as the kingdom of David was virtually replaced by the wider category of the Kingdom of God or the new creation. The early Christians did not, to be sure, find any sharp contradiction between the son of David and the Son of Man, or between the kingdoms of David and of God. But the two images were superimposed in such a fashion that the more inclusive tended to supplant the less inclusive. Notice the juxtaposition in Gabriel's annunciation:

He will be great, and will be called the Son of the Most High; and the Lord God will give to him the throne of his father David, and he will reign over the house of Jacob forever; and of his kingdom there will be no end (Luke 1:32-33).

Here the thought of David's throne becomes more and more inclusive. We should also note that as the image of David's throne receded into the background, it was supplanted not by a more modern or novel idiom, but by an idiom that was even more ancient. As attention shifts to the earlier covenants (e.g., the house of Jacob, the Kingdom without end), the picture becomes more inclusive. The momentum toward universality did not require new images, but movement back through covenant history toward the primal images.

A similar drift in the communal imagination was reflected in the Christian use of the other Davidic symbols. The idea of the Temple of Solomon, a temple made with hands, was absorbed into and in part supplanted by that of the tent in the wilderness and of the heavenly tabernacle; the Levitic priesthood was absorbed into and supplanted by the priesthood of Aaron and Melchizedek. And, as we have seen, all images of the temple were decisively qualified by the presence of God among his people and by the character of the sacrifice. (Cf. [47]-[52]) In terms, then, of their power to mold the New Testament imagination, the Davidic sagas were much less weighty than the Mosaic. There is really nothing strange in this tendency because in both the Davidic and Mosaic traditions the establishment of the city and Kingdom of David had been a fulfillment, however partial and temporary, of God's people-shaping promises to Moses.

In any case, one conclusion becomes clear from our study. The images that pointed to the Mosaic epoch were far more influential in conditioning the New Testament church consciousness than were those which pointed to the Davidic epoch. We could cite extensive proof of this finding, but the tabulation would prove tedious. We have surveyed both the variety and the plurality of such images in the chapter preceding this. Here we may add, however, three foot-notes to the previous discussion.

1. Where other images were substituted for those of Mosaic origin or where other images were superimposed upon them, these images were drawn from covenants prior to the Sinaitic.

2. Wherever the Mosaic images were utilized by the New Testament church, they were interpreted in the light of their eschatological fulfillment in Christ.

3. Whether the Mosaic images were viewed in the light of the fulfillment of the Sinaitic covenant, or whether they were absorbed into the meaning of the earlier covenants, the direction of development lies toward greater inclusiveness and universality.

Two steps in retrogression may show this development toward greater inclusiveness: the movement of imagination back from the Mosaic period toward the covenants that God had sealed with the twelve tribes; and the movement from God's promises to the patriarchs back toward his covenant with all men in the story of Adam, and his covenant with all things in the creation of heaven and earth.

With the use of images drawn from the stories of creation we will be occupied centrally throughout this chapter. We have already dealt with the early Christian employment of idioms drawn from the patriarchal traditions. But at the risk of tiresome repetition we may underscore again this conclusion: whereas in the New Testament period some Gentile Christians were inclined to view God's promises to Abraham as outmoded by Christ and some Jewish Christians were inclined to make the inheritance of God's gift dependent upon membership in Abraham's family according to the flesh, and whereas most modern Christians, Gentile by race and Occidental by imagination, are inclined to view God's covenant with Abraham as abrogated by the opening of his kingdom to all races, the apostolic writings of the New Testament, with a few possible exceptions, express the conviction that in the new community in Christ, God has truly fulfilled his promise to Abraham and to the fathers. There is no contradiction between sonship to Abraham and sonship to God. Instead the contrary is true. In the resurrection of Christ, God has raised up children to Abraham in fulfillment of his promise. Such particularism and such universalism are not mutually exclusive, but quite inseparable and interdependent. This interdependence was in fact implicit in virtually every image that we have classified as political, pastoral, or cultic, every image that we have subsumed under the master image of the people of God.

The rebuilding of the ruins of the dwelling of David is designed to include " the rest of men," " all the Gentiles who are called by my name." (Acts 15:14-18.) The one salvation that God has " prepared in the presence of all peoples " must necessarily take the form of " a light for revelation to the Gentiles and for glory to thy people Israel." (Luke 2:29-32; Acts 26:22-23.) The promise to David, to Moses and the prophets, to Abraham — this one inclusive promise — had from the beginning moved toward a single fulfillment, when God would bless all the families of the earth in Abraham. The glorification of God among the Gentiles was nothing short of the confirmation of all the promises. (Rom. 15:8-12.) Nothing short of such glorification could have confirmed those promises, for the promise to Abraham had specifically said, " In thee shall all the nations be blessed " (Gen. 12:3; 18:18; Acts 3:25; Gal. 3:8).

The images expressive of national and racial identity could, of course, be used to negate this promise of God. And they were on occasion so used by Christians. For example, some Galatian Christians limited the people of God to " the circumcision." But the apostle Paul repudiated this restrictive limitation. " Neither circumcision nor uncircumcision counts for anything." (Gal. 6:15.) Furthermore, in this passage where he repudiated the limiting concept, what Paul added is doubly significant: " Neither circumcision counts for anything, nor uncircumcision, but *a new creation*. Peace and mercy be upon all who walk by this rule, upon *the Israel of God* " (vs. 15-16). Note that it was for the sake of affirming the new creation that Paul negated the category of circumcision. But in adopting this cosmic and universal image, Paul immediately associated with it a term that to him was equally broad: the Israel of God. Elsewhere Paul was quite able, in spite of apparent verbal inconsistency, to claim for the whole Christian community the title " the true circumcision " (Phil. 3:3). This term became fully congruent with the cosmic transformation that had been wrought by the death and resurrection of Christ. (Col. 2:8-15.)

As we begin our survey of the ecclesiological images that articulate the universal and cosmic dimensions of New Testament thought, we therefore do so with the reminder that to draw any sharp distinction between national idioms and cosmic idioms would violate the testimony of the apostles. To them the new creation included the fulfillment of every covenant that God had sealed with his people. To them none of the apparently narrower images (e.g., circumcision, the kingdom of David) excluded the ultimately universal and cosmic dimension. To them both were essential because of the grounding of every ecclesiological image in theological, that is, in ontological and eschatological, reality. God is a *faithful* God; therefore, the creation of the true and final people of God must include the fulfillment of every promise he has made. This faithful God is *God;* therefore his oaths to all the fathers will ultimately determine the shape and scope of the eschatological community. To the apostle, Christ had become a servant to Israel for the sake of the Gentiles; therefore, Paul became a servant of the Gentiles for the sake of Israel. (Rom. 14:8; 11:14.)

[53] The New Creation [1]

We have already cited the clear-cut assertion that the Israel of God is composed of those who live as a " new creation." Now we should note two other expressions of this conviction.

If any one is in Christ, he is a new creation; the old has passed away, behold the new has come. (II Cor. 5:17.)

In the context of this statement Paul located this transition from the old to the new at a single point: the death of all men in Christ's death for all, and the living of all men for him who was raised for all. To the apostle what had happened in Christ simultaneously transformed not only the status of creation but also the vantage point from which this creation must be viewed.

There is a second, though more problematical, parallel in James 1:18.

Of his own will he [the father of lights] brought [created or begat] us forth by the word of truth that we should be a kind of first fruits of his creatures.

This statement suggests the inference that no image of creation can be sundered from the Creator's will and that our very existence implies not only that " we " are a new creation but also that we are only the first installment of those whom God has determined to include within that new generation.

This image of the [54] first fruits (*aparchē*) deserves special attention. It recalls a pattern of Jewish thought in which the first produce, whether of grain, flocks, bread, or children, was specially given by God and therefore must be given back to him as a token of total indebtedness. This conception had played a central role in national festivals and in temple liturgy. In Christian imagination the picture fused together several basic convictions:

1. God's lordship over all and his gift of all.
2. The Passover requirement of the sacrifice of the first-born.
3. Man's dedication to God of all his "produce."
4. The appearance and presentation of the first fruit as a pledge of the coming harvest.
5. The power of the first to represent all others in the series.
6. The power of the first to sanctify and to cleanse the whole series.

These assumptions permeate the following appearances of the idiom in the New Testament: Christ is the first fruits of the dead (I Cor. 15:20-23); the Spirit, which is at work within the Christian community, is the pledge and guarantee, the "down payment" of the coming redemption, which is designed to reach the whole creation (Rom. 8:23; cf. also ch. 11:16); the first converts in a province embody the promise and power of salvation for the whole province (Rom. 16:5; I Cor. 16:15); the Christian community as a whole is begotten in order to serve as the first fruits of all God's creatures.[2]

Although this picture was used rather incidentally by only three New Testament writers, in all three it gives a far-ranging significance to the idea of the church. This idea reflects a strong sense of the church's mission to the world. It locates the historical present of the church as lying between what God has done and what he will surely do. It suggests that God is now active in social history. It identifies Jesus Christ as the agent through whom God's hand is at work. " We are his [God's] workmanship, created in Christ Jesus for good works, which God prepared beforehand, that we should walk in them." (Eph. 2:10.) Christ is the " beginning of God's creation " (Rev. 3:14) in whom, for whom, and through whom all things are created (Col. 1:16). Thus the status as *aparchē* links this community to God the

Creator, to Christ " the first-born of all creation," and to the whole
creation, both " old " and " new." The beginning of the harvest links
the community at once to the Creator and to all of his creatures.
Used thus, the image suggests that there cannot be two creations,
but only one, since the definition of creation itself is conceived in
theological and Christological terms.

But the image preserves a contrast between the old and the new,
at least provisionally. The self-consciousness of the church preserved
its sense of solidarity with the first creation seen, in terms of its beginning and end in God, as good.[3] But the same self-consciousness
placed the major accent upon the newness of creation in Christ.
This newness was defined basically by a contrast with an order
(*ktisis*) that had become subjected to futility through its solidarity
in sin. Worshiping the creature rather than the Creator (Rom. 1:18-
23), it had accepted a " bondage to decay." Its state until now could
be described as the travail of birth. (Ch. 8:12-25.) It lived in tension,
on the one hand, between its " eager longing for the revealing of
God's sons," its desire for the glorious liberty of God's children, and,
on the other, its slavery to fear and its subjection to powers that
effectively blocked the realization of this sonship. (Vs. 12-25.) The
Christian community fully recognized that it shared in this travail.
But it also recognized that it had received " the spirit of sonship ";
it had been emancipated from futility. It knew that this gift was the
first fruit of a harvest that was destined to include the whole creation. So the new creation was the spearhead of transformation which
would rapidly come to pervade all things. Every creature was the
object of the preaching of the gospel. (Col. 1:23; Mark 6:15.) No
creature was hidden from God's judgment or love. (Heb. 4:13.) In
the end every creature would join in singing the doxology to
the Lamb (Rev. 5:13), for God would make all things new (Rev.
21:1, 5).

To this picture of creation and its first fruits belongs the picture
of [55] the new humanity or the new man. The cosmic range of
this picture is inherent in the conviction that the two humanities
exhaust the possibilities. Every person, in the act of decision, incorporates himself in one of the two. There is no third option. Among
many expressions of this idea, one of the clearest may be found in
Col. 3:10. (Cf. [26])

You have put off the old nature [man] with its practices and have put on the new nature [man], which is being renewed in knowledge according to the image of its creator. Here there cannot be Greek and Jew, circumcized and uncircumcized, barbarian, Scythian, slave, free man, but Christ is all and in all.

Limiting ourselves simply to the more obvious implications of this passage, we may recognize five major affirmations:

1. The old humanity is inseparable from its distinctive practices, which fully correspond to the "bondage to decay" as described in Rom., ch. 8. (The parallel passage in Eph. 4:22 strongly suggests that correspondence.)

2. The new humanity is characterized by a continuing renewal in knowledge or, as the Ephesians parallel suggests, in the mind that chooses righteousness and holiness.

3. This choice of one humanity against another, however, is not a matter of private morality, but a matter of choosing a society and a kinship. In one humanity the distinctions between races, religions, cultural and economic classes, remain unbridged and in fact unbridgeable. In the other humanity such divisions have been radically transcended and overcome.

4. The new solidarity of the new mankind conforms to the image of God, an image in the direction of which the renewal causes it to move.

5. This image (a corporate image, let us remember) is the image of Christ, who himself is in all; he is the indwelling principle and the power by which cohesion and renewal are realized. His is the new nature, which has been "put on" by those who belong to him, the mark of this fact being the renewed act of putting on this new nature, "created after the likeness of God" (Eph. 4:24). The character of the new humanity is thus defined by reference to God's activity in Christ, as this activity becomes operative in and through social relationships, and as it becomes effective in the moral decisions of each renewed mind.

A more thoroughgoing description of the position of Jesus Christ as the new Man is provided by two passages: Rom., ch. 5, and I Cor., ch. 15. In both passages he is *a* man and *Man;* he is himself a person and as this person he is the first fruit of that humanity which is created in him and for him. In both passages, the new humanity is described in terms of his role as the second or [56] last **Adam.** The old or the first humanity is represented in and by its progenitor.

As sin came into the world through one man and death through sin, and so death spread to all men because all men sinned. (Rom. 5:12.)

Jesus Christ, like Adam, is "one man." As in the case of the first Adam, the destiny of all men is determined by, in, and through him. But in his case this destiny is "the free gift in grace" which leads to "acquittal and life." All who receive his grace "reign in life through the one man Jesus Christ." [4] This new humanity has been created in the event of his death and resurrection.

As by a man came death, by a man has come also the resurrection of the dead. For as in Adam all die, so also in Christ shall all be made alive. (I Cor. 15:21-22.)

Other men, it is clear, enter into this new humanity when this death-and-resurrection of Christ becomes operative for them. And when is that? The answer is not simple, for it is not a matter of chronological dates but of divine creation. The *when* includes the event on Golgotha, the event of their own dying with Christ, and the event of the redemption of their body. (Rom. 8:23.) This *when* is not determined by the quantitative measurement of decades or centuries but by the qualitative response to "the mind which you have in Christ Jesus." It is this mind which grasps the present moment as the moment when the image of God in the form of a servant produces a movement from one humanity to another.

The dimensions of this transformation as it affects the destiny of the individual are outlined graphically in Rom., chs. 6 to 8. Here death and life are seen as the substance of every decision and act. The old humanity is a community where sin reigns, where law is quite ineffective to do anything but to increase sin's tyranny, and where men's bodies become weapons of sin by the use of which death's claim is ratified. But men can now choose not to be united to the first Adam in a death like his, but to be united to the second

Adam in a death like his. (Rom. 6:5.) Accepting as their own the death of this last Adam, they receive the gift of grace, which enables them in this new humanity to " live to God." Thus to become alive to God and to receive through death his gift of grace is quite impossible except by becoming one with this one new Man and by taking one's place in his humanity.

The proof that this transition transforms the inherited status of societal groups as well as that of individuals is shown by the demolition of what in the ancient culture was the strongest wall of all: " you Gentiles " versus " the commonwealth of Israel."

He has broken down the dividing wall of hostility so that he might create in himself one new man in the place of the two. (Eph. 2:14-15.)

We cannot, therefore, avoid the conclusion that, at least to Paul and his circle in the early period, the Christian community as a whole and in all its parts was viewed as a new creation and a new humanity. This creation appears as the image of God, an image perfectly embodied in Jesus Christ who is the " man of heaven " (I Cor. 15:49), whose image all will bear, and into whose image those who belong to him are already being transformed, from one degree of glory to another (II Cor. 3:18).

It is probable that in the first generation of Christianity a complex fusion took place between the pictures of Jesus as the heavenly Man, as the last Adam, and as [57] the Son of Man. About the exact stages in this process there is endless controversy, which often comes to a focus on two major problems. On the one hand, did Jesus understand himself as the Son of Man, and if so, what was the precise content of that understanding? On the other hand, what were the specific origins and meanings of this phrase and its related Messianic terms? The purpose of our present study does not require the resolution of all these controversies, although they, of course, remain important. We can take the New Testament writings as they stand, without reconstructing all the stages in this mode of conceptualizing history. And we can try to summarize the more certain ecclesiological implications of the Christological imagery. We use the term " imagery " because we have to deal not with agreed-upon titles of clearly defined offices, the various titles being mutually exclusive, but with flexible pictures of a single person, pictures that expressed with varying degrees of success the salvation that his people received in and through him. Because they recognized in him the new creation of a new humanity, or because, in alternative idiom, they hailed in him the inauguration of God's Kingdom, they were naturally more eclectic in their vocabulary than modern theologians can readily tolerate.

The Gospel stories of the work of the Son of Man, taken as wholes, still constitute the most adequate definitions of what that term connoted for the Christian community. In those stories we may discern four recurrent emphases, none of which may be deleted without destroying the integrity of the Gospel portrait.

1. As described by the Gospels, *the Son of Man proclaimed among men the Kingdom of God*. He had been given authority from God to do this. Implicit in this authority (e.g., in forgiving sins and casting out Satan) was a celestial commission; he came from God bearing with him the powers of the Kingdom of God. The majesty and glory that impelled his signs and works, showing through those signs at selected moments (e.g., the transfiguration), linked his work to that of Moses, Elijah, and the prophets, and also to the coming of Final Judgment and redemption. His pre-existence and his postexistence were both implicit in the heavenly origin of his mission.[5] As such he was not a solitary figure unrelated to Israel, but God's chief agent in fulfilling his promises to his people.

2. As pictured throughout the New Testament, *the Son of Man was representative of the many*. He came "emphatically human, deliberately provincial, Galilean" (Boris Pasternak). As a man he was far lower than the angels and shared the temptations and weaknesses of his kin and kind. He came eating and drinking, laughing and talking with his companions of the day. This ordinary role was everywhere considered as necessary to the fulfillment of God's assignment, everywhere viewed not as contradicting his prior and later exaltation, but as embodying it fully.

3. As pictured throughout the New Testament, *the Son of Man* not only took the form of a slave, but he *carried the slave's obedience so far as to die for others*. As the Gospels express it, "the Son of Man must suffer." He came "to seek and to save the lost" and he accomplished this mission supremely in his death. His Passion was the climax and fulfillment of his work as the Son of Man. Virtually

every image of the church in the New Testament reflects the impact of this event: the death was the hidden locus of the world's regeneration.

4. As *the Son of Man,* Jesus *established in and through his obedience a community of the end time.* This new community emerged in the Gospels, in the calling of disciples to share his sufferings and death, and in the covenantal drinking with them of his cup. (Cf. [10]) New Testament writers differ in the precise formulation of how the Son of Man actually had become the "inclusive representative" of God's people. Paul's use of the cosmological thought of the last Adam is one formulation. The Letter to the Hebrews described in terms of Ps. 8:4 the way in which the Son of Man had become one with those whom he sanctified. (Heb. 2:6; cf. [69]) [6] In the Gospel of John the vision of angels descending and ascending upon the Son of Man probably is meant to identify Jesus with Jacob as the ancestor of Israel. (John 1:51.) Throughout the Gospel of John, the term "Son of Man" "retains the sense of one who incorporates in himself the people of God." [7]

In the debates that have raged over the history of this title one fact has frequently been obscured. I refer to the fact that in all of the major conjectured anticipations of New Testament usage the term had included a strongly corporate reference. This was obviously true of the image of the Suffering Servant in Isaiah and of the "saints of the Most High" in Daniel. It was also true of the prophetic use in Ezekiel and of the apocalyptic use in I Enoch. It was equally true of the ancient Iranian myths of the primal man, the *Urmensch,* and of the contemporary rabbinic speculations concerning *Adam.* It was especially true of the various Gnostic myths of the heavenly redeemer. We do not wish to say that the New Testament thought about Jesus as the Son of Man was nothing but an undiscerning hodgepodge of eclectic speculation. We are not avoiding controversy by saying a blessing on all your houses. We do want to say, however, that regardless of the issue of its origins, there lies behind the use of the term in the New Testament a recognition, common to all writers, of the *ultimate* significance of Jesus' work as a suffering, exalted Son of Man, and that this significance carried immediate relevance to the heirs of his Kingdom and final relevance to the origin and destiny of all men. [8]

[58] The Kingdom of God

In the Gospels the mission of Jesus as the Son of Man was comprehended as that of inaugurating God's Kingdom and of bringing it
to fulfillment. This image, in turn, is viewed throughout as a category that parallels the idioms of a new creation and a new humanity.
The fact of parallelism can be most readily underlined by observing
the multiple correspondences between the pictures of the Kingdom
and the Genesis accounts of Creation. These accounts suggest an
order that in the main we will follow.

The Kingdom of God comes as God's creation of a new heaven
and a new earth. It represents the moving of God's Spirit, ordering
and overcoming the enveloping chaos. Here again the Word of God
speaks: " Let there be light "; this light marks the beginning of the
" Day " in which men live as sons of the light. (Cf. [63]) He calls
into being trees and plants. He makes man in his image and gives
him dominion over all the earth. He rests on the Sabbath Day, hal-
lows it, and by implication commands men to enter into this same
Rest. (Cf. [60]) He places man in a garden with the tree of life and
with rivers irrigating the land. (Cf. [66]) He gives to man the power
to name all creatures and to rule them. (Cf. [64]) He also gives to
man a bride, Eve to Adam. (Cf. [23]) The Genesis story is familiar,
of course, but not so familiar as the same story as told in the New
Testament to describe the new creation, which is the Kingdom of
God. To be sure, in the New Testament it is not told as a single story
by a single writer, but some facet of the story appears in virtually
every New Testament book. The writers were not interested in developing an elaborate typology, forcing every item in the Genesis
story to yield its tribute, but they were quite convinced that the Genesis narrative provided an appropriate analogy for revealing the cosmic newness of God's Kingdom in Christ.

In contemporary cultures, to be sure, other visions of the end of
history had been compacted of elements that demonstrated a return
to the primal state of things. In Jewish apocalyptic, Christians found
close at hand a congenial language in which expectations of the coming day were expressed in terms of paradise restored. The New
Testament descriptions of God's Kingdom, however, place the accent
quite differently. Here the end was both like and unlike the beginning precisely as a *new beginning*. The last man is a first-born in

whom a new mankind has its image and solidarity. He has already come and his new creation is an event taking place in the midst of daily routine. From the beginning of the gospel as outlined in Mark, ch. 1, the Kingdom was announced as a force that had already been set in motion toward men. It was in their search for images to describe the experienced reality of life in the new society that disciples found the Genesis accounts helpful. Just as the first Adam corresponded to the last Adam, so there was a correspondence between the story of how God had granted dominion to Adam and the story of how he granted a new kingdom to his kingly servant the Messiah. Each story tells of the beginning of an age that embraced in cosmic terms the character of human society in that age.

There were, of course, decisive differences between these two beginnings, and these were not overlooked. We have noted that the apostle could not compare Christ to Adam without indicating the " how much more " of the last Adam. (Rom., ch. 5.) So too the concept of the Kingdom of God required and provided a way for contrasting the new and the old, contrasts that involved the whole of time and space. We should now examine some of these comparisons in detail.

1. Throughout the New Testament the Kingdom of God was understood in antithesis to its enemy, the kingdom of Satan. The two kingdoms embraced the only two possibilities confronting men. The beginning of the new Kingdom was traced to the victory by Christ over Satan. This victory was accessible to all who would enlist in the same battle and use the same weapons. The community therefore thought of itself as a company of soldiers, [59] fighters against Satan. Their existence was bounded by the course of this dramatic and victorious struggle. Wherever the Kingdom of God came, there this warfare was joined. " If I by the finger of God cast out Satan, then is the kingdom of God come upon you." Between the two kingdoms there could be no compromise or appeasement. The power of God's Kingdom forced man to a radical and final choice between two armies and their two commanders. It was obvious that Christ's soldiers must use the weapons that he provided. (Eph., ch. 5.) To don those weapons was precisely the same as to " put on " the new Man and " put off " the old. (Cf. [26], [55])

This understanding of life in the context of this celestial struggle was rooted in the Genesis story of the Fall, as that episode had been interpreted by apocalyptic seers. Satan had been present and active in the Garden in the form of the tempting and accusing serpent. The same foe had asserted his power in the wilderness of temptation and in the Gethsemane struggle, as well as in every decisive work of the new Adam. To follow this new leader required constant and recurrent participation by the band of disciples in the same temptations and offenses. At the inception of one kingdom, Satan had succeeded by deceit in establishing his reign of sin and death; at the inception of the other Kingdom, Christ had succeeded in replacing the order of deception and futility with the order of truth and life. The two kingdoms, therefore, had similar beginnings, but they were as disparate as the treachery and the faithfulness of the men who represented two humanities.[9]

2. Another analogical connection between the new order and the old was provided by the early Christian description of God's Kingdom as the institution of God's [60] Sabbath, God's Rest. The Genesis story had suggested the creation of the Sabbath as the end of God's work; Jewish apocalyptic had visualized the advent of God's Kingdom as a sabbatical year or as the new Sabbath; the New Testament writers introduced the Son of Man as the Lord of the Sabbath, who therefore asserted his authority over the Sabbath and who gave his disciples access to a community that existed in constant nearness to the Heavenly Rest, freed from the laws of the Sabbath that had characterized the old creation. Here again the Kingdom of God represented a new destiny that was manifested in a new beginning and that linked together the victorious grace of the last Adam and the responding faith of those whom he called into his Rest. By thus instituting a new Sabbath, the divine origin of the first Sabbath was recognized, both its fulfillment and abolition were asserted, and vital interaction was established between every day and the Day of the Lord. Henceforth, whether the faithful continued to observe the Sabbaths or viewed all days alike, their mind was oriented in gratitude to the Lord who had made all things clean and holy. (Rom. 14:1-4.) In their use of the image of the Sabbath there thus developed a symbolism of time that served to articulate the multiple relations between the works and Rest of God and the works and Rest of his people.[10]

3. The Kingdom of God idiom included another temporal symbolism to express both the similarity and the contrast between the new and the old. This was the notion of two ages, God's Kingdom as [61] **the coming age,** of which the church recognized itself as the heir. This picture was based on the assumption that every community and every man was to be understood by the time which it had received from its lord. The kingdoms of God and of Satan both had beginnings; they were of comparable magnitudes; both sought the allegiance of men and societies. But only the kingdom of Satan had an end; the Kingdom of God has no end. The one kingdom was described variously as the old age, the former things, the world that dies and passes away. Conversely, the other Kingdom appeared as the new age, the latter things, the world that comes. Both ages are inherently universal categories, i.e., they pervade and permeate the whole scope of created reality. But the new age is both more primal and more final.[11]

One is the realm where fears, anxieties, and cares reign, where the delight in riches is matched by the futility of such delight, and where all the works of darkness are absorbed into an encompassing and pervasive death. The other consists of the fruits and works of the Spirit: forgiveness, righteousness, peace, joy, and hope.[12] Thus the meaning of the two ages precisely parallels the meaning of the two creations and the two humanities. All these idioms offer a picture of the point where the two orders meet, and of the way of transition from one to the other. The two ages meet wherever the sovereignties of their two kings meet or wherever their sons meet. The mode of transition is everywhere explicated by reference to the story of Jesus. The word of the Gospel exerts the power to orient every human decision toward the claims of the rival kings.

As described in the Gospels the appearance of the king of God's realm offered a challenge to his rival king and provoked a counterattack. He proclaimed both judgment and forgiveness for the sons of the evil one. Through the Messiah the narrow way was opened that leads to life. What had been impossible became possible through his power. He came as the harvester, the collector of rents, the scourge of demons, and the shepherd who gathered again the scattered flock. The two ages therefore met and diverged whenever man entered his service and his army. Having been drawn out of the age that was passing away, they now had their hearts and doings oriented toward the coming age. They presented their bodies as a living sacrifice. Their conformity to the past was broken, and their mind was continually renewed. But this continuing metamorphosis took place on the frontier of the two ages, where each refugee left everything behind as he fled through the curtain of death. Out of the call to carry the cross emerged a community that was bound together and to its King by the common burden. It was in Jesus that they shared with one another in the " tribulation and the kingdom and the patient endurance " (Rev. 1:9).

There is no doubt that the cluster of pictures that centered in God's Kingdom all add to the sense of the mysterious magnitude of that Kingdom, as a reality whose ontological ultimacy is expressed by its eschatological finality. (I Cor. 15:28; Heb. 12:28.) This is a realm of majestic power that precipitates conflict with the realm of Satan and brings that conflict to a triumphant conclusion. This power wields a sword that cuts through all existing human communities and creates a community that is radically different from all other communities. When one asks how this new human community is related to the Kingdom of God, the basic answer is relatively simple. Just as the new creation and the new humanity bear the image of Christ, so too the heirs of the Kingdom of God are related to that Kingdom by its King. The Kingdom of God, where God is all in all, is the source and goal of the Kingdom of Christ. (I Cor. 15:28; Eph. 5:5.) He is the King; his people are its sons and heirs, his subjects and citizens.

The story of how this Kingdom manifested itself among men is the basic theme of the Gospel of Mark. The good news began with God's decision to complete and to fulfill his promise. He anointed Jesus as king, as son, and as prophet, by the descent of the Holy Spirit. The Spirit immediately propelled him into conflict with Satan. In the midst of this conflict he proclaimed the news of God's victory and called men to enter the Kingdom by repentance and faith. As chief fisherman, he called others and trained them as fishermen. Through him, the authority of God acted redemptively in the exorcism of demons, the cleansing of lepers, the forgiveness of sins, the establishment of tablefellowship with publicans and sinners, the spreading of joy and freedom among his companions, the binding of Beelzebub, and the creating of a new family composed of those who do the will of God.

The relation between God's Kingdom and its heirs was described by stories of successive episodes, whether in Mark or in the other Gospels, but the description was thoroughly consistent with more direct affirmations in the letters. The heirs of the Kingdom were the despised, the poor, the meek, the hungry, the helpless, and the persecuted; but these heirs became rich and blessed, beloved and joyful in the Kingdom of their Father.[13] They were invited to the marriage feast and they came from east and west to join the patriarchs at God's banquet table. (Cf. [24]) As they came under the authority of this new King they received a portion of his authority. The receipt of this authority appeared to be quite inseparable from the commission to exercise it in proclamation, in judgment, in forgiveness, in healing, and in allowing the presence of the Kingdom to determine their total behavior. Whenever " righteousness, joy, and peace in the Holy Spirit " controlled their social relationships, there the Kingdom of God was at work. (Rom. 14:17.)

It is important in our reflections on the relation between the church and the Kingdom of God to retain the priority of New Testament thinking. From every standpoint the Kingdom of God retained its essential priority over the human community. Thought must therefore move primarily in one direction: from the Kingdom of God to the heirs and sons of that Kingdom. And this thought must itself be informed and controlled by the perspective and norms of the Kingdom. The only significant comprehension of the church will be a comprehension that views the human community within its native habitat, within the context of God's Kingdom, within the horizons of the new age and the new world. To be sure, the images of Kingdom and of the people of God are not everywhere coterminous, but they can nowhere be separated. There are places where a New Testament writer appears to identify the church and the Kingdom, and other places where distinctions are drawn between the two. But this need not produce confusion if, before one thinks " church," he has already thought " the Kingdom of God," or if one makes the ecclesiological term the predicate in a sentence the subject of which is the theological term. This suggestion may be further illustrated by the other idioms in which certain aspects of the Kingdom are applied to the being of the church.

4. In many passages in the New Testament the idea of God's Kingdom almost coalesces with the idea of his [62] glory. One instance is the passage where Paul exhorts the Thessalonian congregation to "lead a life worthy of God, who calls you into his own Kingdom and glory" (I Thess. 2:12). But Paul was not alone in making this correlation. It is a basic component of all early Christian thinking about "the kingdom, the power, and the glory." God's Kingdom is the embodiment of his glory. But such a statement is meaningless apart from a perception of the meaning of glory (*doxa*).

This word has a long and complicated history with multiple nuances that can never be wholly disentangled, in part because of the mysterious depth of its reference.[14] Long before the coming of Christ, the Hebrew prophets and sages had adopted it as a central category for describing both God and men, thereby referring not to their external appearance but to their innermost being. For them, nothing was more eternal, substantial, or powerful than God's glory. Wherever God engaged in creative or redemptive activity, there his glory manifested itself. Thus Johannes Pedersen, expounding the Genesis sagas, can speak of God's glory as "Yahweh himself, as he appears in all his greatness and might." This word designated "the soul in its highest manifestation of power." "Honor and glory in particular are terms frequently used of the soul of Yahweh as it manifests itself and acts among mankind."[15] The word thus came to refer to God's very being, his aliveness, his powerful activity, his mysterious majesty. When man beheld God he beheld his glory. (Acts 7:55; Rev. 15:8.) When God revealed himself, he manifested his glory. Thus everything that he did was a doxophany, a disclosure of that realm of light and life which constituted his eternal Kingdom. The act of creating man and the act of raising him from the dead were both such doxophanies.

The next step was also very important to Biblical thinking. Whenever God manifested his glory, he conferred glory upon those who received and beheld it. God's glory existed to be shared. And every act of sharing, every doxophany, was intended to lead to a reciprocal act, a doxology, the act of glorifying the giver of glory. "He who receives increases the honor of the giver by acknowledging that he receives." "God has the honor within himself, but through his hymns of praise man renders him honor, strengthens and increases it. . . . Yahweh is enthroned on the hymns of praise of Israel." [16] The glory of God thus was conceived in its wholeness as including doxophany and doxology within a single circle.[17]

It is this circle which was embodied and completed in Jesus Christ. In him was manifested "the glory of our great God" (Titus 2:13). He was the doxophany: whoever has seen him has seen the Father (John 12:45; 14:9; Matt. 11:27). He was also the doxology: "I glorified thee on earth, having accomplished the work which thou gavest me to do" (John 17:4). He therefore was given a body of glory, the spiritual body of the resurrection (I Cor., ch. 15); he ascended a throne of glory, from which he will come in the glory of his Father. His work as king of the new age was therefore rightly described as the way of glory. Through him God glorified his new creation, and the new creation was united by him in glorifying God. (Rev., chs. 5; 6.)

This new creation in the image of God proceeded by way of redemptive conflict with that creation which, having refused to glorify God as God, has become "drunk with self-glorification." [18] It had exchanged the glory of God for the glory of the world. It had enthroned the devil by giving creatures the ultimate sovereignty and majesty. The glory of the Son was therefore embodied in his redemption of other sons from this competing sovereignty. In this work he displayed a far higher degree of God's glory than had been manifested in Moses and the Law. The people of God now beheld the glory of the Lord and in so doing they were changed into his image, a difference as great as that between death and life. (II Cor. 3:7-18.)

Here, then, we discover another profoundly cosmic context for thought about the character of the people of God. They received in Christ the glory of God. And in this gift a pattern of power was released in which we may detect the same components that have already been mentioned.

a. God revealed his glory to the church, and in so doing, shared it with the church.

b. The reception and the sharing took the form of glorifying God by doing the work that he assigned to it, by doing everything to the glory of God.

c. This work of glorifying God proceeded in conflict with the effort of the devil to gain glory and power. This conflict meant that glory for the church was inseparable from the church's participation in the humiliation and suffering of its Lord.

d. During its warfare on earth the church was being transformed from one degree of glory to another, every temporal sacrifice becoming "an eternal weight of glory."

e. The end of this transformation was the inheritance of a body of glory — incorruptible, imperishable, and eternal. (I Cor., ch. 15.)

f. The consummation of the doxophonic-doxological circle would ultimately embrace the whole creation, and therefore mark the final victory over death and the devil.

g. The life and work of the church already was a means by which this coming triumph of the cross was proclaimed to "principalities and powers in the heavenly places" — a clear index to the church's present status as sharing in the heavenly authority of Christ.

This summary of the church's involvement in the realm of glory illustrates what we have already noted about the difficulty in defining what the church is per se and where its boundaries lie. The church derives its glory from a realm that invades it: it expresses its glory by casting crowns before the throne of another. It is neither the whole circle of glory nor merely a segment of it. It is neither the center nor the circumference. Yet its proper being, the core of this humanity, consists of this glory. Because of this substantial definition of its existence, the church is always under the constraint to become what it is. The indicative "God has glorified thee" is the ground for the imperative "Give glory to Him." The truth in these two modes is realized at the point where in spite of the *gloria mundi* the church accepts the form of a servant as its own. This servant, the church is always reminded, "did not consider God's glory as something to be grasped, but emptied himself." Only so could this servant become the judge of all self-glory, which takes the form of a will to power. (Cf. [78])

5. In Biblical language, the glory of God's Kingdom was coextensive with his [63] light. In both Testaments this light was a way of depicting God's creative work. The creation of light marked (or

even preceded) the dawning of the first day. In Christ the new Day dawned, for he was none other than the " light of the world." In the perfected creation of the end time there would be no need for sun or lamp because the glory of God would serve as its light and the Lamb would be its lamp. (Rev. 21:22-24; 22:5.) All nations would walk by this light. Light was therefore one of the powers that constituted this community and set it off from the kingdom of Satan.

First, we may note the more explicit applications of this metaphor to the company of Jesus' followers: " You are the light of the world " (Matt. 5:14). Similar assertions are found both in other Synoptics (Luke 16:8) and in Paul: " You shine as lights in the world " (Phil. 2:15). They are found both in the letters universally attributed to Paul (I Thess. 5:5) and in these often called secondarily Pauline: " You are light in the Lord " (Eph. 5:8). They are found both in historical narratives — " I have set you to be a light for the Gentiles " (Acts 13:47) — and in liturgical formularies — " out of darkness into his marvelous light " (I Peter 2:9). Some writings stress the inward transformation wrought by the light (II Cor. 4:6); others, the outward mission of the light bearers in and for the world (Acts 26:18, 23; I Peter 2:9). It is possible to interpret some of the references as being addressed to individual believers quite apart from the community (e.g., Matt. 5:14-16 is often applied in a moralistic way to personal behavior), but in other passages the community is clearly in mind: " The seven lampstands are the seven churches " (Rev. 1:20; 2:1, 5). It is also possible to link the light image to the distinctive work of apostles (Acts 13:47), but the more frequent reference is to all the sons of the day (I Thess. 5:5; Eph. 5:8), to all who follow Christ (John 8:12).

In all its uses the image of the light presupposes and reinforces the unity of the church. There is but one light, often set over against the one darkness. (II Cor. 4:6; I Peter 2:9.) This light has but one source: it is the light of God's glory, the light that the Savior is and sends. When this light shines in men's hearts it communicates not only a knowledge of God's glory but also fellowship in the light as a common inheritance. (Col. 1:12; I John, chs. 1; 2.) All who receive this new inheritance should recall vividly their previous residence in the night,[19] and should recognize the incompatibility of the light with the darkness. (II Cor. 6:14; I John 1:5-10.) This light which is received through the gospel produces an abundant variety of fruits, which elsewhere are attributed to the Holy Spirit and to the new humanity: love, freedom from slavery to the flesh, " all that is good and right and true," "holding fast the word of life," mutual encouragement and edification, and vigorous work in bringing the light to those who sit in darkness.[20] On the one hand, all these fruits enhance the inner cohesion of the community, because the possession of the light carries its own compulsions to believe in it by walking therein. (John 12:33, 36.) On the other hand, these fruits qualify the church to live as a city on a hilltop (Matt. 5:14-16), to shine in the darkness, and to transform it. This, therefore, became a cogent way of describing the witness and the service of the church. Light is given from the Father of light to the sons of light (I Thess. 5:5; John 12:35) so that they may serve as harbingers of eternal day to all who are blind or dead.[21]

This idiom, so descriptive of the unique character of the church, appears in no fewer than nineteen New Testament writings and in all the major traditions of the early church. It draws upon all the major religious idioms of the ancient Oriental world (e.g., the Old Testament, rabbinic, apocalyptic, Essenic, Hermetic, Gnostic), and it reorients them all around the gospel events and the gospel task. It is even more ubiquitous and more subtly influential than many themes such as the body of Christ or the bride of Christ, which dominate ecclesiological controversy today. But it is quite wrong to set these images over against each other because the image of light is fused with all the other major patterns of thought. What happens in the study of light as an image has happened often in our preliminary exploration: the affiliations of one image lead us in many directions until we are confronted with all the others.[22]

6. One affiliation, for example, is that which links together the Kingdom, the glory, and the light with [64] the name. God's name bears his full authority and power, extending his majesty over his works and carrying his blessing to all who bear it. The prophet John was drawing upon a vast reservoir of meanings when he promised the faithful congregation that they would receive the name of God, the new name of Jesus Christ, and the " name of the city of my God " (Rev. 3:12). An ultimate kinship was represented by the sharing of the same name. When men were baptized they were baptized into

Christ or into the name of Christ, not into the church. It was true of both the person's name and the community's name (ch. 2:17; 21:12) that identity, selfhood, and destiny were vested in the name that is given by God, whether the name of the Beast (ch. 13:17), of Babylon (ch. 17:5), or of Jerusalem. Upon those whom he *named* apostles and those whom he *named* brothers, Christ conveyed a corresponding set of communal obligations. (Luke 6:13; I Cor. 5:11.) All the powers and functions of leadership were presumably carried out in the name of the Lord. (Matt. 7:22.) Every child was to be received in his name. (Ch. 18:5.) Every activity of the church was encircled by prepositional phrases: in, on, upon, through, on account of, into, in behalf of, for, by *the name*. The community whose life was thus bracketed stood under the permanent power of the name of Him who had called it into existence. Name and glory interpenetrated each other, whether thought turned toward the community of men or toward him in whose name every knee would bow.[23] The use of *a* name to designate the church was very rare in the New Testament (e.g., Christians, Nazarenes); much more frequent and adequate as a symbol of the church was the name that Christ himself had shared with it.[24] Whether we deal with God's name or his Kingdom, we are soon forced to deal with the term [65] life.

7. To share the name of God and of his Son was to share their life. (Rev. 3:1; John 20:31.) God's life was understood to be the source and measure of eternal life for man. His Kingdom was so closely identified with his life that the Gospel question "What must I do to inherit eternal life?" is equivalent to "What must I do to enter the Kingdom of God?" (Matt. 19:16). The Fourth Gospel could freely substitute the one category for the other. This life was clearly identified, also, with the new Man and the coming age, where the Son of Man gives life freely to all who belong to him. The church was therefore related to life through the same person who related it to the coming age. He who is life shares it more and more abundantly with all who know him. (John 17:13.)

While it may be denied, with justification, that life is an image, it can hardly be denied that life is constitutive of the church as the apostles viewed it. And there are many various ways for suggesting the intrinsically communal dimension of the life that God shares with men. Thus the prophet John speaks of those whose names are written in the book of life. In I Peter, members of the community are described as fellow heirs of the grace of life (I Peter 3:7). *Colossians* speaks forcefully of Christ as " *our life* " (Col. 3:3), and *Ephesians* views all outsiders as estranged from God's life (Eph. 4:18; 2:12). Behind these expressions one may discern a common conviction: in its relation to Christ, the community is related to God's eternal life. Outside such relationship the church ceases to be the church. That this life is related in analogical fashion to what ordinarily is meant by the word is indicated by the fact that this life begins in death, whereas other life ends in death. Eternal life is sufficiently similar to the more ordinary meaning of the term to justify use of the same word. But it is sufficiently different also to remind us of its metaphorical character. It is as figurative as the other pictures that we have found to be related to the new creation — the new man, the last Adam, the Sabbath Rest, light, glory, and the name. And it is as corporate as the others. It stresses the unity of all who receive it, as well as their distance from those who live in death.[25]

The association between the new community and God's life is portrayed with visual and symbolic power in the image of [66] **the tree of life,** which stands at the center of God's Holy City. If we look for a simple identification of the church with this tree, we will, of course, not find it; but if we ask whether other images of the church (e.g., the city, the temple, both strongly ecclesiological, as we have seen [47], [48]) are qualified by the presence of the tree of life, the answer will be strongly positive. This is most evident in Rev. 22:1-5. Here the prophet describes the city of God as irrigated and cleansed by the river of the water of life, which flows from the celestial throne. Growing along the banks of the river is the fruit-bearing tree of life, with its perpetual harvest of twelve kinds of fruit. Its leaves are efficacious for the healing of the nations. This tree makes eternal life available universally. Such life is characterized by the perfect sovereignty of God, by the perpetual worship of the community, by unending light, by the continuing vision of God, by permanent identity with his name, by unqualified victory. All this is to say that the covenant that has been sealed by God and the Lamb will produce perfect communal relations among men and among all the nations of men. Because each symbol in this picture bears manifold meanings, no brief summary can include them all; we have suggested only a few of the more assured emphases.

Implicitly, yet quite certainly, this view of final fellowship is related to the tree of life in the Garden of Eden. (Rev. 2:7; cf. [53]) The assurance of eating fruit from this tree is given to every believer or church that conquers in the earthly warfare. This tree had been planted in the Garden for the sake of Adam and Eve (Gen. 2:9) who had been free to eat of it. But their sin had impelled God to drive them out of the Garden, to cut them off from the tree of life. The seer visualizes a holy city in which that curse, with all its dread entailment, has been removed. (Rev. 22:3.) His word to the congregation at Ephesus links the inner decision of that congregation to this New Jerusalem. By faith the parish at Ephesus eats fruit from the tree of life, a tree that stands both at the beginning and at the end of creation as the symbol of God's gracious purposes and power. By faith the results of Adam's sin have been overcome in the results of Christ's love.

In the later pictorial art of the church, the tree of life became a prominent motif. Often the tree was pictured as growing out of Jesse's loins, showing how readily Christians identified it with the root of Jesse, i.e., with Jesus Christ. This correlation does not appear explicitly in the New Testament, but there may be found within the New Testament itself three further correlations. (a) The fact that some writers came to picture Jesus in his death as hanging from a tree may indicate the fusion in their minds between the cross and the tree of life. (b) The symbol of the tree was closely connected to the symbol of the lampstand. In early synagogue art the seven-branch candlestick was often depicted as a tree with seven branches. (c) The tree of life and the lampstand are both associated with the olive tree in Rev. 11:4-13. Here the olive trees represent the prophetic witness, the prophetic victory, and the conjunction of death and life in their work.[26]

Thus the tree of life conveyed a shifting pattern of associations which exerted an important influence upon the perception of how God's life indwells and sustains the witnessing community, the tempted but triumphant church. Although the mode of expression makes it difficult for us to reduce the perception to any set of prosaic definitions, it is clear that God's life is constitutive of his city and that this life is a profoundly corporate reality that links every historical epoch to the beginning and to the end. By itself the figure of the tree is only of minor significance, but the life is undoubtedly of ultimate significance, and the visualization of this life as a tree shows how imaginative the whole pattern of thought was.

8. Inseparable from the same network of eschatological symbols was the conception of the church as the [67] communion in the Holy Spirit. One popular way of expressing this is to speak of Pentecost (Acts, ch. 2) as the birthday of the church. This location of the birthday is to some degree erroneous. The book of The Acts does not use this term. Unless many of the images thus far surveyed are totally false, we should not think of the church as coming into existence for the first time on the one Day of Pentecost. Nevertheless, the picture of God, pouring out his Spirit and fire upon all flesh in fulfillment of Joel's prophecy, rightly stresses the church's dependence upon this gift of God for its unity, its mission, its power, and its worship. To be sure, *the Spirit* is no metaphor, but Biblical writers made free use of metaphors to signify its presence. The writer of The Acts no doubt had a typological analogy in mind — the contrast between the confusion of tongues and the fragmentation of community at Babel.[27] Other writers associated the movement of the Spirit with the wind, its descent with the dove, its judgment with the sword, its purifying power with the fire. The Spirit was active not only in the birth and baptism of the Messiah but also in the birth and baptism of all the sons of God. It was active not only in the creation of the church but also in producing all those fruits which signified the continuing creation.

This dependence of the community on the Spirit is often recognized by considering as a definition of the church the apostolic benediction: " The grace of the Lord Jesus Christ, the love of God, the communion of [*koinōnia*] the Holy Spirit " (II Cor. 13:14). We have seen and we will notice subsequently many images that articulate the work of the Spirit among men (e.g., the sanctification of the saints, cf. [69]), and when we come to expound the term " the body of Christ " we will observe the virtual equivalence of the phrases " one body " and " one spirit." (Cf. [89]) Here, then, it may be sufficient simply to underscore two accents that radiate through New Testament thought. (*a*) Reference to the Spirit is always thoroughly eschatological. Wherever the Spirit moves there is detected God's new creation of the new humanity. Wherever the powers of the Spirit draw men within the realm of God's Kingdom, there the new age comes. This life-giving Spirit makes men sons of God and sharers in God's eternal glory and life. The community that is created by this Spirit becomes a partnership in the epoch of consummation, receiving the first fruits of that epoch and bearing within itself the pledge of the redemption of all things. (*b*) This image of the Spirit as the substance and power of the eschatological realm expresses the conviction of ontological reality. This is the same Spirit that brooded over the face of the waters in the beginning, the same heavenly purpose and power that are implicit in the foreknowledge and preexistence of the sons of God. As shareholders in the one Spirit, Christians are linked to the creative word and power of God. Their dependence on the Spirit is total; by this dependence their life in space and time receives the stamp of transcendence, both primal and final.

9. Among the communal marks of the Spirit's activity, none was more strongly emphasized in the New Testament than [68] **the bond of love.** Whether or not this term is a pictorial one, its value in describing the church should not be denied. Because it was so frequently part of the content of the images of the new creation, all those images must be interpreted as simply, as concretely, and as corporately as love. Because they are so frequently linked to love, it must be interpreted as imaginatively, as subtly, and as radically as they. In New Testament thought the Kingdom of God is coextensive with God's love. To be sure, when theologians seek to deal with cosmic ultimates they often ignore love as such an ultimate, and when moralists seek to expound the duties and works of human love they, too, often pass over any thought of love as having metaphysical weight. But in the New Testament the new creation was considered coterminous with the realm where God's love was in fact extending its power among men. His followers described this creation as proceeding both from and toward the fullness of his love. They detected in the works of love that the Spirit produced a primary key to the mystery of ultimate reality. Consequently, in their thinking about the church as the society wherein Christ's love was being channeled into and through human hearts they were simply drawing the necessary corollaries of a new cosmology and a new anthropology, both

derived from a new theology and a new eschatology. As one index to this fact we observe this: when they sought to distinguish between life and death, glory and shame, the Spirit of God and the spirit of the devil, the two kingdoms, the two ages or the two men, they had recourse, sooner or later, either to Christ's love or to his love operating through his people. (I John, chs. 3; 4.) From this perspective the first and great commandment became far more than a "moral imperative." It was seen as veritably the law that operates with final power throughout the new creation. As such it was a symbol of the Final Judgment and mercy under which the church stands, and of the final power of the Messiah to extend his Lordship over every creature. Those who belong to him, i.e., the church, receive his love, abide in it, and by exercising it allow it to abide in them. As Boris Pasternak has written, "The idea that underlies this is that communion between mortals is immortal, and that the whole of life is symbolic because it is meaningful." [28]

In the next chapter we will review the ecclesiological images that describe further the mutuality produced by this love. There we hope to discover what it is that makes the inner solidarities of this community so distinctive. Before terminating this chapter we may remind the reader once more that the images that we have termed "cosmic" are by no means antagonistic to those which are national and cultic. For example, the glory of the Kingdom of God does not exclude the glories of the kingdom of David. Those who now bear the name of God also bear the name of the City of Jerusalem and of the patriarchs. Oneness in glory and life, in the name and in the Spirit, in the new age and the new humanity — all this characterizes God's people from the beginning. God has done a new thing, he has made all things new. Yes. But all this is in fulfillment of the promise made to his people. It is in faithfulness to God's former covenant that he has sealed a new one. Therefore, each of the universal images must be understood in harmony with the particularistic images. The new age continues to be an order of concrete historicity and contingency, embodied in persons, events, societies. And conversely, the conception of the new society as the twelve tribes or as the temple is faulty unless this concrete particularity is related to its context in the eternal mystery and majesty of God's new creation.

THE FELLOWSHIP IN FAITH

[69] The Common Life of the Sanctified

WHEN THE APOSTLE addressed a letter to the church of God in Corinth he used two phrases that characterized this and other congregations: "to those sanctified in Christ Jesus" and "called [to be] saints" (I Cor. 1:2). His address is typical of a widespread New Testament habit, reflected in no fewer than one hundred passages in eighteen different writings, of speaking of individual members of the church as *saints*. Another tendency is the use of both the noun and the verb in this description, so that when the noun "saints" appears, its content is defined by God's action in sanctifying the company, and when the verb "to be sanctified" is used, the reader knows that the sanctification has as its result the creation of saints. We need not pause to defend the statement that this is one of the most prevalent and characteristic designations for Christians. A glance at any concordance will furnish numerous passages that bespeak almost universal use of the term "saints" in the first century.

Perhaps, however, some evidence should be suggested for the explicit reference to the church as "the saints." The terms, we must admit, are not always interchangeable. The terms "holy one" (*hagios*) and "holy things" were applicable to persons and things that did not directly pertain to the church, and conversely, "ecclesia" could be applied to groups not considered saints. (Acts, ch. 19.) Yet in a large number of cases, to say "the saints" was equivalent to saying "the ecclesia." Moreover, these cases appear in at least seven different writers.[1] Almost never is *hagios* used in the singular as referring only to an individual member of the church. (Rev. 20:6 and 22:11 are

136

rather doubtful exceptions.) Because this connection between the church and the saints is so close, the analysis of the latter term has major ecclesiological significance. And this analysis should include all the words based on this root: holy one or saint, *hagios;* to sanctify, *hagiadzein;* sanctification, *hagiasmos;* holiness, *hagiasunē;* the Holy Spirit, *pneuma hagion.*

The analysis of these terms discloses, first of all, that the life of the saints belongs within the context outlined in the chapter just preceding. As the company of saints, the church is ultimately dependent upon the continuing activity of God. It is in his holiness that the church shares. (Heb. 12:10.) Because he who called is holy, the church must be holy. (I Peter 1:15-16.) To God, the Trisagion of worship is rightly directed. (Rev. 4:8.) The Son of God is also spoken of as *ho hagios,* which might even be translated " the saint." It is regrettable that the English translation could not preserve the links that the Greek suggests between the Christ as the Holy One and the church as holy ones. Only when the translators deal with the Greek verb do they make the line of connection clear: " He who sanctifies [that is, *the* saint] and those who are sanctified [that is, the *saints*] have all one origin " (Heb. 2:11; John 17:19). This process of saint-making is everywhere related to *the* saint's Passion. " We have been sanctified through the offering of the body of Jesus once for all." (Heb. 10:14, 29; 13:12; Eph. 5:26.) It was in his death that the Messiah became in fact our sanctification. (I Cor. 1:30; 6:11.) The dual relation of the saint to the holy Father (John 17:11) and to Christ, the Saint, is a relationship accomplished by the Holy Spirit. Consequently, wherever the church is spoken of as the saints, the power of the Holy Spirit is assumed to be at work within it. The community of saints has been born of the Spirit and baptized into this one Spirit. On this community the Spirit is poured out; within this community as a temple the Spirit dwells. Thus the life of the saints is at every point circumscribed by the Holy Spirit, and determined and empowered by it. In this holiness lies the unity and power of the church. Herein also lies its participation in the new creation, for, as we noted (cf. [54], [55]), the coming of the Spirit signals the coming of the Kingdom and the new creation. Herein also lies the continuity between the saints and the people of God from the beginning, since the first brooding of the Spirit " over the face of the waters." (Gen., ch. 1.) This ecclesiological category, therefore, serves as a useful summary of both our previous chapters.[2]

In the present chapter, however, the focus of our attention falls upon patterns of thought that illuminate the fabric of human relations within the church. Does the church's sainthood or holiness say anything about the structuring of communal activity? What implications for its *ethos* are provided by its partnership (*koinōnia*) in the Holy Spirit? It is clear that everywhere in the New Testament the gift of sainthood is the gift of a task. " Be holy, as I am holy." (I Peter 1:16.) This is one of the central axioms of this community. In Pauline terms, the gift of the Spirit is intended to produce in the saints a daily " walking according to the Spirit." (Rom., ch. 8.) Does the New Testament offer a more specific description than that? This question is embarrassing, for the answer includes virtually the whole of the New Testament. It would not be difficult to show that every demand placed on this community is a demand implied by its status as a fellowship of saints. But time and space will not permit so exhaustive an exposition here. A few representative samplings may, however, suggest the outline of such an answer.

1. The sanctification of the church confers upon it the task of witnessing in the world. Saints are sent by him who sanctified them; this oneness in mission and in love is what unites them under the one name, the one glory, and the one truth. (John 17:18-26.)

2. In this mission to the world, as the book of The Acts pictures it, the Holy Spirit goes before the apostles and " falls on " men, making them saints and compelling other saints to recognize them as such. It is thus that Gentiles are first added to the number, the Holy Spirit erasing " the distinction between us and them." The church is therefore under obligation to accept such new developments and not to add any new requirement to what the Spirit has demanded of the new " saints." (Acts 10:44-47; 11:15-18; 15:6-11.)

3. Within the church, the Spirit that creates saints also confers on them whatever gifts are needed for their equipment in the work of ministry. (Eph. 4:12.) The ordering of the various gifts so that no rivalry and no anarchy will appear is the work of the same Spirit. Because every gift is Spirit-bestowed, every gift is designed " for the common good." Because God apportions the gifts " individually as he wills " the exercise of the gifts must proceed according to the

measure of grace. (I Cor. 12:1-11; Rom. 12:3-9.)

4. The company of saints is fully qualified to provide arbitration when disputes arise, albeit the need for such arbitration indicates a failure to live by the common sanctification. Saints should not defraud one another; they should even be defrauded rather than become involved in disputes that demonstrate the absence of the standards of the Kingdom of God. (I Cor. 6:1-11.)

5. As saints they must regard holiness as something to be "perfected in the fear of God" (II Cor. 7:1), an accomplishment attained daily by presenting their bodies as a holy sacrifice (Rom. 12:1) or by putting on the new humanity (Col. 3:10 f.). To be saints they must act as saints, with compassion, meekness, patience, forgiveness, and love. Perhaps the most inclusive list of actions required of saints is found in I Peter, where every exhortation can be viewed as an inference from the rule "You shall be holy, for I am holy" (I Peter 1:16). Just as there is no use of saint in the singular, so too there is no private or individualistic ethic in the New Testament. Every demand for holiness was a demand placed upon all the saints by him who, in sanctifying them, created a single community with a single mission and gave to that community gifts designed to build up "the common good." To be a saint was to become a participant in this common good, an action requiring of all saints to become what the Spirit had already made them. When this requirement was fulfilled, every action could be judged as a fruit of the Spirit. These fruits supplied the norm of social judgment for the saints; they provided cohesion and growth for the church as a human society.

The Common Life of the Faithful

According to Paul's confession as recorded in The Acts, the Lord Jesus revealed that it is "by faith in me" that men receive "a place among those who are sanctified" (Acts 26:18). No one could express his faith that Jesus is Lord except by the Holy Spirit (I Cor. 12:3), and no one could receive that Spirit except by faith (Gal. 3:2). It was therefore entirely normal for the same congregation to be addressed simultaneously as "saints and faithful brethren" (Col. 1:2). The same term in the Greek (*pistoi*) can be translated by the two nouns "believers" and [70] the faithful.[3] More frequently used was the participial form of the Greek verb: *those who believe*. Very frequent also is a phrase used to indicate the distinctive power of the common faith (*pistis*) over those who believe, indicating that both they and their actions are born of faith and produced by it. Here again the evidence compels the conclusion that such terms as "believers," "the faithful," and "those who have trusted in the name" were often used as inclusive descriptions of the entire community.[4]

When we ask what was the context for such a conception of the church we are turned toward the key convictions of the Gospel. The God who is the object of this community's trust has proved himself absolutely faithful; he is, therefore, the faithful one (*ho pistos*). If he should prove not to be worthy of this trust, the whole structure would collapse.[5] So too, the Messiah in whom the believer's trust is vested is known as the faithful one (*ho pistos*).[6] Belief in this faithful one introduces a person into a family in which he is a son of Abraham (Gal. 3:9) and a pilgrim in the long file of exiles (Heb., ch. 11). Thus the company of believers in any place is linked to the total past and future of God's work of salvation through Christ.

In this segment of our study, we must now ask whether the category of "the faithful" contributes anything to our understanding of the inner cohesion of this community. How does faith affect the structure of human relations? The question produces the same embarrassment as in the case of sainthood, a fact that is not surprising since all believers were considered saints. The act of believing (which, of course, receives its content from its total context) creates a new man who lives in a new community in a new age. It would be contradictory indeed if believers did not find themselves bound together with quite new bonds. But what are those bonds which are disclosed by the participation of believers in the faithfulness of God? For answer, consider two very different pictures of the community of the faithful.

1. In Acts, ch. 4, the narrator described the "life together" of the five thousand who believed (v. 4). This life was characterized first by the boldness with which those "who had been with Jesus" proclaimed salvation in the name of Jesus. No threat could restrain or silence the word that faith constrained them to proclaim. (Vs. 10-20.) The power at work within them was also expressed in the unanimity of praise and prayer. (Vs. 23-31.) "The company of those who

believed were of one heart and soul." (V. 32.) This experienced oneness of loyalty, of love, of wonder, and of courage seems to represent the center of gravity of the narrator's story. The fellowship was marked by " great power and great grace " (v. 33). Among the results of participation in this power and grace was a transformation in the idea of property. Being possessed by the same spirit, they no longer considered their own possessions as their own, but, as the story runs, they had everything in common. Consequently, none of them was needy. This is the picture. The modern reader can hardly avoid the suspicion that this is a highly idealized picture, far from the actual story of conditions in that band of believers. He may even sympathize with the rebels, Ananias and Sapphira, whose story demonstrates that it was no simple thing to establish or to administer such a community. (Acts 5:1-11.) Nevertheless, even though the face value of the story is discounted for the sake of historical realism, there remains a testimony to the conviction on the part of the author that believers were introduced by their faith into a radically new kind of fellowship, which rightly should confer upon them all a freedom from fear of external enemies and from the tyranny of private possessions.

2. In Rom. 14:1 to 15:13 a photograph is found that begins with a more detailed appraisal of the tensions existing among believers. So sharply divided were these people that they could not eat together or agree on a day on which to worship together. When they did meet, they became embroiled in disputes in which mutual condemnation and mutual condescension destroyed the fabric of faith. They had little comprehension of the nature of the new home that had been given to them in faith; therefore, they did not perceive the hospitality that this faith demands. (Cf. [32])

What were the marks of this hospitality in faith? A common standing before the same judge who had welcomed them all; a common loyalty, however great the divergence between their behavior patterns, to the same Lord; a common thanksgiving to God, whether in eating or in abstaining; a common destiny that quite obliterated the line between life and death because of the power that Christ's dying and living had exerted over the living and the dead; a common status as property of this owner. (Rom. 14:1-12.)

What were the marks of that mutuality which was intrinsic to their status as believers but which must, according to the apostle, become explicit in new attitudes and actions? Within their community they must welcome one another in the same way and to the same depth as both God and Christ had welcomed them. (Chs. 14:3; 15:7.) They must yield to God the work of Final Judgment and thereby cease their mutual judging and despising. (Ch. 14:4, 10.) They must treat every brother as one for whom Christ died, and accordingly they must avoid any action that would injure him. (Vs. 13-15.) They must give priority to the common good, to God's work of building his household, rather than to self-esteem and self-interest. They must, to the degree that they are truly strong in faith, bear the full burden of those who are weak in faith. (Ch. 15:1-3.) They must cease measuring the faith of another by their own faith, but must respect both the independence and the interdependence conferred by the common faith, knowing that the only thing that now ranks as sin is the attitude and action that does not spring from faith, and knowing as well that this sin is nothing less than a defilement and destruction of the work of God. (Ch. 14:13-23.) They must live in such harmony with one another that they can glorify God with one voice. (Ch. 15:6.)

It is important to note also that certain things were not mentioned as being essential to faith's common life. Nothing was said about a structure of offices and officials whose authority must be recognized by believers. Paul did not even urge the community to adopt a single day for worship or a single set of rules concerning clean and unclean foods. There may, indeed, have been no single Eucharist where these Roman Christians could share in one covenantal food and drink. If so, then the absence of any requirement of a single table becomes significant.[7] Paul did not view agreement on the points at issue between the contending parties as necessary to securing "the one voice" in worship. It was not by a process of eliminating one faction or by devising an acceptable compromise between them that they would begin to "act from faith." The righteousness of the Kingdom (ch. 14:17) was not interpreted as requiring a set of acceptable standards and laws; nor was its peace defined by a superficial conformity for the sake of expediency. Its joy was not contingent upon that kind of communal self-satisfaction which emerges from social congeniality and the homogeneity of moral customs. Faith was not presented as a short cut for eliminating deep differences of conviction among believers. Rather was it viewed as a power that creates communal bonds strong enough to thrive on all the difficulties that had ensued from God's avowed intention to bring Jews and Gentiles into the same community. (Ch. 15:7-13.) This did not imply that the coherence created by faith was vague and tenuous. To the apostle the communal bonds produced by faith were much more powerful and demanding than would be true in a community where desire for greater cohesion had produced the adoption of a table of bylaws, a ladder of recognized authorities, and a working code of social amenities. Yes, faith in Jesus Christ carried within itself the essential structuring of the common life of believers. Given this faith, all believers received a given unity. But distinctions were possible and necessary between degrees of strength in faith. To Paul, the stronger the faith (i.e., the more it was actually defined by the faithfulness of God in Jesus Christ) the more steadily the community of believers would allow its interdependence to be shaped by " the righteousness and peace and joy " of God's Kingdom.

It is not surprising to find in the apostle Paul the use of the title [71] the justified (*dikaioi*) to designate the company of believers, for one of his central convictions is that faith in Jesus Christ as Lord justifies (*dikaioun*) the believer. The faithful are those who are justified. Here again the Greek with its cognates of the verb (*dikaioun*) preserves the interdependence of the categories more clearly than the English, and here again the accent falls upon the righteousness (*dikaiosunē*) of God. God himself is the Just One; as such he is the standard and source of righteousness.[8] Therefore he alone can make men righteous and declare them to be so. This is what he has done in Jesus Christ. (Rom. 3:26.) Therefore Jesus Christ is also called the Just One, who justifies men and himself remains their justification.[9] The Holy Spirit also is frequently spoken of as actively securing the forgiveness and justification of men. (Rom. 8:4-30; I Tim. 3:16.) It is within this galaxy of convictions that the central appellation of " the just " or " the righteous " is applied to the church. In many contexts the noun presupposes the verbal action: the righteous are those who have been justified.[10]

The use of this term for Christians accented their solidarity with all just men from the beginning.[11] Nor did this plural indicate a numerical collective, the aggregate of separate individuals who were righteous. All had, in fact, been bound together as the unrighteous for whom Christ died (Rom. 5:7); all had been bound together in the impossibility of self-justification (ch. 3:10); all had been bound together in the righteousness of God who justified them in Christ; all had been bound to a living Christ who became their justification. Consequently, their justification or their righteousness was a single inheritance in him. This was what constituted their community as a fellowship of the justified.

In this fellowship every person incurred obligations of mutuality. With a new rigor and a new relevance the judgment of God was exercised over this very community. And this judgment was needed to uncover the subtle drift toward self-justification and self-righteousness. (Luke 15:7; 18:9; 20:20; Rom. 10:3.) God's justice (his *dikaiosune*) could readily be made the excuse for complacent alibis. (James, ch. 2.) Therefore his righteousness as defined by Christ must be allowed to produce its intended fruits among the people of God. Genuine righteousness was something received and sought and enacted. (I John 3:7.) It could not be separated from walking according to the Spirit. (Rom. 8:4 f.) The Kingdom of God was just such " righteousness . . . in the Holy Spirit " (ch. 14:17). Thus righteousness was given in heaven to the people of God in order that it might become the goal of their earthly struggles. Jesus Christ was known as " our righteousness " both as heavenly source and as heavenly goal. The inner life of his saints was empowered from this source to move toward this goal. (Matt. 5:6, 20; Luke 1:75.) As justified, their bodies became weapons to be used to this end (Rom. 6:30), for they had become " enslaved to righteousness " (v. 18). Righteousness was something that the justified pursued, something that they loved, for it was in fact embodied in the First Commandment. The church, then, as the justified or the righteous, recognized that the Messiah who had justified them was continuing to wage war with a double-edged sword. (Rev. 19:11.) Justification did not therefore refer primarily to the moral or social or psychological aspects of the community's existence, but it first of all related the total history of the community to its eschatological ground. But this very fact enhanced its power over the social and moral behavior of the justified. The creative act of heavenly forgiveness, the gift of righteousness, must be allowed to produce its earthly fruits among them, lest they face the most devastating heavenly judgment. (Matt., chs. 18; 25.)

Before proceeding to other descriptions of the distinctive bonds of mutuality, we pause to observe several features that these three designations — saints, believers, the justified — have in common. In the first place, they are all used normally in the plural. This fact might be construed to signify that they do not belong among descriptions of the *church*. Obviously applicable to the *members* of the church, do they apply to the *community* itself? The evidence we have reviewed makes a positive answer necessary. The meaning of each term in its New Testament usage refers to the common ground of reality in God's action. A saint becomes a saint only through what God accomplishes through his Son and his Spirit. This action creates and sustains a single *koinōnia* that can be addressed as a unit by the plural: saints, believers, the justified.

In the second place, these plurals encourage the inference that the duties of sainthood are primarily conceived as individual virtues to be cultivated by each member on his own. But, again, the evidence points in almost the opposite direction. It is precisely these duties, these fruits of the Spirit, which characterize this community as God's people, and which therefore constitute the cohesive integrity of this people.

In the third place, none of these plural designations impresses us as being metaphorical, analogical, or figurative. Yet when seen in their full context, each one requires imaginative reflection, a reflection that will perceive behind the *nouns*, not a state of being but the action and interaction of spiritual potencies, which are constantly at work far below the surface of institutional behavior. These same features will recur in some of the following paragraphs.

The Disciplined Community

According to all four Gospels, the work of Jesus Christ as God's Messiah entailed his calling of men to be his [72] followers, as soon as he had received the authority of the Spirit. The men who responded became [73] disciples. In these images of following and learning was pictured a relationship to a common teacher, paralleled by the contemporary custom of speaking of the disciples of John the

Baptist, of the Pharisees, or of Moses. Now it would be easy to limit these terms to the period before Jesus' death, thereby removing them from the field of ecclesiological inquiry, were it not for two factors. In the first place, scholars are increasingly convinced that in the early church the stories of the disciples were normally understood as archetypes of the dilemmas and opportunities that later Christians experienced. Each Gospel pericope became a paradigm with a message for the church, because each Christian had inherited a relationship to Jesus similar to that of James and John and the others. Moreover, this connection is explicitly recognized within the Gospels themselves.[12]

In the second place, Christian habit in writings other than the Gospels indicates that at least in some circles Christians continued to be called both " disciples " and "followers." This practice, to be sure, may not have been general. The adoption of " disciples " as surrogate for both individual believers and the totality of believers is recorded only in the book of The Acts,[13] and the designation as followers (in the verbal form) is recorded only in the book of Revelation (Rev. 14:4; 19:14). But these two cases are sufficient to impel us to ask what light these terms may throw upon the structure of Christian community. This becomes all the more imperative when we read in Matthew that the risen Lord commanded the eleven to make *disciples* of all nations (Matt. 28:19) and when we observe that in several of the letters it is stressed that the believers must *learn* from Christ (Eph. 4:20-21; Heb. 5:8-9).

We are thus fully justified in asking whether the self-image of the Christian church as a company of disciples may give any clear clues concerning the fabric of social relatedness. Quite obviously the major content of the term is defined by the relationship to the teacher, but that has been true of practically every image we have examined and has not prevented a mental picture from divulging suggestions concerning the relation of disciples to one another. For such suggestions we are quite dependent upon the Gospels; the book of The Acts, although it uses the title frequently to designate the church, limits itself to the more casual kind of designation, e.g., "the disciples were increasing in number " (Acts 6:1). In citing Gospel passages we will restrain ourselves to those sayings of Jesus in which there is implicitly a generalized reference that supported demands that were accepted as normative by the Christian community after his death.

First, we may well note sayings in which Jesus associates loyalty to him as teacher with attitudes toward other disciples. For example, there is the famous parable addressed to his disciples in which the climactic warning is: " As you did it not to one of the least of these, you did it not to me " (Matt. 25:45). Herein is defined a basic social component of discipleship: to regard the least, whether or not he is naked, hungry, sick, or an outcast, as the Lord incognito. This principle is quite clearly expressed in other than parabolic form. To receive an apostle is to receive the one who sent him: to give a little one a cup of cold water because he is Jesus' disciple is in fact a gift to the lord of the disciple. (Matt. 10:40-42; John 13:20.)

Secondly, the Gospels record blunt utterances in which Jesus lays down the requirements for being a disciple. Among such requirements, stated without qualifying or ameliorating conditions, are these: to take up the cross, to lose one's life for his sake, to reduce to secondary status obligations to kinfolk, to refuse to count the cost in advance. " Whoever does not renounce all that he has cannot be my disciple." [14] Now, although it is clear that such a demand cuts across the whole range of societal obligations and was intended to do so, it should also be clear that a band of disciples, all of whom have " died out " to all other claims, will have as a " posthumous community " a character far different from that of other communities.

Thirdly, the claim of this imperious Master is not designed to increase his own formal glory by multiplying the number of minions who have cut themselves loose from all other obligations. It is this Master who, in line with his redemptive mission in the world, protests against the emptiness and treachery expressed in shouts of " Lord, Lord." The true test of total allegiance to him is total obedience to the will of God, whose great command is love of neighbors. So if he detaches the disciple from all that he has, it is for the purpose of sending him into a community of servants. (Cf. John 15:8-27.)

Fourthly, the Lord establishes rules for superiority among his disciples which belong to an entirely new kind of human society. On the one hand, the fact that the disciples have but one father, one master, and one teacher places them all on one level of genuine equality in relation to the teacher. " You are all brothers." (Matt.

23:8-9.) On the other hand, the fact that as disciples they must learn from a master whose rank as first was realized by his becoming last sets before them a permanent revolution in standards of inferiority and superiority. (Mark 10:35-45; Matt. 23:10-12.) Henceforth the supreme ambition for the disciple is simply to be like his teacher. (Matt. 10:25.) The social dynamics of a society where such a revolution is central are bound to be radically different from that of societies where other measurements of greatness and authority prevail. (Mark 10:42.) It is clear, then, even from this limited sampling of the Gospel definitions of discipleship, that this picture of the Christian family has far-reaching ecclesiological implications.

Both in Matthew and in Luke the teacher, speaking to the company of disciples, concludes his initial summary of prerequisites for discipleship with a call to enter the narrow gate and to follow the difficult road that alone leads to life. (Matt. 7:13-14; Luke 13:23-24.) In choosing this figure of [74] the road or the way (*hodos*), Jesus was continuing a manner of conveying God's absolute demand, which had been adopted in both the Law (Deut. 20:19) and the Prophets (Jer. 21:8), a method of instruction that has been used by a host of teachers both before and since his day. The image of the narrow road is explicitly set over against that of the broad. One leads to life, which in the context of the Gospels is equivalent to the Kingdom of God; the other leads inevitably to death. The presumption is clear that this is God's threat and promise and that Jesus is its mediator. The implication is inescapable that the narrow gate is the one that Jesus the teacher has himself entered and that to be his disciple one must join him and follow him on this steep path. Another implication, not, perhaps, so obvious, is that his road to the Kingdom leads him to Jerusalem and that, accordingly, their journey will also lead them to the same destination, which is at once mundane and celestial. (Cf. [47]) Thus far the image of the road merely includes and brings to a focus all the requirements for discipleship as preserved in the Gospel records. Thus far the ecclesiological reference is present only as a potential development.

Its development in one direction appeared in the book of The Acts, where in six separate episodes the identification of the community of believers with "the road" was unmistakable. (Acts 9:2; 19:9, 23; 22:4; 24:14, 22.) Those who "belong to the Way" were

quite clearly identified with " the disciples of the Lord." (Ch. 9:2.)
We should observe, however, that this use of the term was restricted
within certain limits. In all six episodes the center of attention was
the story of Paul who first persecuted " the Road " and then defended
it before magistrates and kings. All six episodes contrasted " the
Road " to the Jewish community among which its members had first
emerged. Others called these disciples a " sect," but Paul carefully
rejected that term in preference for " the Way " (ch. 24:14). The
term therefore aided in distinguishing Jewish Christians from their
Jewish compatriots. Yet this distinction was viewed as extremely
important, for it meant, as it had meant also to the members of the
Qumrân community, a claim to the status of being the only true
fulfillment of God's covenant with Israel and therefore the only gate
through which contemporary Israelites might enter the Kingdom of
God.[15]

This was the only road of salvation and hence the only genuine
fulfillment of the hope of the fathers. (Acts. 24:14-15.) Therein lay
the reason both for the hostility of the Jews and for Paul's loyalty as
a Jew. To both Jews and Gentiles he defended the Way as the genuine and sole channel through which the resurrection of the Messiah
had conveyed life to Israel. Having observed these positive nuances,
we must observe some negative aspects of the reference to the church
as the Road. The image itself did not, in The Acts, throw light upon
the interdependence among disciples. The contexts do not contribute
anything new to the more general and colorless term " disciples
Moreover, only in one passage was the image used, perhaps inadvert-
ently to suggest the relationship between the church and the living
Christ. When Paul trekked to Damascus to arrest members of the
Road, he was stopped by a strange epiphany of the Lord. When Paul
asked for his identity, the answer came, " Jesus, whom you persecute " (ch. 22:8). Jesus of Nazareth had identified himself with
those whom Paul was hounding. That was an important accent, because it was repeated in all three narratives of the incident. (Chs.
9:5; 26:14.) But the more negative observation is justified; this identification of the Lord with the persecuted was not a constituent element in the metaphor of " the Road." The image in The Acts was
primarily an objective designation of the Christian Jews and only
secondarily a figurative description of the inner fabric of common

life and only by remote association a picture of Christ's continuing activity.

In the Gospel of John, however, the center shifted. Only once did this writer refer to *hodos*, but this reference was extremely rich in symbolism. (John 14:4-6.) Here the primary accent fell upon the person of Jesus: "I am the true and living Way." In this context two corollaries appeared: (1) "No one comes to the Father but by me." This identified the Way as the mode of access to the Father and it implied that the "coming of men to the Father" was the basic objective of Jesus' work. His existence as the Way was inseparable from providing such access for others. (2) To know him, to know the Father, to know the Way to the Father — all these were made dependent upon knowing "the way where I am going." This knowledge of where he was going is presented as an enigma. It is an ultimate truth about ultimate life, but it mystified Thomas, Philip, and the other disciples. They knew it and yet did not know it. They must see the Father first; yet, as Jesus insisted, in seeing him they had seen the Father who dwells in the Son. (Vs. 9-11.) But they still did not know where he was going. Why not? Because the way to the Father was the way to the cross. In this Way the destination was made inseparable from the going, the whither was manifested in the direction of walking. It was in laying down his life for them (ch. 13:37) that he showed "the way where I am going." This was why they could not follow him then and why they would follow him after he had gone. (Ch. 14:2-3.) This Way which Jesus is, is his love-expressing, life-giving death. To know this Way is to know him, to know his Father, and to follow him by obeying his command: "Love one another, even as I have loved you" (ch. 13:34). Thus in John's Gospel the image of the Road was permeated by profound meanings, which were simultaneously and interchangeably Christological and ecclesiological, because the *Road* articulated the ultimate meanings for the community of the passion of the Father's love.[16]

We should note, therefore, that the image of the Way in the Fourth Gospel merged into another image that was more frequently used: the double phrase "whence I come and whither I go." This phrase compressed into one image of [75] coming and going the three interlocking stories: of Jesus, of the Spirit, and of the church.

All were contrasted to the story of those who had an opposite origin and destiny.

With the greatest brevity we will try to sketch this complex pattern of thought. First the story of Jesus. He came from God, having been sent to do God's work. All his works had originated in God's work. (John 6:33-38; 7:28-29.) This "coming from" determined the "going to." (Ch. 3:13.) In loving his disciples to the end he was lifted up on the cross, ascending to his Father. The whole of his redemptive work, all that he had done between descent and ascent, derived its truth and its life from this beginning and this end.

To recognize his whence and his whither — this was the mark of his disciple. Only through such a recognition could a man truly follow him. But this knowing and following was not accomplished by one's own insight or determination. (Ch. 8:14.) Only a person who had been born from above and who therefore had received the Spirit, which comes from above, had access to this knowledge. (Ch. 3:3-9.) This disciple's witness and works must have the same origin as his teacher's. (Chs. 1:13; 3:11; 6:37.) Disciples must be sent by him as he was sent by the Father. This new sending created them as sons who shared a new destination. Where did he go? To Jerusalem to be lifted up on the cross, to wash their feet, to give his life for others. That is where they would go: to wash one another's feet, to feed his sheep, to bring others into the same fold, to complete the task of loving as he loved.

This knowledge and mission could in the nature of the case be fully communicated only after he had followed that Road to the end. Power to be born again into this new way required the Holy Spirit, whose coming and going no one can trace. (Ch. 3:9.) The Spirit was given by the risen Lord, with his own commission. In ascending to his Father he revealed to them their Father (ch. 20:17); so also they would come from and journey toward the same place, abiding in him with one another. Their works would become the Father's works, greater even than those of their Lord, because they would be works stemming from his power as crucified and ascended. And these works would be done "in the world" where his had been done.

Consequently, the hostility of the world was inevitable. The world had hated him who was the true and living Way because the world had a divergent origin and direction of movement. Those who were of this world were "from below." Their father, whose works they did, was the devil. In him there could be no life and no truth. (Ch. 8:23-44.) The kingdoms of the world constituted a realm of fighting, deception, hatred, and death, all because of this different whence and whither. For men to follow Jesus, therefore, required standing in the world where the two lines of descent-ascent collide and to accomplish at that point the works for which they had been sent. Thus the figures of coming, of going, and of following in the Fourth Gospel conveyed almost endless insights into the correlations among the interlocking stories that together constituted the history of creation.

When we read the Synoptic Gospels in the light of John it is intriguing to ask whether John's idiom was a development out of Synoptic teachings concerning the ways of life and of death (Matt., ch. 7) or whether John's idiom, which clearly had been long in developing, had in subtle ways colored the Synoptic references to those who met Jesus on the Road. It was typical in the Synoptic narratives for men to be confronted by Jesus on the road. This was a place where men were forced to a decision (Luke 9:57 f.), a place where they were compelled to reply to the imperious query, "Who do you say I am?" This was a place where the movement of Jesus toward Jerusalem became filled with mysterious potency and where he instructed his followers concerning his Passion and theirs. This was a place also where the risen Lord, unrecognized except in the burning heart, opened the Scriptures to make clear the divine promises fulfilled in his death. (Ch. 24:32-35.) This was where such companions as Peter, James, John, and the rich young ruler learned how narrow is the gate; it was where Paul and the Ethiopian eunuch detected who Jesus really was. (Acts 22:4; 8:26 f.) It is admittedly difficult to control the exegesis of such an image. Yet there are enough common traits to justify the conclusion that in many circles of the early church the mental picture of the road evoked a sense of the bonds between the teacher and his disciples and of the corresponding ties that knit disciples together in their obedience to him in serving the world.[17]

This same complex of convictions became articulated in the picture of the church as a [76] witnessing community, a community in which every believer gave his testimony (believing and witnessing being quite inseparable) and the oneness of the common life was constituted by the common confession. In the Pauline thought the controlling image was that of dying with Christ as a slave of Christ. In the stories of Luke–Acts the terms for witnessing (*martys, martyrein*) were reserved primarily for those leaders within the church on whose testimony to the resurrection the origins of the congregations depended, i.e., the Twelve, Stephen, Paul.[18] In two major writings, however, the category of witnessing was used to describe the whole church in so far as it was faithful.

Looking first at the book of Revelation, we are immediately confronted by two factors that have induced many to conclude that the conception of the witnessing in the Apocalypse should not be applied to the community as a whole. We have to deal with a vocabulary that is permeated by apocalyptic conventions that demanded of the prophet that he use heavenly symbols to describe earthly phenomena. Furthermore, we have to deal with the fact that the word for witness (*martys*) was in the process of absorbing the meaning of martyr. Those who hesitate to associate martyrdom with the work of every Christian must accordingly hesitate to make the word " martyr " applicable universally to the church. These considerations would terminate further examination were it not for the fact that in several passages the prophet John made the wider reference quite inescapable.

Then the dragon was angry with the woman, and went off to make war on the rest of her offspring, on those who keep the commandments of God and bear testimony [*martyria*] to Jesus. (Rev. 12:17.)

The vision equated the bearing of testimony to the keeping of God's commandments. Moreover, this activity was true for all of the offspring of the woman, since the phrase " the rest " was a way of relating " the male child " (the Messiah, v. 13) to his brothers. We notice, too, that " the woman " was clearly a figure for the Messianic people as a unity. (Cf. [21]) This unitary conception was underscored by the fact that the dragon (Satan) and the woman were engaged in a world-wide war in which it was " the testimony to Jesus " that had enraged the dragon. If he could destroy that testimony, he would win the war. His campaign was waged against the saints as a community who constituted the only ultimate challenge to his sovereignty. (Ch. 13:6-7.)

Because the very target of the dragon's fighting was the testimony to Jesus, the clue to victory over the dragon was the fearless enunciation of this testimony. Conquest for the saints as individuals and as congregations depended upon maintaining an identity between "the blood of the Lamb" and "the word of their testimony" (ch. 12:11). This identification would have become quite impossible should their self-love have triumphed at any point in the battle. Death as a martyr (one meaning of *martys*) was only a final test of their work as a witness (the other and basic meaning of *martys*), a test of the sincerity and strength of their love for Christ. Their self-love had been provisionally overcome in their initial witness to Jesus as Lord. The dragon's objective was to reverse that initial witness. Should they, as the battle reached its climax, "love not their lives even unto death," they would thereby prove the power of their initial witness and thereby vindicate the power of "the blood of the Lamb" (v. 11). It was their unwavering hold on Jesus' own witnessing that made them his brothers, fellow servants of one another and kindred to both the prophet and the angel who disclosed "the true words of God" (ch. 19:10).[19]

This context of thought may enable us to comprehend still another passage, that which voices the cry for vindication by the souls of those who have been "slain for the word of God and for the witness which they had borne." In reply to their cry "they were each given a white robe and told to rest a little longer, until the number of their fellow servants and their brethren should be complete, who were to be killed as they themselves had been." (Ch. 6:9-11.) Out of context this appears to assert that only martyrs who had suffered a bloody death were included within the community of the end time. Yet in giving full weight to the event of death, which manifested the power of the persecutors and of the dragon, we should not forget that earlier event which had elicited the persecutor's power, that is, the earlier witness to the "word of God." It was this which provoked the testing, not the testing that produced the witness. It was the validity of the witnessing that created the solidarity with brothers and fellow servants. Viewed from this angle, the prophet John expressed the same understanding of following Jesus (chs. 14:4; 19:14) as that which lay behind the Gospel's definition of discipleship: "Whoever would be my disciple must deny himself" (cf. [73]) and the Pauline definition of baptism (Rom., ch. 6; cf. [56], [86]). He also made the story of each disciple conform to the story of Jesus as unfolded in the Gospels. Jesus' death as witness had served to disclose the power of his earlier decisions in Gethsemane, on the Mount of Transfiguration, in the wilderness of temptation, and even in his baptism.

The entire story of Jesus also informed the concept of witnessing in the Gospel of John. On his last evening with his disciples as he was preparing them for his death, Jesus disclosed many truths that would become clear only after his death.

When the Counselor comes, whom I shall send to you from the Father, he will bear witness to me, and you also are witnesses, because you have been with me from the beginning. (John 15:26-27.)

This declaration may, of course, have been limited to the apostles and to their distinctive function within the church. But it may also have been addressed to them as the representatives of the believing community. The latter is altogether probable. In their witness as apostles the witness of the church had been embodied. It was the church that so frequently adopted the plural pronoun in John:

We speak of what we know and bear witness to what we have seen. (Ch. 3:11.) That which we have seen and heard we proclaim also to you, so that you may have fellowship with us. (I John 1:1-4.)

It was this common witness to the coming of God's son as Savior of the world which created the community and disclosed the presence within it of God's abiding love. By believing, every man "had the testimony in himself" (I John 5:10). Unless he made this testimony vocal and active he would never know the common joy that God imparted to the community through a love that could drive out all fear. (Ch. 4:11-18.) Thus witnessing is as constitutive of this community as love. Love that could not be translated into the shared witness (v. 14) and the shared martyrdom (Rev. 12:11) could not be translated into the other modes of communal action.

A similar conception of the church lay behind the words [77] confessors and confession. The church was the "we" who made confession in trial situations where it became tantamount to martyrdom.[20] Because the two patterns of witnessing and confessing are so similar we will move directly into another area of inquiry.

The Common Slavery [21]

Very often in the New Testament the church was described as the [78] slaves of God and of Jesus Christ. It was as slaves (*douloi*) that authors frequently introduced themselves to their readers.[22] It was also as slaves that they addressed those readers.[23] Thus they recognized common ground between themselves and all the members of the churches. The basic axis that constituted this slavery was, of course, the relationship of allegiance to the same master. "No one," Jesus had taught, "can serve two masters." Here and in many other teachings he stressed the exclusive demand that God makes of men.[24] There was no more constant motif in the parables of Jesus than the varying stories of slaves.[25] In these parables it was taken for granted that the relation of slaves to masters provided an entirely fitting analogy for the relation of men to God.

Now it must be admitted that this is not a popular way of visualizing the church. Men have never, whether in the first or the twentieth century, whether in Africa or Indonesia, relished this image of themselves. In fact, what country today is not fighting against slavery of one type or another? Our deepest sense of human dignity, our greatest longings for our nation, our strongest demands on the future — these come to a focus in the one word "freedom." There are, of course, countless types of slavery and countless conceptions of freedom, but we are all psychologically disposed to shout and to work for emancipation. And did not Jesus the Christ begin his ministry to man broadcasting the good news of God — "release for the captives" (Luke 4:18)? (That very term "ministry," of course, disguises the more rugged and menial Greek word for the service of a slave.) How, then, could the early church accept a band of slaves as an accurate picture of itself?

It was impelled to do so by the very picture of its Savior. Jesus the Messiah was pictured as both slave and lord, the two quite interdependent. As slave he had become lord, as lord he had become slave. His story epitomized this essential, though mysterious, interdependence. Through his mission as lord/slave he had "bought" many slaves, so that all belonged to him in the sense that property belongs to its owner. There was a tendency, therefore, for this picture to coalesce with many others. Slaves were members of the same household and family. They had died to the old creation, with its law of sin and death, and had " put on " the new Man. Slaves of Christ were his witnesses and confessors. However, the slave image had its own importance, for it appears in at least fifty New Testament passages in no fewer than eighteen writings.

We must ask, therefore, how this status as a company of slaves affected the church's sense of its inner cohesion. Did this idiom throw light upon the kind of mutuality that characterized the church's members? The apostle Paul was most explicit in giving answers to such a question. For example, in Phil., ch. 2, he sought to show how the slave's obedience on the part of the Messiah should produce one mind between every Christian and his lord, and how this same mind should dominate the community, producing the love and humility in which each would count the others better than himself. In writing to the Corinthians the apostle suggested that those who preached Jesus Christ as Lord must regard themselves " as your slaves for Jesus' sake " (II Cor. 4:5). Those *for* whom Christ had become a slave were bound by his death into slavery to *all those* for whom he had died. His love turned them into slaves of one another. (Gal. 5:13.) Moreover, this slavery had no humanly defined limits, since Christ had died for all. This is why his loyalty to Christ forced the apostle to become a slave to all. (I Cor. 9:19.) It was recognized throughout the New Testament that slavery to God immediately transformed one's relation to every other man. Every obligation toward the Messiah was immediately transferable into attitudes and actions toward one's fellow men.[26]

The interpretation of this idiom would go awry, however, should we suppose that this slavery destroyed freedom. In becoming a disciple, the Christian did not move from a prior freedom into slavery: he moved from one slavery to another. Serving the one Lord ended the old frustrated effort to serve many masters. The only alternative to serving Christ was the effort to please men (Gal. 1:10; Eph. 6:6) or to safeguard one's own prosperity, security, or honor. These various alternatives in the end merged into one, although this one bore many names: slavery to fear, to the law, to the flesh, to the world, and to the devil.[27] Freedom from all of these was assured in the new bondage to Christ. If in legal terms a man were the property of another man, he might as a Christian remain bound to him. In fact, Paul thought he should remain so, unless the owner should offer liberty. But were he to remain enslaved to this earthly master, even this slavery was transformed by the new slavery to Christ. Now he would obey his earthly master not to please him or to evade his penalties, but to please his heavenly master. By doing this he became free in relation to his earthly owner, but a slave of his new owner.[28]

There are two passages in which New Testament writers seem to have repudiated this image by saying, "No longer a slave, but . . ." In Galatians what follows the "but" is the word *sons*. (Gal. 4:1-7.) In saying this, however, Paul did not deny the applicability of the term "slave" to Christians. (Cf. Gal. 5:13.) For in Galatians the opposite of sonship was bondage to "the elemental spirits of the universe" (vs. 3, 5, 8). Sonship in Christ was not opposed to slavery to Christ, but to the old yoke of the law. Even so, however, the passage is a reminder that the symbolic aptness of the idiom of slavery depends upon remembering which is the master to whom these slaves belong.

The other passage, often cited to show a rejection of the metaphor, is found in the Gospel of John, where Jesus reassured his disciples: "No longer do I call you slaves, . . . but I have called you [79] friends" (John 15:15). The fact that in the same Gospel Jesus approved the title *doulos* for his disciples (chs. 13:16; 15:20) shows that this Gospel does not deny that disciples are also slaves. In fact, these "friends" become friends only through their obedience. "You are my friends if you do what I command you." The obedience was measured by the laying down of Jesus' life. This was his command. If they obeyed, they were slaves.

Although we cannot use John 15:15-20 to negate the picture of the church as slaves, we can use it to secure a conception of what is meant by being friends of Jesus (*philoi*). For here is a minor but interesting church image. In addition to the component already mentioned (a friend = obedience = love = self-denial) at least one other component is stressed, in direct contrast with the use of *doulos*. Whereas the slave does not know what his master is doing, the friend does know. He knows because Jesus has revealed it to him. The friend knows how God works among and in men; he knows how the fruit produced by Christ and his disciples is in fact the work of

God. Abiding in love, he abides in God and comprehends what God is doing so intimately that he can ask anything in the name of Jesus and it will be done. (Vs. 9-11, 16-17.)

This picture of the disciples as friends is reflected in fragmentary ways elsewhere. In the third letter of John (III John 15) one congregation greets another as friends to friends. If there was a link in the Evangelist's mind between the noun for friend (*philos*) and the verb to love (*philein*), then there may be significance in the reference to Lazarus as Jesus' friend (John 11:11) and to the disciple whom Jesus loved (ch. 20:2). For Jesus to call his followers " friends " was perhaps suggestive of their love for him and his love for them. (Ch. 16:27.) We might even suggest as a translation of Jesus' question to Peter: " Simon, are you my friend? " (ch. 21:16).

There may have been other circles in which the term " friends " was a surrogate for church. In the Synoptic Gospels, Jesus on occasion addresses his disciples as " my friends " (Luke 12:4) and tells parables in which the presence of friends would give the story added weight in congregations where this was an accepted title for Christians.[29] The complaint that Jesus was a friend of publicans and sinners (Matt. 11:9) may well have carried intimations of the distinctive nature of the Christian fellowship. The special comment that Abraham had been called " the friend of God " may have been prompted by the fact that in Christian thought friendship, servanthood, and sonship were so closely allied. (James 2:23; cf. Isa. 41:8.) Also within the range of possibility is the interpretation of two passages in the book of The Acts as identifying friends of Paul with Christian believers. (Acts 19:31; 27:3.) At such points we cannot speak with confidence, but the conclusion is justified that if *philoi* were a genuine church image, it neither contradicted the more frequent image of slavery nor contributed significant nuances on its own.

We turn now to other terms for servanthood, terms that are perhaps not so shockingly menial as the term " slave," but that have similar associations. Important among these is the picture of [80] servants (*diakonoi*). It must be recognized that this term was sometimes used to designate a special ministry within the church.[30] But scholarship is quite agreed that the more general use preceded the more technical. The Greek words were flexible enough to fit many types of servants and many forms of service. As in the case of slave, here too Jesus Christ was both the lord who is served and the servant who provided the archetype for all servants.[31] Every disciple and believer was *ipso facto* a servant. (Mark 9:35; 10:43; John 12:25-26.) Service to the Lord took many various forms, but in them all the Lord was actively serving other men through these servants, as well as being served by them. Thus servanthood was a gift;[32] those who mediated this gift did so by the strength that God supplied. (I Peter 4:10-11.) The alternative was to become servants of Satan. (II Cor. 11:15.)

Not only did all members thus participate in this ministry, but each congregation was judged by its service. (Rev. 2:19.) More than this, the whole church was both a recipient of the dispensation (*diakonia*) of the Spirit, an instrument in the work of ministry, and a fellowship that was nourished and built up by the service of all. (II Cor., ch. 3; Eph., ch. 4.) The image thus reflects a complex process of interaction by which the Lord, through the Spirit, ministers to the church, and the church, through the Spirit which activates all of its members, ministers to the Lord by ministering to the world.[33]

At first glance the passages that we have been collating seem to be little more than a series of platitudes. They strike us as far removed from effective tools for analyzing the inner structure of a community. Even so, these analogies may have quite realistic implications for societal organization. The pictures of servanthood transformed the meaning and purpose of freedom in community life. They reversed the normal conceptions of humiliation and glory. They articulated vivid criteria of greatness and excellence. They dominated basic ethical and liturgical patterns of behavior. They qualified the exercise of human authority, since the power of an apostle was traced to his weakness and no achievement on his part could transcend the confession "unworthy servant." They were the index to a social fabric that was woven by mutual loyalties and gratitude, mutual suffering and worshiping. They constituted first-rate evidence that this society had at its core, at least in conscious awareness if not in actual accomplishment, the memory of the cross and with that memory the awesome presence of a living and judging master, as severe as he was gracious.

Moreover, this slave-church was quite aware of the " sociological " importance of its "theological " norms. It knew at first hand the hostility of other societies that could not exalt the same standard of greatness nor accept as their own the demands of a servant-lord. The Christians were too free and too subservient to escape the sharpest kind of conflict with groups that were less free because they were less subservient. The very idea of a Savior in the form of a slave was ridiculous; it was, when embodied in communal bonds, entirely too sharp a challenge to the type of mutuality that binds families, classes, and races together. By his servanthood the Master had made his community more inclusive than any other. By the same token, by the cross-shaped demands of his love, he had made it more exclusive than any other. And since he remains ever its final judge, qualified as such by God's approval of his slavery, he remains a Grand Inquisitor whom the church itself can face only with the greatest trepidation. The New Testament church was quite aware that it had not actually embodied his standard of authority, his criteria of greatness, his inclusiveness and exclusiveness. But all this is simply to say that the church's confession of faith in him remained all too relevant to its own common life in him, and all too relevant to its vocation in the world as a slave of all men.

The Prepositions of Mutuality

In planning this chapter of our study, we expected to survey those images which would throw the greatest light upon the intrachurch dimensions and upon the distinctive quality of its human relations. Actually this kind of division has proved to be impossible. The images draw their basic meaning from the central relationship to the work of Father, Son, and Spirit, and not from their immediate social components. Actually, none of them is drawn directly from the stock of analogies by which the cohesion of social groupings is normally indicated. What do the analogies, whether of saints, of disciples, of the Way, of slaves, say intrinsically about the interstices of community life? Almost nothing in themselves. It was only by the application of these analogies to the field of human relations that their social values became apparent. This application of the images was determined neither by the mental picture conjured up by the words nor by adeptness in rhetorical juggling, but by the total tradition of the message and mission of Jesus Christ. Only as he was allowed to define each picture did that picture become relevant to the daily social contacts within the Christian community.

The texture of community life was often reflected more effectively, if more subtly, by the use of prepositions than by the use of nouns and verbs. Perhaps, then, by tracing the use of one of these prepositions we may get a further clue to the sense of community. Several such prepositions might be chosen: through, into, in, by, for, for the sake of. Later we will have occasion to consider the force of some of these. Here we will indicate the results of a survey of the use of the preposition [81] with (*syn*). The appearances of such a link word are so numerous that we cannot cover them all, but it may be of some value to conduct a preliminary test drilling into the substratum of meanings by looking at the verbs that the New Testament writers have compounded with this preposition. Even when limited in this fashion, the task remains an extensive one, because there are at least forty-five such verbs in the New Testament that have reference to the Christian community. We can note here only a few conclusions from a preliminary survey of these compound verbs.

The largest concentration of these compounds is located in the Pauline corpus, a fact that shows that thinking about the community in terms of prepositional relationships was a primary characteristic of Paul's mind, although he was by no means the only writer who habitually thought in this way.[34] The study of prepositions corroborates our previous survey in this regard, that at least ten of the images already covered are echoed in the use of this preposition of mutuality. Christians share equally with one another as joint heirs of the Kingdom and as fellow slaves. They share in the olive tree, in the fish net, in the flock, in election, in witnessing, in the work of building, and in the inheritance of glory.

One primary use of the preposition is to show the mutual dependence of the community on Christ. The preposition points to a bond with Christ so strong that nothing can destroy it. (Col. 3:3-4; Rom. 8:32.) The understanding of the name Immanuel as God-with-us is paralleled by the understanding of the church as we-with-the-Lord.[35] We may note that it is the plural pronoun — we, us, our — that is normally linked by the preposition. When we ask about the verbs used in the compound relationship we find that they are those which link the community to the event, supremely important, of the Lord's death and resurrection. Note the variety and yet the similarity in the following list:

to die with him	— to live with him
to suffer with	— to be glorified with
to be crucified with	— to be raised with
to be baptized with	— to be made alive with
to be buried with	— to sit with
to be planted with	— to rule with
to be conformed to	— to come with

This communal bond is by no means limited to the present membership in the church. All creation groans and travails together. (Rom. 8:22.) All men are imprisoned and locked together in disobedience. (Ch. 11:32.) And all things hold together in Christ. (Col. 1:17.)

A great many of the verbs compounded in this fashion focus attention upon the solidarities among the citizens of the new age. These have a direct bearing upon the concerns of this chapter. Many of these suggest ways in which participation in Jesus' death created a similar mutuality with one another. If one Christian was imprisoned, all were to consider themselves as actually imprisoned with him. (Heb. 13:3.) They suffered persecutions and oppositions together. (II Tim. 1:8; 2:3; Heb. 11:25.) By their share in Jesus they were made sharers together in both tribulation and endurance. (Rev. 1:9.) They lived in one another's hearts, they died together (II Cor. 7:3), together they carried on the struggles incident upon a shared mission (Rom. 15:30).

This mutuality in suffering and dying, produced by the common dependence on the Master's death, was paralleled point for point by a mutuality that flowed from the Master's life into all the interstices of human relations. All Christians, for instance, shared in life-giving grace. (I Peter 3:7; Phil. 1:7.) In the fullest sense they participated as joint heirs in the single promise (Heb. 11:9; Eph. 3:6) and in the joy that God's love brought into their hearts (Phil. 2:17-18; I Cor. 1:6). Mutuality was expressed at the depths of intercessory prayer (II Cor. 1:11) and of intercessory action.[36] Consolation, strength, and nourishment from a single source permeated their life together. (Rom. 1:12; Eph. 4:16.) If some of them were rulers, then, by the logic of the new age, all must be rulers with them. (I Cor. 4:8.) To the degree that one imitated Christ, others should also share in imitating him. (Phil. 3:17.) To the extent that a common heart and mind appeared, to that extent the mind of Christ was manifested among them. (Ch. 2:2.) In short, all who were conformed to the new humanity found their mutual relations transformed from the center outward.

The processes of inner cohesion and interaction, which marked this community, were rather vividly expressed by one of the images already mentioned. Let us say a further word here about the work of [82] edification. (Cf. [17]–[19]) The Greek student will immediately recognize that the same Greek word (*oikodomē*) is translated by the English nouns " building " and " edification." To most English ears there is a sharp contrast between these. When we hear the latter word we seldom visualize a company of stonemasons engaged in cementing stones into a structure. But to edify is to build, to join stones and timbers into a strong house. What edifies the church builds the church. It is edification thus understood that has significance for communal integumentation. Whatever edifies the brother does far more than improve his moral behavior; it strengthens him in his position in this structured society. The commission of the apostles to build a house was no different from their obligation to edify the church.[37] The same obligation falls upon all forms of ministry, since each gift had been intended for building up the body of Christ. (Eph. 4:7-12.) We may remark in passing that the symbol of building a house (edification) made virtually the same impact as the symbol of the growth of a body (v. 16). Quite naturally then, love must be spoken of as the most excellent gift, because it provides the greatest cohesive force, whether the community is imagined as a growing body or as a building under construction. (I Cor. 8:1; Eph. 2:21; cf. [68]) It was by the standard of what is edifying that Christian worship should be ordered (I Cor., ch. 14), that liberties should be controlled (chs. 8:1, 10; 10:23), and that such activities as kindness and sincerity should be treated as the most appropriate sacrifices. The processes by which men are " built into a spiritual house " (I Peter 2:5) thus become a virtual definition of the church itself.

Where men edify one another, there the church is alive and growing.

This image thus welds together important convictions about the church: the co-operation of God, Christ, the apostles, and all the " living stones "; the integumentation of the community through the daily embodiment of gifts of grace in works of love; the recognition of both the joy and the discipline of shared responsibility; the combination in the total structure of moral with ecclesiastical forces; the preservation of the dynamic and spiritual aspects without the loss of the more stable structural conception. All in all, one must say that contemporary thought has given far too little attention to the positive implications of this pattern of thinking for ecclesiology.[38]

In Greek the verb for " building " is a compound based on the noun for " house " (*oikos*). Moreover, the New Testament quite frequently brings the two ideas into direct conjunction by way of a redundancy, " to house-build a house." [39] We must therefore give more extended attention to a cluster of images centering in the [83] **household of God** and the family of Christ. This consideration will also enable us to summarize the major constellations thus far studied.

The Household of God

In our third chapter we studied several constellations of analogies that related the church, by comparison and contrast, to the national, racial, and cultic traditions of Israel. The wide range of meanings expressed by those analogies meets us again in the New Testament picture of God's household. We may cite the example of I Peter. It was axiomatic for this writer to think of the church as the household of God (I Peter 4:17) and equally axiomatic to identify this house with the temple, the Kingdom, the race, and the nation (ch. 2:5-10). The same was true for the author of Hebrews. In his mind the household of God over which Jesus was set as a Son is to be understood by its relation to the household in which Moses had been the representative servant. (Ch. 3:1-6.) So, too, the temple or sanctuary that was " set up by the Lord " is the fulfillment of a new covenant, a covenant that God had made with the house of Israel and of Judah, a covenant that is fulfilled in the perfection of the knowledge of God on the part of this people. (Ch. 8:1-13.) Because of the interchangeability of these terms — people, temple, Kingdom, house — we must assume that none of the figures was intrinsically more or less political or nationalistic or cultic than the others.[40]

That this idiomatic identification of household or family with Israel was fully congenial to Biblical patterns of thought should be readily affirmed by anyone familiar with the Old Testament. The pattern of associations has been well summarized by Johannes Pedersen, and we therefore allow him to remind us of the structure of that pattern. When the Hebrew sought to refer to all men, it was natural for him to speak of "all the *families* of the earth" (Gen. 28:14; Zech. 14:17 f.). This was natural not alone because every man was a member of a particular family, but also because the idea of the family "is the basis of all definitions. . . . It immediately presents itself whenever the Israelite wants to define a community."[41] Inseparable from the thought of the family is its father, its patriarch whose story *is* the story of his family.

He is at the same time the tribe and its father, and to everyone who joins the tribe he thus becomes a father. . . . The patriarchs are neither merely individuals nor the personifications of tribes; they are fathers who take part in the life of the tribe. . . . [Each father] is not removed by death from his tribe, but continues to live in it and share its adventures. . . . All the great events happening to the tribe are ascribed to them.[42]

What therefore provides the cohesion in the society is participation in the continuing life of a common ancestor, a life that is mediated by the historical saga that weaves together the story of the patriarch and the story of his family. The common story was more clearly definitive of the community than external evidences of biological descent. In fact, Pedersen insists that one cannot define family as a "materially limited quantity." To be sure "common flesh and common blood" are descriptive of what we might call biological continuity, but the chief thing in kinship is "common character." "The family extends as far as the feeling of unity makes itself felt. Therefore the line of distinction must necessarily be fluid."[43] So we find that while the idea of family is "the basis of all definitions," the definition of what constitutes the family is extremely flexible. There is "no external definition" of kinship, but the "chief feature" in it is "whether one has the common stamp in oneself." Wherever a social whole bears "the impress of a common character" there the term "family" is legitimately used. For example, those who are guilty of the same transgressions form one family, which comprises "all of the same stamp throughout the ages." [44] The homogeneity of the family, the element of kinship, stems from a psychic bond that discloses the fact that contemporary mutualities actually spring from a common source. "Wherever a man goes, he takes his 'house' with him." [45]

The character of a man's house will be indicated by his actions vis-à-vis his particular associates. His history, in terms of his enacted kinship, derives its true stamp from the character of the family whose history is also enacted in it. Having a common stamp is the same as having a common history and as being one people. If this homogeneity is destroyed, the people is destroyed or it becomes a "nonpeople," which is the same as "to perish." On the other hand, wherever homogeneity appears, whether in evil or in good, there appears also a family, a people. [46] It is clear, then, that the pictures of the family, of the household, and of the people tend to coalesce, since all articulate a flexible sense of kinship, a realistic homogeneity in which the "common stamp" of a contemporary community is understood as its participation in a common tradition, a history understood as the continuing life of a common ancestor. This, stated all too briefly, is the cluster of idioms that permeates the New Testament identifications of the household of God with the house of Israel and of David, with the covenantal promises and the faith granted to the fathers.

But the same cluster relates the New Testament picture of the church to more cosmic and universal categories. Abraham is the father of the saints, but so too is God, for whom all human families are named. In this conception of household and family, therefore, may be summarized all that was covered in our fourth chapter. To early Christians nothing was more distinctive of their common life than their existence as [84] sons of God. As sons they had been born again into the new creation; they were molded on the pattern of Jesus Christ, the new humanity; they were sons of the Day and sons of the Kingdom. The opposite sonship was pictured in terms of the night, the wrath, the curse, the evil generation, Gehenna, the devil. [47] We are obviously dealing with an ultimate distinction. The question "Whose son are you?" is a question that must be asked of every man, and the answer bears tremendous weight.

The same kind of imagination pervades the Old Testament. Again Johannes Pedersen is a helpful guide:

> Wherever those of one mind form a community round a common leader, they are a house; the leader who stamps it with his personality is its father, and those who join him are his sons.

As instances Pedersen notes the fact that members of a community of prophets are called sons of prophets. Jonadab who founded the house of the Rechabites becomes their father. A wise man is " the son of the wise "; so, too, a wicked man belongs to the house of the wicked.

> All living beings consist of this kind of unities, and the various characteristics and possibilities of every individual make him a part of many wholes. A man may at the same time be the son of his own father and of Jonadab ben Rechab, while he is also the son of the shepherds, of the just, etc., all his characteristics making him a part of wholes, and it depends upon circumstances which of these at the moment is most important.[48]

For our purposes several points in this outlook become important. In calling an individual a son, he is simultaneously designated as a member of a community. That which makes him a son also makes this community what it is, a whole that is embodied in this representative. The unity of the son in the family binds both him and the family to its leader, its father, who represents the whole family par excellence. What distinguishes an individual most sharply from others is the unity that lies at the deepest source of his choices and actions. He belongs to many families, but presumably one of these sonships is the most determinative and enduring. In this basic context belonged the conception of Israel as God's son or daughter. A corollary was the association of God as the father with the king of Israel as his son in a special sense. Other corollaries include the conception of the prophet and the priest of Israel as sons of God. All these idioms are interrelated and some of them are no doubt extended into the New Testament, even though the degree of extension is a matter extremely difficult to determine.

What is the element that constituted Israel as the Son of God? Many scholars today will agree on a single answer: the covenant.

> The doctrine of the covenant implies, therefore: (1) the absolute recognition of the reality of a true communion between God and man [people]; (2) the absolute recognition of God as the Holy One, the Supreme, who

has established and who guides this relationship; (3) the acknowledgment of the rules of the covenant.[49]

It is the definition of family by reference to this covenant that "makes Israelites brothers," that enables writers to speak of Israel as God's son, and to speak of God as the Father of Israel.[50] The same covenant idea made it incongruous to speak of all men as sons of this Father. Professor Vriezen, whose conclusions I have been adducing,[51] stresses the conviction that this father-son image should not be taken in a "generative sense," but wholly in the sense of the covenant relationship. It has a symbolic meaning also when divine sonship is attributed to the kings of Israel. It is therefore important to remember that from beginning to end, whether dealing with human sons and fathers, with Israel as God's son, or with the king of Israel as Son, the substratum of associations consists of a historical community in which kinship is a corollary of covenant. If this is true of the thought of Israel under the old covenant, it is all the more true under the new. To that covenant we now turn.

We need not argue the point that in the New Testament this covenant is intended for all men and that God's household, accordingly, is designed to embrace men from every tribe, tongue, people, and nation. The life of this family was grounded solely upon the action of its Father. This is expressed very succinctly in Matthew. "You have one father, who is in heaven." (Matt. 23:9.) Everywhere in the New Testament it is presupposed that sonship is a fruit of the mission of Christ through whom comes the power to be children of God. (John 1:12.) It is he who gathers into one the scattered children. (Ch. 11:52.) Accordingly, sons of God are those to whom it can be said, "You have one Master, the Christ" (Matt. 23:10). Some writers link the existence of this sonship to the descent and indwelling of the Holy Spirit. Some speak of its inception as a new birth from above. All ground the existence and source of sonship in the formation of the new covenant.

We come now to the final value of this idiom of household — its effectiveness in summarizing our observations concerning the inner cohesion of this community. Pedersen has reminded us of the essentially qualitative conception of kinship. The New Testament as a whole spells out this qualitative conception, as do also many separate passages. Consider a few of the ways by which sonship is defined:

by obeying God (Mark 3:35; I Peter 1:14)
by work of reconciliation (Matt. 5:9)
by the love of enemies (Matt. 5:41-45)
by loving the brothers (I John 3:10-11)
by walking as children of light (Eph. 5:8)
by living free from fear of death (Heb. 2:15)
by being sanctified in Christ (Heb. 2:11)
by watchfulness and soberness (I Thess. 5:5 f.)
by drawing and accepting the hatred of the world (John 15:18 f.)
by imitating God (Eph. 5:1)
by walking according to the Spirit (Rom. 8:14)
by conquering temptation (Rev. 21:7)
by the acceptance of discipline (Heb. 12:15 f.)
by living in freedom from law (Gal. 4:5)
by coming to Jesus for forgiveness and healing (Mark 2:5)
by hoping in God (I John 3:1-3)
by relying solely on faith (Gal. 3:26)
by continuing the mission of Jesus to the world (John 17:18-23)

All these are marks and fruits of sonship; more than this, they are the very substance of kinship to God. And each is corporate in its reference, i.e., it reflects, elicits, and expresses the interdependence that makes this community the family of God. Sonship is a gift of the Father to the whole community and therefore a command addressed to that family as a family. Taken together these components of sonship form the very fabric and texture of the family's cohesion; they help to define the nature of fatherhood, the work of Jesus Christ as first-born son, and the structure of this unique society.

They also serve to suggest the battle lines in the history-long struggle between the realm of God and the realm of the devil. This last point warrants an added comment. According to the New Testament the devil has sons, a family, a household, a kingdom. The conflict between the two communities forms the very structure of the eschatological vision of history. Between the two solidarities there can be no compromise. As was true of the Old Testament, so also the New Testament does not speak of all men as now belonging to God's family. The definition of family does not permit that.[52] But as in the Old Testament, God's covenant promises include the vast range of

" all the families of the earth." Therefore the church as one family is the harbinger of the reunification of all families. The definition of family requires that!

The communal implications in the status of the sons are, of course, made explicit in the references to the church as a [85] brotherhood. Although this term *adelphotēs* appeared only twice (I Peter 2:17; 5:9), the idea is much more pervasive. Shared by this brotherhood was unity of spirit, suffering, sympathy, humility. (I Peter 3:8; 5:9.) The salutation "brothers" was in the New Testament the most natural (and therefore most quickly conventionalized) way to address fellow Christians or a congregation as a whole. But the salutation reminds us that the birth of the brotherhood was explicitly traced to the work of " the first-born of many brethren." Brotherhood referred to the mutuality of sharing in his sanctification, his suffering, his death, his spirit, his Kingdom. (Rom. 8:39-40; Heb. 2:11 f.)

The term " brother " did not by itself invest the relationship with its meaning; quite the contrary was true. The relationship invested the word " brother " with its pattern of meaning. This shift of priorities in logical order is underscored by two passages in the Gospels. There Jesus explicitly identified his brothers as those who do the will of God. (Mark 3:35.) And he threatened the usual obligations of brotherhood by insisting that his followers must surrender all existing family ties if they were to receive " in this age " new brothers a hundredfold. (Ch. 10:29 30.) It was this exchange of families which educed the radically new meaning in the term " brother." In the new family Jesus Christ was identified with every brother in his need of food, clothing, or friendship. (Matt. 25:40.) Within the new household the existence of estrangement required immediate action by the estranged persons and by the family as a whole.[53] Kinship now required a shared humility and eliminated jostling for superiority. (Ch. 23:8.) If particular brothers were given a special commission, this task was designed to strengthen their brothers. (Luke 22:32.) [54] The definition of brotherhood by the love that " bears all things, endures all things, hopes all things " indicated that the very existence of such brotherhood was viewed as a clear sign of the resurrection. (I John 3:1 to 5:5.) Such affiliations of meaning were intrinsic to the Gospel's radical conception of sonship and equally intrinsic to the conception of the church as the household of God.

Our discussion of this category brings to a close the study of the church as the people of God, as the new creation, and as the fellowship in faith. As we have seen, the texts themselves relate the household of God to the house of Abraham and of Israel, to the temple, and to the flock of God. For early Christians this imagery of brotherhood was not so distant from the political and cultural images as for modern Christians. Just as the picture of household was drastically revised by the experience of communion in Christ, so the same revision extended to the whole gallery of racial, cultic, and political pictures. The picture of sonship suggests that every picture needs to be understood anew by reference to the Son of God, even though that understanding radically revises priorities among the component elements in race, nation, and temple. But we have also noted how the thought of God the Father, revised in the light of the cross, gave universal and cosmic status and scope to the thought of the church. Again, these cosmic dimensions were required by the revelation of true sonship in the work of the Beloved Son. His love was nothing less than the power of the new creation, the new humanity, the Kingdom of God. Finally, this cluster of images — father, household, sons, brothers — constituted perhaps the climactic articulation of that new fellowship in faith whose bonds were as strong as the power of the cross. Through our whole discussion we have been impelled by the images to rethink the essential structure of the community in terms of such simple constituents as faith and obedience, grace and forgiveness, hospitality and love. We should not overlook this important corollary: because the people of God must be defined in terms of such qualitative human relationships as are indicated by hospitality and forgiveness, these very relationships must be reconceived in terms of their sociological, ecclesiological, and ontological implications. To give a cup of cold water becomes much more than an instance of private morality; it becomes an event in the creation, edification, and redemption of human community. This simultaneous redefinition both of ecclesiological structure and of personal decision will be fully documented in the ensuing analysis of the image of the body of Christ.

VI

THE BODY OF CHRIST

W E HAVE NOW completed the second stage of our project, having reviewed the uses of some eighty analogies and designations for Christian community in the New Testament. Only one major configuration of thought awaits exploration — that which oscillates around three terms: body, members, head. The objectives of this book have made it desirable to defer this configuration until last. These objectives now make it desirable to attempt a more detailed and thorough exposition of the relevant passages, paying heed both to the contrasts and to the associations with the other images. Such is the task of this chapter. Our investigation of this image will be confined to the Pauline letters, because in them alone is the church explicitly described as " the body of Christ." Other writings, to be sure, make scattered and indirect allusions to this mode of thought,[1] but the decisive passages are those located in the Pauline corpus.

Given the current situation in the Christian world, any appraisal of the meanings of this image will be highly controversial. We will not attempt to avoid disagreement, but we will continue to look for the more certain deductions on which some degree of ecumenical consensus may be expected. Many discussions go astray by beginning with the less certain and the more tendentious theories at the expense of overlooking the more certain and obvious meanings. In many passages the major thrust of the apostle's argument is relatively clear, and we should begin with those passages.

Beginning there, we will quickly learn that the phrase " the body of Christ " is not a single expression with an unchanging meaning. Paul's thought remains extremely flexible and elastic. Here the term

173

" body " has one meaning; there it has quite another. Here the term " members " signifies one thing, there another. Rarely can all the nuances of a word be systematically organized into a single pattern. In some passages the church is explicitly identified with Christ's body, but in other passages this identification becomes very tenuous indeed. This variety of usage should warn us against seeking to produce a single inclusive definition of the image, and against importing into each occurrence of the analogy the range of meanings which it bears in other passages.

Redemption from the Body of Death Through the Body of Christ

We will begin with the central passage in the letter to the Romans, ch. 5 through 8. Two key verses may serve as justification for choosing this passage: (1) The apostle summarized his understanding of the human situation apart from Christ with the exclamation: " Who will deliver me from the body of this death? " (Rom. 7:24). Here we seem to have a trenchant statement of the antithesis to belonging to the body of Christ, and if so, we may learn the content of the latter by its contrast to the former. (2) The apostle summarized his understanding of deliverance from one body to the other by the assertion, which he addressed to all the believers in Rome: " You have died to the law through the body of Christ, so that you may belong to another " (v. 4). Postponing for a time the direct consideration of the church, we must seek to comprehend the background in Paul's thought for these two statements.

What is the content of the phrase " the body of death " and how does it throw light upon its presumed opposite [86] **the body of life?** [2] The question calls for us to look again at the material covered earlier (cf. [56]) in which Adam and the Messiah are pictured as the " inclusive representatives " of the two humanities. Those who lived in solidarity with the first Adam constituted one body; those in solidarity with the " one new Man " constituted another. These two bodies provide the only two solidarities that are open to men; in their inherent opposition lies the clue to the character of each. The two are universals and yet are mutually exclusive. To summarize the previous discussion we will tabulate the major formulations of this single antithesis as they appear in Rom., chs. 5 to 8.

In Adam	*In Christ*
all die	all shall be made alive
death rules	all reign in life
all sin	all receive gift of righteousness
sin rules	grace rules
men's bodies are instruments of wickedness	men's bodies become instruments of righteousness
the law of sin and death enslaves men	the law of the Spirit frees men

The first solidarity is embraced in the term " the body of this death " (ch. 7:24); the opposing solidarity is variously described as " life through the one man Jesus Christ " (ch. 5:17), union " with him in a resurrection like his " (ch. 6:5), " eternal life in Christ Jesus " (v. 23), those who are " in the Spirit " (ch. 8:9) or those whose spirits are alive because they are in Christ and Christ is in them (v. 10). Participation in Christ Jesus is participation in an order wherein eternal life rules.

The alternate and antithetical character of the two realms should be clear. The conflict between them is not only analogous to the two humanities but also to the two creations, the two kingdoms, the two ages, and the two sonships, which earlier sections of our study have explored. (Cf. [53], [58], [61], [84]) In dealing with the body of death and its opposite, we are in touch with the cosmic and universal categories of early Christian thought.

We must now turn to the second key verse: " Likewise, my brethren, you have died to the law through the body of Christ, so that you may belong to another, to him who has been raised from the dead in order that we may bear fruit for God " (ch. 7:4). In this verse, which is very strategic on many counts, there are two features that are very important for our discussion: the character of the community whom Paul addressed and the character of the transition from one realm to another.

It is clear that Paul was addressing the church: " *Brothers.*" (Cf. [84]) The *you* refers to all the believers. Of them, three specific things are said. They have died to the law. They belong to the risen Christ. Their new function is to bear fruit for God. These three are not incidental but fundamental to their existence as a community.

They cannot understand themselves as church apart from understanding their death to the law, their new belongingness, and their new vocation.

"You have died to the law through the body of Christ." This is a description of their own death through his body. He had died. "The death he died he died to sin, once for all." (Ch. 6:10.) They too had died to sin. (V. 2.) They had been "baptized into his death" (v. 3). Their newness of life in his resurrection had presupposed burial with him into death. (V. 4.) In this passage Paul stresses both the total dependence of the community on Christ's death and their total interdependence in this event. (Cf. [81]) He also stresses the present significance of the past event. Through baptism they had been united with him in both his dying to sin and his living to God. Now they must consider their "bodies [sic] as dead to sin and alive to God in Christ Jesus" (v. 11). Participation in his body (ch. 7:4) thus means participation in both his dying and his new life. Through this door, they have broken away from the binding servitude to the law. They have been released from slavery to sin and from the death that is sin's rightful wage. (Ch. 6:20-23.) They have been delivered from the wretched existence in the body of death. (Ch. 7:24.) All this had happened "through the body of Christ."

Such a transition could, of course, not be completed until the coming redemption of the body, an event toward which the whole creation moves (ch. 8:23). But this redemption has already been guaranteed by the gift of the Spirit and has already been inaugurated in the power of the Spirit (vs. 9-11). Nevertheless the redemption of the body has yet to be fully realized. Solidarity in the Spirit means, therefore, participation in a living hope that embraces all creation (vs. 21-25).

In his discussion of the two solidarities Paul made use of both the singular and the plural — "body" and "bodies." Whenever the unities and solidarities were of central importance, whenever Paul was considering the mutually exclusive universals (this is his dominant angle of vision) then the singular was more appropriate. (Chs. 6:6, 12; 7:24; 8:13, 23.) When he was adopting the standpoint of an individual agent whose struggles of decision give an inalienable particularity to his own existence, then the distributive plural was more appropriate (ch. 8:11). Thus, the term " body " enabled him to convey, almost in shorthand fashion: (1) the universal solidarity of all persons in one man, whether the old or the new, (2) the particular selfhood of each person with his separate decisions, (3) the diverse acts by which a person was transferred from one humanity to another, and (4) the overarching promise and hope of a single consummation for the whole creation.

This use of the term " body " also underscored the identity between the people-creating work of Jesus Christ and the people-empowering work of the Holy Spirit (ch. 8:10-13). The needs of the situation did not demand any sharp distinction between the two nor did the character of their work permit it. Although the term " body of Christ " as such appears but once (ch. 7:4), there is no doubt that the Kingdom of life in the new Adam was assumed to be identical with the realm of solidarity created and sustained by God through the continuing work of the Spirit of holiness. For example, note these two descriptions of the same act: through *the body of Christ* you have died to the law (v. 4); by *the Spirit* put to death the deeds of the body (ch. 8:13). The meaning would not be greatly changed if we reversed the two phrases: in the body of Christ put to death the deeds of the body; through the Spirit you died to the law. Bondage to the body of death (i.e., the total nexus of relationships to Adam) had been broken by participation in the Spirit of life, a participation synonymous with dying to the law through the body of Christ (i.e., the total nexus of relationships to the new Man). The new bondage within the new body is the realm over which the grace of Christ rules. The solidarity of the church is thus constituted by oneness in this Kingdom, oneness in redemption from the body of death through the dying body of Christ. In this context the use of the phrase " the body of Christ " accented the actual mode of transition by which the community had been delivered from the old kinship to the new (ch. 7:4).

We should note that the relationship between the church and the body of Christ in this passage is not one of simple identity. Ernest Best has reminded us that the majority of commentators find in the phrase " the body of Christ " only a reference to Christ's crucifixion. " The primary reference is to the death of Christ." [3] It is entirely true that it would distort the meaning if we should write the verse thus: "You have died to the law through *the church*."[4] On the other hand, we cannot eliminate the thought of the church. It is present throughout the verse and the whole passage. Dr. Best himself uses the passage extensively to establish the concept of Christ as an "inclusive personality," as the second Adam. One basic meaning of the church as a community *in Christ* is provided by the shared event of dying to the law through the body of Christ. Only thus do believers belong to Christ and therefore to one another. To Paul the only means of deliverance from the body of death is the body of Christ. To be sure, the primary reference is to his crucified body, but it would violate Paul's thought in this passage to disjoin the church from this body. Such a disjunction would probably indicate that our presupposed definition of the church is still remote from Paul's thought. For Paul, death and life are *primary* categories for ecclesiology, and the death and life of Christ were the primary clues to the fundamental choice: either a living death (ch. 7:24) or a dying life (v. 4). The church had its existence at the point where that choice was seen and made.

[87] *The Bodies of the Saints as Members of Christ*

In a very different passage, Paul's mind is brought to a focus upon the same choice, but from the standpoint of the believer's treatment of his own body. How should a Christian think of his own body in its role as a member of Christ? This is the central question in I Cor., ch. 6, where a problem had been created by the practice of flagrant sexual immorality on the part of a Corinthian Christian (ch. 5:1). This act had in turn received the approval of the congregation, which had defended the approval as a demonstration of its new liberty in Christ. To Paul it should have mourned over this appearance of old leaven in its midst (ch. 5:2-8; cf. [6]). The church had supported its approval by an elaborate theological rationalization based on the truth that the Kingdom of God had freed them from law. Thus the action of the individual was defended by the action of the community, and both were based upon a false understanding of life in Christ. The apostle set himself to correct this understanding. According to his analysis their confusion sprang from a false notion of their bodies. The fact that they had been "united to the Lord" had not as yet converted their attitudes toward their own bodies or toward their common obligations as a congregation. We should study carefully the whole passage, noting especially the eight appearances of the term "body."

"All things are lawful for me," but I will not be enslaved by anything. "Food is meant for the stomach, and the stomach for food" and God will destroy both one and the other. The *body* is not meant for immorality, but for the Lord, and the Lord for the *body*. And God raised the Lord and will also raise us up by his power. Do you not know that your *bodies* are members of Christ? Shall I therefore take the members of Christ and make them members of a prostitute? Never! Do you not know that he who joins himself to a prostitute becomes one *body* with her? For, as it is written, "The two shall become one." But he who is united to the Lord becomes one spirit with him. Shun immorality. Every other sin which a man commits is outside the *body;* but the immoral man sins against his own *body*. Do you not know that your *body* is a temple of the Holy Spirit within you, which you have from God? You are not your own; you were bought with a price. So glorify God in your *body*. (I Cor. 6:12-20.)

The first step toward comprehending Paul's understanding of bodies as members of Christ is to locate collateral descriptions of the same relationship. This passage abounds with them, especially if we include the preceding discussion of the same problem. In this preceding section (chs. 5:1 to 6:11) Paul had brought within the circle of reference a long series of church images. Those who are members of Christ have been washed, have been sanctified (have become saints, cf. [69]), have been justified in the name of the Lord (cf. [71]) and in "the Spirit of our God" (cf. [67]). They have been made heirs of the Kingdom (cf. [58]) and of the Day (cf. [63]). They have become the unleavened bread (ch. 5:7; cf. [6]) for whom the Paschal Lamb has been sacrificed (v. 7; cf. [52]). Their assemblies are therefore occasions for celebrating the Passover of the exodus. (Vs. 4, 8; cf. [41]) They have become separated from "the immoral of the world" by having become brothers (v. 11; ch. 6:6, 8; cf. [84]) and by their participation at the same table (v. 11; cf. [8]). Accordingly, they are fully qualified to serve as judges in enforcing community discipline. (Vs. 12-13.) Here no fewer than twelve collateral images contribute to the description of the Christian congregation.

The list of associated images is extended still farther in the passage cited above. This community was viewed as standing under the power of the risen Lord. (Ch. 6:14.) Their body (the singular may be significant) has become a temple established by the indwelling Spirit. (V. 19; cf. [48]) They are men who have been bought as possessions of a new master who had paid their ransom price (cf. [78]). Accordingly, the glory of God must produce its glorification of God in their body (notice the singular "*body*"; cf. [62]). This whole range of images constantly fed Paul's thoughts, yet he was quite unconscious of the rhetorical clumsiness of mixing metaphors so freely. The commingling of the images accents the unity and solidarity pertaining to a congregation that exemplifies "one spirit with the Lord." One supposes that Paul might have conveyed his message without referring to members and bodies.

He did, however, place at the center of argument the picture of the body of each believer as a member of Christ (ch. 6:15), and the reason for this is not far to seek. His wayward followers, in their self-defense and corporate rationalizations, had appealed to a popular slogan, "Food is meant for the stomach and the stomach for food." They had turned what to them was no doubt a Christian understanding of the functions of the body into a justification of harlotry. It was the form of their delusion that conditioned the form of the apostle's therapy. Paul furnishes us here with several clues to his conceptions of both the believer's body and the Lord's body, in their separateness and in their interdependence. Let us observe the clues and attempt to draw conclusions therefrom.

One clue is provided by Paul's rejection of the slogan, "Food for the stomach and the stomach for food." Both the food and the stomach, insists Paul, will be destroyed by God. But the body must not be confused with the stomach. The stomach will be destroyed, but the body will be raised through Christ's power. The body represents the person's whole self, inclusive of will and heart, soul and mind. The point at issue is the believer's body, not the physical organs such as the stomach.

A further clue appears in the substitution of an alternate slogan, "The body for the Lord, the Lord for the body." Instead of the complementary relation of the stomach and food, the believer must recognize the complementary relation of the body and the Lord. Here may be discerned both a comparison (the same dative is used in both slogans) and a contrast (the body does not consume the Lord). What is the import of this alternative slogan? The context suggests the following paraphrase: the Lord is *for the body* because he has died for its redemption; he has become its true servant and Lord. He wills to accomplish unity with it. The body is *for the Lord* because it has been claimed for inclusion within his redemption of all things (his power is the means of its resurrection). As his member, the body is obligated to serve him, to manifest union with him, to become his instrumentality.

Still another clue emerges when we notice the nature of prostitution as Paul saw it. Prostitution implied that the body had become the instrument of immorality, not of the Lord. It substituted one union for another, union with the prostitute instead of union with the Lord. The alternatives were sharply defined: either " one body with her " or " one spirit with him." This alternative is made all the more rigorous by the use of the same verb to denote being united to the harlot and being united to the Lord. Each union is complete: the two become one. Therefore each union excludes the other. In one case the situation is *one body* with her; in the other *one spirit* with him. It is probably impossible to recover the reason why Paul should shift from one body to one spirit in this contrast. But surely he was seeking to emphasize the character of the bond between Christ and his members. (Ch. 6:15).

This oneness of spirit with the Lord makes every person a temple, a dwelling place of God in which the recognition of total indebtedness yields the proper act of total self-giving in glorifying the new owner. The gift of Christ produces the obligation; unity with Christ in the Spirit empowers the fulfillment of the obligation. This oneness of Spirit links together the fact that God had raised the Lord and the fact that he " will also raise us up by his power." To Paul there was no sharp conflict between spirit and body. To be joined to the Lord as his member is to be one spirit with him. (V. 17.) Body is not defined per se, nor can it be so defined, apart from this body-Lord relationship. Man's use of the body simply discloses the character of this relationship as one of reciprocal loyalty and action. In other words, the body is he whom the Lord serves, the Lord is he whom the body serves. Everything that a person chooses to do through his body becomes subject to his status as a member of Christ.

In this passage, of course, Paul does not use the phrase " the body of Christ," nor does he speak directly of the church; this pattern of thought is not absent, however, because he speaks so strongly about the bodies of all believers as members (*melē*) of Christ. It is impossible to visualize members apart from the body to which they belong. As members they are forbidden to do anything that might embody any other sovereignty; any subjection of the will to another (here to the harlot) becomes a sin against the body and thereby against the Lord. The Messiah will not tolerate this kind of prostitution of his own members. Harlotry is idolatry.

Other Pauline passages corroborate this set of attitudes toward the ways in which the believer treats his body as a member of Christ. He must present it as a living sacrifice. (Rom. 12:1.) It must be pommeled and subdued, disciplined and trained. (I Cor. 9:27.) It is the means by which the believer manifests both the dying and the living power of the Lord Jesus (II Cor. 4:10; Gal. 6:17), the means by which he magnifies Christ (Phil. 1:20). In this context we deal not so much with the church as Christ's body as with the believer's body as a member of Christ and " one spirit with him." Although the emphasis in this chapter is on the individual saint and on his body as the meeting place of reciprocal loyalties, a necessary presupposition of the argument is the membership of all believers in the one body of Christ. To be a member of Christ thus defines and determines the totality of one's existence vis-à-vis other men.

Perhaps this is the place for a footnote regarding the Pauline idea of members. In our day the term has lost its figurative force, even in our thought about the church. The church is a membership organization; i.e., persons become members of it. In Paul's thought, Christ (as body) has members, i.e., men and women whom he has incorporated within himself as belonging to him. Only as a corollary of this basic image could they be visualized as members of the church, although this corollary was never used during the New Testament period.

[88] *Partnership in the Body and the Blood*

We now turn to two passages where Paul was impelled by problems in the Corinthian church to remind the congregation of the meaning of their common meal. These problems are sufficiently different to call for a separate analysis of the two passages.

In the first (I Cor., ch. 10), Paul attacked the misuse of liberty on the part of the "spiritualists" in Corinth. The problem was occasioned by the purchase of meat that had been offered in sacrifice at a pagan temple, together with the fact that Christians were eating meat with unbelievers in such a way as to offend the conscience of other believers. More than this, they were openly flaunting their emancipation by eating with unbelievers at the festival meals in the pagan temples. Paul did not deny the cleanness of the meat (vs. 26-27), nor did he demand the termination of tablefellowship with unbelievers. He denounced the practice of placing one's own advantage above the neighbor's (v. 33) and the related practice of worshiping idols. Both contradicted the interdependence of the Christian community as symbolized by their joint participation in the Lord's table. To eat at that table should have eliminated such practices.

The cup of blessing which we bless, is it not a participation in the blood of Christ? The bread which we break, is it not a participation in the body of Christ? Because there is one loaf, we who are many are one body, for we all partake of the same loaf. (I Cor. 10:16-17.)

Immediately we notice that the figure of the body is not the only index and instrument of oneness. The body of Christ and his blood are complementary channels of the unity. The blessing of the cup of blessing is a participation in the blood of Christ just as truly as the breaking of the loaf is a participation in his body. The oneness of the body and blood, in turn, was also paralleled by the oneness of the table. (V. 21; cf. [7]-[10]) Participation at one table had a double implication: it expressed a single communal entity ("we who are many are one body"), and it recognized the Lord's exclusive sovereignty over this entity. It conveyed his power and his right to total obedience. The covenant sealed with him at this table was assumed to be absolutely binding and absolutely exclusive; it articulated the unity in plurality of this participation.

When we seek for analogies to this unique table, we find two in the context. The first is provided by "the practice of Israel" (v. 18). In Paul's thought, partnership in the loaf and cup was comparable to Israel's partnership in the altar sacrifices. Paul even carried further the analogy provided by Israel's history. The covenantal oneness in the Eucharist paralleled the covenantal oneness of Israel, of "our fathers" in the wilderness sojourn. The bread corresponded to the exodus manna and the wine to the water from the Rock. (Vs. 3-4.)

All ate the same spiritual food and all drank the same spiritual drink. For they drank from the spiritual Rock which followed them, and the Rock was Christ.

This was far more than a casual comparison, because Christ *was* the Rock from whom all "our fathers" drank. Christ had given unity to Israel through the eating and drinking, as much in Moses' day as in Paul's. (Cf. [41]) In both covenants this unity was mediated by spiritual food and by spiritual drink from the spiritual Rock, i.e., by the gift of the Holy Spirit to Israel. (There is presumably some connection between this spiritual food and the use of the same adjective *pneumatikos* to describe the risen body of Christ and the Christians in I Cor. 15:44-46.)

It was this continuity in one table which enabled Paul to speak so trenchantly of the dangers of making the Lord jealous. (Cf. I Cor. 10:9 and v. 22.) In spite of eating the spiritual bread, the fathers had become idolaters, undisciplined dancers, self-willed grumblers who "put the Lord to the test" (vs. 6-13). Precisely the same temptation attacked their sons who ate at the Lord's table. Only at one point did Paul distinguish these two tables. The fathers and their sons lived in two different periods. "We," wrote Paul, "are those upon whom the ends of the ages have come." (V. 11.) It was participation in the new age (cf. [61]) that gave greater urgency to the demand for wholehearted allegiance and threatened greater peril to those who provoked the Lord to jealousy. Partnership at his altar carried with it the extremest hazards of playing with his Final Judgment and grace.

Another instructive parallel was provided by the practice in heathen temples. As might be expected, the contrasts here overshadowed the similarities; Paul gave no hint of any continuity between the two communities. Nevertheless, there remained a similarity. Just as the cup of demons made men "partners with the demons" (v. 20), so too the cup of the Lord created partnership with the Lord. The validity of this comparison alone validated the contrast; partnership with the Lord was absolutely incompatible with partnership with demons.

The two sovereignties were mutually exclusive.

In referring, then, to both heathen and Jewish practices, Paul accented the power of Christ and of the Spirit to establish, through the covenantal meal, a community that should embody corporate dependence on God and the interdependence of its members. Paul also used the analogies to stress the fearful hazards of betraying this dependence and interdependence. The Corinthians defied their oneness in the body of Christ not alone by overt worship in the pagan temples but more significantly by injuring their brothers. When a Christian sought his own good at the expense of his brother, Paul saw this as nothing less than idolatry. Selfish indifference to the brother effectively denied both the Lord's Lordship and body's unity. The basic choice for every Christian was whether he would participate in the building up (v. 23; cf. [82]) of the Lord's house. Eating this bread with gratitude freed the eater to eat all sorts of food, but it also bound him to do everything to God's glory (vs. 30-31), and God is glorified when a person seeks the neighbor's good. (Cf. [62]) Paul thus showed how participation in the one loaf and cup was intrinsically linked to participation in the works of love, which alone could demonstrate the power of this Lord over his own body. As Bishop John Robinson so succinctly says: " The body is built up and cemented not by baptism but by love." [5] Cup — loaf — blood — body — table — the symbols varied, but the emphasis remained the same — the interdependence of the one community in its *koinōnia* in the one Lord. Accordingly, participation in this body constituted a covenant of dying with Christ and of loving one another. *Sōma* and *koinōnia* are used in this passage in such a way as to explain each other.

As in the earlier passages, it would distort Paul's thought here to make *church* and *body* interchangeable or identical terms. Yet the community's participation in the Lord's body is seen to be intrinsic to its life. Its unity stems from the oneness of the loaf and cup. Its interdependence stems from its dependence on the Lord's death. And communion in this death excludes the thought of idolatry, of divided lordship. The sacrament demonstrates the strength of the Lord to destroy all other lords (v. 22). Moreover, participation at his table is not limited to the liturgical action itself. The communion extends throughout the whole range of the believers' activity. This

Lord jealously watches everything his people do. We may note, finally, that in this context there is no need to introduce the idea of members. The body is not visualized as having members, but the body and blood, both symbols of sacrificial death, are visualized in the form of bread and wine.

There is a second passage that deals with the Lord's table, but that bears upon a different situation in Corinth. (I Cor. 11:17-34.) In this case the defiance of love took as its occasion the assembly of the congregation for the Lord's supper. It appears that the individual believers brought their own baskets and ate from them, often without waiting for one another. There was no genuine sharing of the food; some gorged themselves while their brothers remained hungry. (V. 21.) Paul saw such gluttony as a clear case of " despising the church of God." Men treated their brothers in a way precisely the opposite of God's way. Instead of enriching the poor, they put the poor to shame. This is in fact the equivalent of despising God's church. (V. 22.) " Therefore," said Paul, drawing the only possible conclusion, " this meal which you eat is not the *Lord's* supper." It was not the supper of which he was the lord, the host, and the food; not the partnership in the one loaf.

To make clear the contrast between such meals and the Lord's table, Paul quotes the tradition which he had given to this congregation:

The Lord Jesus on the night when he was betrayed took bread, and when he had given thanks, he broke it, and said, " This is my body, which is for you. Do this in remembrance of me." In the same way also the cup, after supper, saying, " This cup is the new covenant in my blood. Do this, as often as you drink it, in remembrance of me." For as often as you eat this bread and drink the cup, you proclaim the Lord's death until he comes." (I Cor. 11:23-26.)

We can state the primary issue behind Paul's thought in these terms: when was the common meal the Lord's table and when was it not the Lord's table? We have already seen the negative test. It was not the Lord's table when participants despised God's church and profaned his house by putting their own good above their neighbor's. The positive test was more complex because several criteria were woven together. The table was the Lord's when it was a living remembrance (a re-enactment, a moment when the past event ruled the present) of the night when Jesus was betrayed by his disciples. The table was the Lord's when men proclaimed and renewed the power of Jesus' thanksgiving. It was the Lord's when the bread that was broken and given was his body, broken and given, and when the cup was his blood of the new covenant. It was the Lord's when the present moment was subjugated by it to the power of the coming Lord, whose death revealed the present operation of judgment and mercy. What made it the Lord's supper was the presence of him who said, "This is *my* body." By giving his body and blood for others he had bound them into a covenant of self-giving. By sharing in his body, they affirmed this covenant which had been sealed by his death — and theirs.

Why did Paul appeal to this liturgy which was already familiar to the Corinthians? What relevance did it have to their disputes? What light did the liturgy and the disputes throw upon the church as Christ's body? There were divisions, factions, smugness, and gluttony. The liturgy was a form of judgment by the Lord, a judgment that produced either chastening or condemnation. (V. 32.) Only these two results are mentioned, because no third alternative is possible. There is no mention of any blessing available that is free from chastening or condemnation. Each must judge himself as to which of these verdicts pertained to him. Paradoxically the oneness in the body and blood of Christ increased the danger that this congregation and its members would be condemned with the world. (V. 32.) The hazard was very great that they should " come together to be condemned." Most trenchantly stated, " Whoever eats the bread or drinks the cup of the Lord in an unworthy manner will be guilty of profaning *the body* and *blood* of the Lord." (V. 27.) This warning appears to be exactly the same as another: " Anyone who eats and drinks without discerning *the body* eats and drinks judgment upon himself " (v. 29). There were doubtless in Paul's mind many ways of profaning the body and blood (or the table or the new covenant), but the specific way that he described here was that of humiliating companions at this table. (Vs. 21-22.) Factions and divisions in the church may have been inevitable (v. 19); even so, the behavior at the one table placed them all under a scrutiny in which " those who are genuine among you " might be sifted out. These genuine partners presumably were those who accepted chastening (v. 31) and who applied to themselves a ruthless self-examination (v. 28). They were also, although this remains conjectural, those who ate in a worthy manner, those who discerned the *body*. Disputes have raged over what constitutes an unworthy manner, over what is the body to be discerned and how such discernment proceeds. No solution is yet in sight, and v. 30 will probably always defy exact explanation. " This [failure to discern the body] is why many of you are weak and ill and some have died." The context, however, emboldens me to venture two comments. Eating in an unworthy manner does not establish the rule that only the sinless should sit at this table; rather, it establishes the principle that this is the place where in self-judgment the participant must recognize the Lord's judgment. (Vs. 31-32.) To discern the body includes the discernment of their communal solidarity in Christ. Such discernment produces mutual courtesy, mutual concern, and an active sharing of resources by those who have with those who have not. (Vs. 21-22, 33-34.) This discernment can be produced only by genuine participation in the body that has been broken for others. The absence of dying to self-interest and of living for others profanes the body and blood of the Lord. Therefore the body that must be discerned includes this nuance: it is such an interdependence of the Crucified with his own that a denial of *koinōnia* with them is in fact a denial of *koinōnia* in him. It is noteworthy that in all four pericopes we have analyzed, social behavior can belie membership in the one body or participation in the Lord's table. Believers may be members of harlots, they may eat at demon's tables, they may not discern the Lord's body, but they cannot negate the sovereignty of the one Lord or evade his jealousy.

Are we now in a position to summarize the attitudes toward the church which pervade Paul's remarks concerning the Eucharistic body? We acknowledge that the use of the term " body " is at many points problematical. The interpretation is extremely difficult. I believe, however, that there may be at least a limited agreement with the more obvious inferences I have drawn. Controversy flames up when exegetes try to deduce from the separate passages a systematic doctrine, when on the basis of this doctrine they press all the nuances of meaning into a precisely defined, conceptualist mold, and when they then mechanically transfer to the church whatever Paul has said about Christ's body. In the passages thus far analyzed Paul was not attempting to provide for exegetes any of these things — a systematic, coherent doctrine concerning the nature of Christ's body or the nature of the church. Neither Christological nor ecclesiological nor liturgical questions stood at the center of Paul's concern in I Corinthians. He appealed to the body image in a flexible fashion, always associating it with other images. In all contexts the power of the Spirit was inseparable from the oneness of the body. In all, the exclusive sovereignty of the one Lord was taken as constitutive of this body. In all, participation in the body was in fact a participation in Christ's death, participation that when genuine, transformed from within all human relationships. This transformation produced a societal interdependence that was accorded an unquestioned reality. Those who belonged to Christ participated as one in this revolution. Wherever an image of solidarity was used, it pointed to the fact and mode of the transformation wrought by Christ's vicarious dying. Accordingly, the central images are: body, blood, loaf, cup, covenant, altar, temple, sacrifice. In none of the Eucharistic passages did Paul have recourse to the cognate images of members and head. These cognates were not needed to explicate Paul's meaning. In fact, they would have disturbed the more basic thought of one loaf and the common participation in the one death.

In his thinking, Paul does not appear to have isolated the image of the body for special emphasis; when he appealed to this figure it was the contours of the church's confusions that made that image especially germane. In I Cor., ch. 6, the communal defense of fornication impelled Paul to explain the meaning of Christ's Lordship over the believer's body. In I Cor., ch. 10, the proud participation by Christians in the tables of demons provoked his exposition of partnership in the table of the Lord. In I Cor., ch. 11, the selfish individualism at the Eucharist itself required a warning against the danger incurred in profaning it. In all three situations Paul's thought diverged sharply from that of his adversaries. They were guilty of more flagrant defiance of the Lord and of the Lord's people than they had supposed. Therefore, he knew that they must discern the living, judging presence of the Lord within his community before their pride would be humbled and their individualism overcome.

[89] The Diversities of Ministries in One Body

The Pauline use of this cycle of images leads us now to the twelfth chapter of I Corinthians. Here we must note that, although the explicit use of *sōma* is limited to some sixteen verses (vs. 12-27) the whole of ch. 12 to 14 is a single unit, and the interpretation of any one sentence must be congenial to the whole unit. We must also remember that throughout these chapters Paul was grappling with a single situation in the life of the church in Corinth. That community was being demoralized by the profusion of spiritual gifts, a profusion that was most apparent when the church gathered for worship. This profusion of gifts encouraged recipients to draw invidious distinctions among themselves and to claim for one gift preeminence over others. Thus was produced a bedlam of sound and a competitive spirit that were destroying the fabric of fellowship. All this was rationalized and justified by an appeal to the Holy Spirit. The anarchy in the employment of the various gifts had reached a crisis that demanded the most careful reassessment of the nature and function of all gifts.

In Paul's mind the issue resolved itself into a matter of understanding the full correlation between the oneness of the Holy Spirit, as the source of all gifts, and the oneness of the church, as the area where the gifts were apportioned individually. This resolution of the question was presented in the first eleven verses in such a way as to embrace the argument of all three chapters. At the outset (ch. 12:1-3) the apostle established the inseparability of the Spirit of God from the confession of Jesus' Lordship. No spiritual gift could have come from God if it did not support this confession, nor could this confession be affirmed apart from the instrumentality of the Spirit. The same God, the same Lord, the same Spirit — these were actively co-present in all genuine gifts. No form of spiritual expression could be authentic which did not serve all and which was not empowered by all. God was at work in all the varieties of working. The Lord was serving and being served in all the forms of service. Therefore in every spiritual gift there must be oneness in source and goal, a oneness that was itself manifested by the variety in the gifts themselves. Unity was not uniformity; it was neither the source of uniformity nor served by it. "There are varieties of gifts, but the same Spirit." This constitutes the basic axiom to the whole argument.

On this axiom rested the corollary: every gift had been dispensed for the sake of producing the common good. The thought of Paul was here focused not upon the individual believers, but upon their separate gifts, services, and accomplishments (*charismata, diakoniai, energata*), i.e., not upon a particular prophet but upon the work of the Spirit in prophecy. This distinction has both doctrinal and practical import: doctrinal in that the link between the Holy Spirit and the individual was formed by a gift that was shared by many persons, practical in that the zealots among the Corinthians were concealing their private ambitions behind the primacy that they claimed for that spiritual gift in which they were proficient (e.g., glossolalia).

We may note that in this opening paragraph Paul dealt with the matter without summoning to his help the picture of the church as the body of Christ. I do not suggest any disjunction between the reality of the Holy Spirit and the reality of Christ's body. But a distinction may be drawn between alternate ways of describing that one reality. This passage demonstrates the fact that Paul was quite able to deal with the dynamic interdependence of all the gifts within the church without explicitly using the somatic terms: members, body, head. In fact, the apostle seems to introduce the body image as a supplementary way of conveying the truth that all the gifts " are inspired by one and the same Spirit, who apportions to each one individually as he wills " (v. 11). Observe how the pneumatological note dominated the Christological: " By one Spirit we were all baptized into one body . . . and all were made to drink of one Spirit " (v. 13).

" All baptized into one body " — this baptism had displaced the solidarities of race and class: " Jews or Greeks, slave or free." In this context, however, the reference to racial and economic barriers was quite parenthetical, included no doubt because Paul was using material that had been formulated in another connection. He does not develop the theme of the changes in social stratification but hurries on to apply the picture of the body to the realities of congregational animosities. Because their animosities stemmed from pride in the superiority of certain spiritual gifts, when Paul spoke of the body's members in this context he was thinking still of the Spirit's varied gifts to the church rather than of individuals who had received those gifts. It was probably not the individual believer per se who said, " Be cause I am a foot, but not a hand "; rather, it was the believer whose gift was being belittled by his fellows whose protest took this form. The answer to the protest, accordingly, was an answer relevant to all to whom God had apportioned either an inferior or a superior gift. All gifts and services must be regarded as essential to the one body. In fact the more lowly forms of service had properly received from God the greater honor. Pluriformity of gifts, services, and achievements was necessary; exclusive claims for any one of them were impossible. Thus discord among the recipients of the various gifts was ruled out by their interdependence in the Spirit, in the Lord, and in God. No recipient who was proficient and energetic in the use of any *charisma* could appeal to the superiority of his gift over that of others.

We have drawn a distinction between a spiritual gift and its recipients. Quite obviously this distinction was not disjunctive. Every gift was manifested through particular individuals and no individual entered this community without participating in a gift. (Vs. 1-3, 13.) When Paul spoke of members of the body he probably had in mind both gift and person.

Just as the body is one and has many members, and all the members of the body, though many, are one body, so it is with Christ. (V. 12.)

Now you are the body of Christ and individually members of it. (V. 27.)

In this verse just quoted we come to the first occasion on which Paul directly described the church (you) as the body of Christ, and where each individual was simultaneously viewed as a member of that body. Moreover, the context indicates the motivation and meaning of this description. Paul's basic concern was to restore the sense of unity in the Corinthian congregation by restoring the sense of interdependence among the believers. And this restoration required a true sense of their mutual relation to Christ. To say " one body " was to say " the common good " (v. 7) or to say that the members " have the same care for one another " (v. 27). The apostle reached a climax in his argument by concluding: " If one member suffers, all suffer together; if one member is honored (*doxadzein;* cf. [62]), all rejoice with it." The one body means absolute solidarity in suffering and glory. The image of the body articulated the reality of unity in the plurality of suffering and glory, and attributed both unity and plurality to the service of Jesus, the work of God, and the gifts of the Spirit in the new age.[6] (Cf. [67], [68])

So much by way of comment on ch. 12. But Paul did not cease discussing this interdependence of the body when he concluded the chapter. To be sure, the term *sōma* was left behind, but the character and work of the Spirit remained the subject of the next two chapters. In ch. 14 the apostle sought to replace the anarchy of spiritual gifts in the assemblies of the Corinthians with the order intended by " the God of peace." (Ch. 14:33, 40.) The congregation must apply to the exercise of all gifts the axioms of ch. 12. In effect, this meant that those spiritual gifts must be coveted and preferred which produced upbuilding, encouragement, and consolation. The edification of the church became a strategic test of the authenticity of each gift. (Ch. 14:3-5.) This criterion not only replaced the goal of self-enhancement and self-satisfaction, but it even reduced the importance of speaking to God or of understanding the mysteries of the Spirit. (V. 2.) The excellence that counted most was excellence " in building up the church " (v. 12; cf. [82]). To discern the body of Christ in the assemblies for worship was tantamount to the discernment in all the gifts of their true function in serving the community. Those who have been baptized by the Spirit into one body (ch. 12:13) must zealously utilize whatever gift the Spirit had apportioned, but this necessity must be controlled by the truth that the building up of the church (ch. 14:12) continues to be the overriding intention of the Spirit.

Paul had prepared for the explicit commands of ch. 14 by characterizing that gift which more than all others accomplished the nourishment and growth of the body. This gift, the gift of love, was given with every other gift and was superior to them all. No other spiritual gift profited anyone if its exercise had been divorced from this gift. (Ch. 13:1-3.) Paul intentionally contrasted love to those gifts which had engrossed the congregation and which were more obviously effective. By contrast with the other gifts, love belonged intrinsically to the Kingdom that never ends. No consummation of God's redemption would ever render love obsolete (unlike even prophecy and martyrdom). We cannot expound the compressed verses of this chapter, but we must not fail to suggest that Paul intended this description of love as an exposition of the meaning of the one body (ch. 12) and the building up of the church (ch. 14). The works of love (ch. 13:4-7) were the primary means for enhancing the inter-dependence of the body's members. Consequently, this love defined what it meant to be the *sōma*, whether as individual believers or as recipients of such gifts as prophecy. Love was that which, being itself a gift of the Spirit, produced the varieties of gifts and simultaneously unified them in the service of, shall we say, the brothers? Yes, and the world and the Lord also. It supremely illustrated what lay behind Paul's words in his opening summary: varieties of gifts, the same spirit; varieties of service, the same Lord; varieties of working, the same God. (Ch. 12:4-6.) First Corinthians, ch. 13, must therefore be interpreted as having major ecclesiological importance. The gift and service of love was the manifestation of the pluriform unity of the members in the one body. The image of the body and the image of love should for all significant purposes be considered one image; they cannot, in fact, be considered otherwise, since the primary content of both is determined by the image of Christ. (Cf. [68])

The cluster of ideas in I Cor., chs. 12 to 14, appeared again in an abbreviated fashion in Rom., ch. 12. The situation was probably different, although in Romans it is difficult to reconstruct the connection between the teaching and a specific need of the Roman congregation. There are two minor variations in the statements concerning the body. (1) In I Corinthians, Paul had written, " You are *the body of Christ* and individually members *of it* " (I Cor. 12:27). Now he writes, " As in one body we have many members, and all the members do not have the same function, so we, though many, are *one body in Christ*, and individually members *one of another*." (Rom. 12:4-5.) Some students have detected a wide difference between saying one body *in* Christ and saying the body *of* Christ. This difference seems to me to be largely verbal and due to the native flexibility of Paul's mind. There seems no reason to doubt that Paul had but one truth in mind and that the two forms of expression should be kept quite interchangeable. (2) In Romans we find the supplementary statement " individually members *one of another*," which adds a nuance not found so explicitly in I Corinthians. It is an important nuance, however, even though it renders the initial picture more difficult to visualize. Each person is not only a member of the one body in Christ; he is also, within the same body, a member of all the other Christians and all of them are members of him. Paul wanted to stress the interdependence of the members, and it is this intention which led him to stretch the analogy almost beyond recognition. Yet even this stress upon being members of other members, even their compresence in one another, is found over and over again in I Corinthians, although there it is more aptly couched in terms of building up the church by building up one another.

Two other variants may be noted. One primary motive in Romans for using this traditional pattern was to correct a Christian's attitude toward himself: he must not regard himself more highly than the measure of faith permitted (Rom. 12:3). And another variant in application was due to the absence of the same setting in services of worship, confused by excessive zeal for ecstatic speaking. As a consequence of this absence, the list of functions did not follow the order of "platform leaders," but moved quickly into the less dramatic gifts, like the acts of mercy, which were equally spiritual but less easily associated with formal offices in the church. Proportionately more attention was given to those gifts which by nature were intended to be universally exercised by all the body's members. In fact, it is difficult to detect just where Paul terminates this list. He may not have intended to include the work of overcoming evil with good (v. 21) in the list of gifts that begins with prophecy and *diakonia* (v. 6); yet, he surely meant to include the gift of love (ch. 12:9; 13:8-10). And if love belonged on the list, can the other things mentioned in the chapter be excluded? It would appear that the unity of the body and its many functions was understood by the apostle to cover a vast range of activities and attitudes, stretching out through every believer toward the farthermost boundaries of his willing and doing. In I Corinthians the immediate horizon was sufficient: the "service of worship" of a single congregation. In Romans it became clear that no limits could be placed, nor boundaries drawn, around the operation of the spiritual gifts that found their cohesion in the one Christ.

The Spiritual Body

We began this section of our study with the goal of surveying the central connotations of the Pauline images of the body of Christ, and the members of that body. Already we have noted the wide variety of nuances, and the extensive range of cross references to other images. Before proceeding to a new passage, we should recall *one* of those cross references which has appeared in every passage thus far. At every step we have encountered evidence that oneness in the body is paralleled by oneness in the Spirit. In the examination of the body of death we learned that to die to the law through the body of Christ was for Paul equivalent to serving " in the new life of the Spirit." (Rom. 7:4-6.) In his attack upon fornication Paul insisted that every member of Christ had become " one spirit with him " (I Cor. 6:17). In resisting the practice of drinking the cup of demons, the apostle appealed to the precedent of Israel, which had eaten the spiritual food and had drunk the spiritual drink from the spiritual Rock (Christ). He thus stressed the spiritual character of the Eucharist, and thereby the spiritual character of the solidarity of the community. (Ch. 10:1-22.) So too when he was dealing with the strident divisions within the church (ch. 11:18) as it gathered for the Supper and the worship, he made it clear that the discernment of the body was linked closely to the discernment of the oneness of the Spirit (ch. 12:1-11). It was by *one* Spirit that they had been baptized into one body. (V. 13.) It was this same Spirit, at work within the community, which gave the guarantee of the ultimate " redemption of our bodies " and thus provided the ground of hope for all creation. (Rom. 8:18-27.)

This continuous interaction of body and spirit in defining the character of the church reaches climactic clarity in the concept of the [90] spiritual body as expressed in I Cor., ch. 15. We should therefore take a special interest in this chapter, and be specially alert to the possibility that any reference to Christ's body or to the Spirit may have a bearing upon the idea of the church, and may throw light upon the other passages that we have surveyed.

It seems utterly foolhardy to attempt an exposition of I Cor., ch. 15, merely as one small section of a survey of church images. A dozen complex issues, all unsolved, meet us in this chapter, and scholarship is far from agreed on their proper statement. It would be a great convenience to any expositor if he could avoid entanglement in the intricacies of this nest of problems, but unfortunately almost every basic theological issue sooner or later leads to such entanglement.

To be sure, many general readers and even many scholars read this discussion of the resurrection as if it had nothing to say on ecclesiological matters. Presumably the argument of the chapter centers in the effort to answer two questions: Is there a resurrection of the dead? If so, with what kind of bodies do the dead rise from the tomb? At first glance, such questions have nothing at all to do with ecclesiology. As death and resurrection are usually defined the answers to these questions, while naturally important, are not integral to the nature of the church. Conversely, whenever the church is conceived apart from its Christological and pneumatological substance (and hence in a very un-Pauline way), then the discussion of death and resurrection becomes quite irrelevant. We are prevented from adopting this dichotomy because already we have seen that the participation by the church in the death and resurrection of Jesus Christ is native to its existence qua church.

Reaction against the dichotomy has led some scholars to contend that whenever Paul discussed the body of Christ he also discussed the church. Therefore the spiritual body (*sōma pneumatikon*) of I Cor., ch. 15, must be identical with the church. The risen body of Jesus Christ is actually coterminous with his elect community. In raising up the church, God has given a new form and mode to the dying body of the Savior. Accordingly, ch. 15 is not simply ecclesiological by implication but is totally dominated by the idea of the church.[7] When a scholar has eyes for only this one church image, when in exploring the Pauline literature he discovers the unvarying realism in Paul's use of *sōma*, and when he assumes that the apostle always used this term consistently, then he is practically forced to this conclusion.

Our interpretation of the image of the spiritual body may provide an alternative both to this verbalistic monism and to this hasty dichotomy. It is true that Paul's argument in I Cor., ch. 15, has many important implications for his doctrine of the church, but it is very doubtful if we should make the church coterminous with the risen body of Christ. Paul's use of the body image was too flexible to justify such an equation. His reliance upon many images should warn us not to rely unduly upon one; his avoidance of systematic conceptual equations should discourage the making of such equations on our part. His pastoral concern for specific issues should remind us that our thought also is perforce conditioned by the existential situation.

Let us look, then, at the problems posed for Paul by his adversaries in Corinth, who were probably the same group of spiritualist libertarians whose Christian faith had offered a theological justification for sexual license (ch. 6), for continuing to eat in idol's temples (ch. 10), for self-gratification at the Lord's table (ch. 11), and for uncontrolled spiritual frenzy in the services of worship (chs. 12 to 14). Several of their questions are explicitly mentioned in ch. 15 and others are mirrored in Paul's answers. (1) " Some of you say that there is no resurrection of the dead." (V. 12.) (2) Some were perhaps saying in effect: because there is no resurrection " let us eat and drink because tomorrow we die " (v. 32). (3) Their skepticism concerning the resurrection stemmed in part from their inability to answer *how:* " With what kind of body do they come? " (v. 35). It may have been encouraged by Paul's own insistence that " flesh and blood cannot inherit the Kingdom of God " (v. 50). (4) It may also have been bound up with the doctrine that man's spiritual body had been created before the natural body and therefore was not affected by the death of the latter. (V. 46.) Since this was true, they argued that victory over death did not require that the mortal put on the immortal. (V. 53.) (5) From the foregoing convictions they had drawn the inference that faith in Christ did not require " dying daily " (v. 30), daily work in the Lord (v. 58), or strenuous labor according to the grace that he had bestowed (vs. 10, 58).

Paul was abrupt and harsh in his rejoinder. Such convictions marked the questioners not as wise men but as fools. (V. 35.) They were not truly " spiritual " men nor were they acquainted with the elemental mysteries. (V. 51.) They prided themselves on a faith that was vain, because they believed themselves to be freed from sin when they were in fact still bound by sin. (V. 17.) Paul set himself to answer their basic questions concerning the fact and mode of resurrection, but behind his answers we discern his attack on a skepticism of action that was more deadly to him than this skepticism in thought. Here we will attempt to examine the points where church images entered his mind and qualified his thought.

The apostle testified that in Christ's resurrection a new creation had already begun, a harvest of which Christ himself was the first fruits. (Cf. [54]) Christ has become the last Adam (vs. 20-22), in whom all men would be made alive. "Thus it is written, 'The first man Adam became a living being'; the last Adam became a life-giving Spirit." (V. 45.) We have already seen how importantly this conception of the two Adams influenced ecclesiology. (Cf. [56]) Those who belonged to this last Adam, those who received his image, were united with him in the Kingdom of the life-giving Spirit. (Vs. 45-49.) The image of the new creation here coalesced with the image of the Kingdom of God. (Vs. 24, 50.) Christ had already begun his reign, had begun to dethrone "every rule and authority and power," and those who belonged to him already shared in the results of that victory. (Cf. [58], [59]) The future consummation of this new order still lay ahead, but those who belonged to this "heavenly Man" would certainly share in his coming (v. 23), as they already shared in his image and reign. The apostle could not tolerate any ultimate division here; Jesus' own resurrection guaranteed the resurrection of the dead (vs. 12-18). The denial of his resurrection meant that in the future other dead men would not be raised; it also meant that even now "your faith is futile and you are yet in your sins" (v. 17). The bondage to the body of sin and death had not in fact been broken by the body of life and righteousness. (Rom., chs. 5 to 8; cf. [86]) This being so, the mark of futility would rest on everything: "our preaching," "your faith," the grace and gift of apostleship, baptism for the dead, the daily dying of the believer, and all the work done in the Lord by all believers. (I Cor. 15:14, 29, 31, 58.) Everything would relapse into the futility of a creation as yet undelivered from slavery to sonship by the power of God. (Rom., ch. 8.) Only if those who belonged to Christ shared in his resurrection would they avoid being the most pitiable creatures of all. (I Cor. 15: 19.)

Having been raised as a spiritual body, the Messiah had become a life-giving Spirit. This Spirit was not something unknown to the Christian community, for they had already been given, through the same Spirit, communion in his life. God has created many kinds of bodies. What is at stake is the kind of body that God has chosen to give. What is at stake is not the physical body but the spiritual body (v. 44), the body of "those who are of heaven" (v. 48). The character of this body calls for a decisive change: "For this perishable nature must put on the imperishable, and this mortal nature must put on immortality. When the perishable puts on the imperishable, and the mortal puts on immortality, then shall come to pass the saying that is written: "Death is swallowed up in victory" (vs. 53-54). The final transformation is clearly assigned by Paul to the time of "the last trumpet." Nevertheless, the description of that change utilizes idioms that were quite intelligible to Paul's readers. The image of putting on the new Man, the new clothing, was one of the standard idioms for describing both the baptism and the daily renewal of the Christian man. (Cf. [25], [26]) Moreover the marks of life-from-the-dead were the very marks of the daily working and walking of the believer. (Cf. [62], [67]) At the outset of the chapter, in his famous summary of the kerygma, Paul had used a series of the essential verbs (died, buried, raised), which were precisely the verbs that he so frequently compounded with *syn* to indicate the present participation of all believers in Christ. (Cf. [81],[55], [65]) Their baptism with Christ and into Christ had been in fact a dying with Christ. It was to this correlation of baptism and death (vs. 29-31) that Paul appealed both as a ground for understanding the mystery of resurrection and as a practice that lost all meaning and relevance "if the dead are not raised." The certainty of sharing in Christ's rule over every enemy and of coming again with him in his return — this certainty was grounded in the church's experience of solidarity in him with one another, and inseparable from the labor that now linked them to the work of this Lord (v. 58).

The whole point at issue then is the character of Christ's death and resurrection, and the character of Christian participation in that event. Paul was trying to convey a radically new understanding of what death is and of what life is. If death is a reality that is to be understood as the bondage to sin and the law (v. 56), then victory over death has been given "to us" by God "through Jesus Christ our Lord." And the character of the church ("us") is wholly to be understood by reference to his victory. It is this understanding of Christ's resurrection which makes it profoundly ecclesiological. As Markus Barth has said: "The resurrection of Christ cannot be spoken of or attested, unless we recognize that his resurrection is a miracle which affects our being as radically and miraculously as it affected him who was buried in the garden." [8]

One prerequisite for understanding Paul's thought is to keep in mind the close links to his argument in ch. 13. In particular, let us point to two: (1) Paul appealed to the resurrection of Jesus Christ as the justification for his own fighting with wild beasts. (Ch. 15:32.) If the first were denied, the second became futile; if the first were affirmed, the second became logically necessary. But in ch. 13, Paul had written, using the first person, "If I deliver my body to be burned, but have not love, I gain nothing." Only by participation in Christ's love does a person participate in the "life-giving Spirit." (2) Again, in ch. 15, Paul attempted to solve the riddles posed by Corinthian skeptics by appealing to his prophetic knowledge of a heavenly mystery (ch. 15:51). Yet in ch. 13 he had insisted, "If I understand all mysteries . . . but have not love, I am nothing." Surely this means not only that love is essential to understanding the mystery of resurrection, but also that the action of love is itself an expression of the power of the resurrection, a manifestation of "the spiritual body."

From this perspective we must ask what specific human actions Paul had in mind when he spoke of sowing a body.

So is it with the resurrection of the dead. What is sown is perishable, what is raised is imperishable. It is sown in dishonor, it is raised in glory. It is sown in weakness, it is raised in power. It is sown a physical body, it is raised a spiritual body. If there is a physical body, there is also a spiritual body. (Ch. 15:42-44.)

By sowing did Paul mean the act of laying a corpse into a grave? Was this what he meant by being planted together with Christ (Rom. 6:5) and by being buried with him (v. 4; Col. 2:12)? Was this comparable to the planting of a plum seed in order to produce a plum tree? Was this the act that paralleled the creation of Adam as a living being? (I Cor. 15:45.) Was burial in a tomb to be the moment when for the first time we bear the image of the man of dust? (V. 49.) To be true to Paul we must answer all these questions in the negative. (V. 36.) But we must qualify this negative, for Paul certainly had in mind also that man of dust whose image was not only one of present corruption and mortality, but also one whose physical body would be laid in a tomb. When Paul referred to the body that was sown, he had in mind the whole of man's existence in "the old age." Man's existence as a whole, whether communal or personal, is ruled by law, stung by sin, and therefore both permeated and terminated by death. The church participates in this sowing of the body, and its solidarity with the Lord's spiritual body does not break its solidarity with the man of dust. Of this body Paul said clearly: "What you sow is not the body which is to be" (vs. 37, 42); when this body dies, it comes to life in a new form, a form given by God (vs. 36, 38).

There are two bodies, and the contrast between them is great. Yet there is a necessary link between the dying of one and the manifestation of the other. The link is not to be discerned by dissecting the old to find the germ of the new; the link is provided in Christ, in God's creation of a new Man whose image all will bear. It is therefore the real and present unity in the new Man, whose life-giving Spirit has already been given to them, which constitutes their hope. They are joined in solidarity with him in the "body that is sown." They are joined to him in his spiritual gifts and fellowship, which motivate their dying daily with him. They are joined to him in a spiritual body, the heavenly body of incorruption, glory, and power, which through him God will give to them "at the last trumpet." Thus we can agree with J. A. T. Robinson[9] when he includes within the primary meanings of the phrase "the body of Christ," the three modes of Christ's activity: the incarnate body, the crucified body, and the risen or spiritual body. Those associations were undoubtedly present in Paul's thought. But I would again suggest that it is hazardous to rely upon a simple equation: the church = the body of Christ. In none of the passages does Paul appeal to the church as indicating the character of Christ's incarnate, crucified, or spiritual body. In all the passages Paul appeals to Christ's person and work as the basis for understanding the character of the church's participation in him. The church is *not* definitive of Christ's death and resurrection, but the latter *is* definitive of the church. The order is important; the central reference is decisive. One strategic contribution of I Cor., ch. 15, is its emphasis upon the *spiritual body*. This should encourage us to recognize the mysterious character of this reality and the flexibility of Paul's thought in dealing with it. It should also convince us of the necessity of dealing with the Spirit in any consideration of ecclesiological issues.[10]

The Head of the Body

The Corinthian church, as we have seen, was deeply confused by the questions of how Jesus Christ could have overcome the power of death and what kind of body men would use to escape their "last enemy." They could not, therefore, be as confident as Paul was of the final reality of a spiritual body that would inherit the Kingdom of God as a single body of heavenly glory, a body through which the victory of Jesus was shared with a humanity whose suffering seemed to confirm the power of death rather than of a life-giving spirit. The problems that disturbed the Colossian church were formulated in a different fashion. Consequently, the form of the answers varied. In surveying the ecclesiology of Colossians, therefore, we must first present the problems and then sketch the outlines of the answers. Because, unlike I Corinthians, the whole of this epistle attacked a single problem, we will attempt to expound the ecclesiology as a whole, ordering our treatment around the separate facets of meaning in the two terms "body" and "head."

Whether or not Paul wrote Colossians is a matter that may be waived here because our central interest lies in New Testament church images. No one challenges the fact that Colossians and Ephesians belong within the New Testament or the fact that the image of the body plays a dominant role in both. Some expositors appeal to the altered meanings of this image as evidence of non-Pauline authorship. There are important differences, to be sure, but whether the contrasts in ecclesiology require us to posit separate authorship is becoming increasingly dubious to me. Be that as it may, our concern is with the content of the basic idioms and not with their authorship. If in citing these letters we speak of Paul, we do not thereby wish to beg the question of authorship, but only to adopt the most convenient designation.

The aberrations in the Colossian church become visible to us as the author mentions certain practices within the church and the rationalization of those practices. Some brothers continued to insist upon the necessity of observing dietary regulations. Wishing to obey all legal demands, they were cowed by the prohibitions, "Do not handle, do not taste" (Col. 2:21). They were also very careful to honor the Sabbath, the new moon, and other festivals. These behavioral patterns were tied to a " self-abasement and worship of angels," which were viewed as " elemental spirits of the universe." Salvation necessitated a circumcision of the flesh, a regimen of devotion, and severe control of the body. This paraphernalia of religious and cultic observance was supported by a prevailing philosophy, a " human tradition " that esoteric knowledge of the elemental spirits appeared to vindicate. These spirits were assumed to be more powerful than men because they shared in the fullness (pleroma) of the Godhead. Between the most high God and men was stationed a whole galaxy of mediators: " thrones, dominions, principalities, authorities " (ch. 1:16). Each of these thrones exerted control over some aspect of human life: each helped to determine man's destiny; each must be appeased. To make his eternal destiny secure, man must have a chart of this celestial hierarchy and must accept whatever form of self-abasement would satisfy each " throne," each heavenly lord. Thus knowledge of the ladder of angelic authorities, supplemented by this subjection of the body, became the essential key to salvation. To be sure, Jesus Christ must be honored, but only as one of the " thrones " set up between the highest heaven and earth; faith in him was accordingly but one of the disciplines that men must adopt. Neither was his authority all-inclusive, nor were acts of obedience to him all-sufficient. He belonged to the angels, of course, but in worshiping him man simply placed him in the pantheon of invisible powers and added to his other religious practices such demands as Jesus might levy. In effect, this was a confession of Christ's impotence to emancipate his people from all other dominions. The human participation in his dying and rising did not confer full freedom from alienation. Therefore those who entered his community were not excused from their former traditions and duties. They must continue to enhance their spiritual security by progressive self-abasement to the *stoicheia*. It was in countering such convictions, whether explicit, or implicit, that the author of Colossians expounded the " headship " of Christ and the " bodyhood " of the church. We must ask what he meant by speaking of Jesus Christ as the *head*.

[91] Head (Kephalē) of the Elemental Cosmic Spirits

" In him the whole fullness of deity dwells bodily, and you have come to fullness of life in him, who is the head of all [or every] rule and authority." (Col. 2:9-10.) This text itself indicates that the head is something that exercises authority and lordship over something else; the body is that over which such dominion is exercised by the head. For the fullness of the Godhead to dwell in him bodily means, with other implications of course, that all invisible and heavenly powers, of whatever status in the chain of God's rule over creation, are subjected to him, and therefore that all their claims to human obedience and all their power to affect human destinies are subordinated to his claim and included within it.

In establishing the primary meanings of headship it is well to look for parallel descriptions. One of these parallels is the designation: the first-born (prōtotokos) of all creation. This suggests several related truths. As the first-born he is the first principle (archē) in and through whom " all things were created," including every invisible ground and seat of authority. As one who " is before all things," he retains sovereignty over everything created after him. He is the archetypal pattern that gives them their reason for existing. In him they find their end as well as their beginning, for they gravitate toward him as the fulfillment of the purpose of God. Consequently, they find in him that which holds them together, that in which they cohere. If there is warfare and competition among them, as there is, they find their reconciliation and their peace in him. (Col. 1:20.) Christ's headship is thus a way of pointing to his status as first principle, as first-born, as primal image, as the source and goal of all things, and as the legitimate ruler of all other spiritual rulers. Whatever men may need to know about them, they can learn from him. (Ch. 2:3.) Whatever truth concerning divine authority may be seen fractionally elsewhere may be seen totally here in their head. Whatever action of God may operate elsewhere fractionally operates fully and finally in " the word of Christ " and " the peace of Christ," for he is " the All in the All " (ch. 3:11, 14-16). Or to return to our text, he is the head of all other authorities because the fullness of the deity dwells in him.

It might seem that this line of thought is entirely Christological rather than ecclesiological. Where does the church appear in this cosmological speculation? Three suggestions are offered. First, we note that Paul's reference to the whole fullness of deity in Christ appears in connection with the assertion " *You* have come to fullness of life in him " (ch. 2:10). It is surely valid to infer that this life which the church receives would not have this fullness unless Christ were in fact the head of every other authority. Because he is the head of all things, the life received from him by the church has a comparable fullness of glory and freedom. Only thus can the deliverance from the dominion of darkness be a final emancipation. (Ch. 1:13.) Only thus can the forgiveness of sins received through him be unqualified and complete. Only thus is Christ able to " present you holy and blameless and irreproachable " before God (v. 21). In short, the headship of Christ over all other authorities guarantees the sufficiency of his atonement to free the church from legal bonds and from subservience to the elemental spirits. (Ch. 2:13-19.)

Second, Christ's headship over all other heavenly rulers implies that he is head over all the men who now live in subjection to those rulers. He is the head of every man, whether that man believes in Christ or not. If we allow this conception to condition our picture of the church, we will be forced to agree with Markus Barth that the church " includes virtually all who are still unbelievers." [11] P. T. Forsyth stated this rule in a different form: " Every soul is born for the church. For every soul is born for society; and it is also born for redemption; and therefore it is born for the society of redemption." [12] This is the necessary corollary of the doctrine of the universal headship of Christ. Because he is head of all, his power of reconciliation extends to all. (Ch. 1:19-20.) If this reconciliation becomes operative in one society, this society will bear within itself the secret of all society. In short, the image of headship asserts the sufficiency of Christ's atonement to redeem all men from their bondage, and sets the church in the midst of the world as the sign of that sufficiency.

Third, if Christ had been merely one of the heavenly powers and not their head, it would inevitably follow that his society (i.e., his body) must be viewed merely as one of many human societies, one religious group among all the others, comparable to them and competing with them. But because he is the head, his society participates in his full sovereignty and thereby receives from him a quite unique function with regard to all other human communities. His headship means that his body continues the work of reconciliation (ch. 1:19), continues its participation in his sufferings (chs. 1:24; 3:5 f.), continues his ministry of love (ch. 3:14) as a sign to the world of Christ's victory over all its gods.

[92] Head of the Church

What does it mean to say that Christ is head (*kephalē*) of the church? What major nuances does this figure of headship carry? It is obvious that the answer will follow point by point the exposition of headship over all things. To say head was to say creative source, first principle, first-born, image, king, lord, the pre-existent and the pre-eminent one. It would seem clear that this one figure carried a meaning equivalent to that of many other expressions. At no point is the author drawing his analogies from the visual image of a human head connected by the neck to a human torso. At every point he appears to have in mind the total saving work of Jesus Christ. Let us summarize the functions of the head vis-à-vis the church. He is:

the first principle, the beginning, the archetype (*archē*), the One in whom and through whom and for whom the church is created. the king by whom this community is delivered from " the dominion of darkness " (Col. 1:12-13).
the redeemer in whom this community is forgiven and freed from the realm of sin. (V. 14.)
the One through whom the treasuries of wisdom and knowledge are accessible and manifested " to his saints." (Vs. 26-28.)
the first-born from the dead (*prōtotokos*), i.e., *first-born* in the sense that all his brothers are born according to the same image; *from the dead,* in the sense that the church is composed only of those who die and are raised with him. (Chs. 1:18; 2:12, 20; 3:1, 5.)
pre-eminent over the church in everything. As a result, all the cosmic powers that operate over these men (in the same way as over all men) are in this body and through this head reconciled to God. (Ch. 1:22.)
the source of nourishment and growth and harmony within this realm where his rule is recognized and shared.

the life of the community, its principle of cohesion, its indwelling peace and glory. (Ch. 3:4-10.)

The thought of Jesus Christ as head thus articulates the perception of a single sovereignty with multiple threads binding him to his community. His Lordship is not a double matter, for there is no contradiction between serving as head of " his body, the church " and serving as head " over all things." It is significant that Colossians gives no place to a picture of *two* bodies. Because redemption " in the Kingdom of his beloved son " is unconditioned, the citizens of that Kingdom can trust in his power to " reconcile to himself all things, whether on earth or in heaven, making peace by the blood of his cross " (ch. 1:20). Those who are now " knit together " in his body, who now know " the riches of the glory of this mystery," know that in him and in his cross " the fullness of the Godhead " has extended its power of reconciliation over all things on earth and in heaven. His body the church is the living confession of his present position as " head of all rule and authority " (ch. 2:9) and the provisional embodiment of a society destined to include all societies.

The image of the head requires the correlative figure of body. But this requirement does not spring from the need for preserving the anatomical wholeness of the *tertium comparationis,* nor from the need for literary or aesthetic consistencies. It springs rather from the redemptive work of this head. Or, to state this in theological terms: every Christological figure has ecclesiological corollaries because the divine will embodied in the work of Jesus Christ was directed at producing a harvest throughout creation. The term " first principle " requires " all things " as its corollary; the term " firstborn requires as its complement the humanity that is born according to his image. So too with the figure of headship. Each of the truths expressed in this figure is a truth concerning the church, which is the body of this head. Behind every heretical ecclesiology lay a heretical Christology. It was by correcting the Colossian misconceptions of Christ that the author sought to correct their misconceptions of the church. For example, the fact that Jesus Christ had accomplished forgiveness of sins *as the head* gave to those forgiven both the confidence that this forgiveness was final and the assured hope that the process of reconciliation will be completed. (Ch. 1:14, 18-23.) It was

because of Christ's headship that the church could continue stead-
fastly in the hope of the gospel. But now we should look at other
meanings implicit in this body status of the church.

[93]   The Body of This Head

The writer of Colossians used the term " body " to refer to the
church in several ways. Among these ways two are perhaps most
notable. First, he spoke of the body of flesh (*sōma tēs sarkos*) which
they had " put off " in " the circumcision of Christ." (Col. 2:11.)
This was a mode of existence described as a living death. " You . . .
were dead in trespasses and the uncircumcision of your flesh." (V.
13.) It was an existence dominated by the absence of full forgiveness,
by unpaid legal demands and debts. (V. 15.) It was an existence in
which men anxiously give final allegiance and self-abasing devotion
to inferior " angels " or to the " elemental spirits of the universe,"
making frantic but futile efforts for salvation by soothing the flesh
or by flaying it. The body of flesh was coextensive with the dominion
of darkness, and was ruled by thrones and principalities that enslaved
men by their laws and regulations, and yet were unable to deliver
men from death. But Christians were reminded that Jesus Christ had
used this very body of flesh for his saving work. (Ch. 1:22.) Through
it he had established solidarity with all men. It is clear, as we pointed
out in earlier discussions, that this body had a quite universal scope.
But by confessing the reality of " this body of flesh " the church confessed the power of the crucified Messiah over it.

Second, the author spoke of the body of Christ, explicitly calling
it the church. (Vs. 18, 23.) The church's transition from the body of
the flesh to the body of Christ had come through his death. (V. 22.)
His dying was called his circumcision. It was in his circumcision that
they had " put off the body of flesh " when they had been " buried
with him in baptism." (Ch. 2:11-12.) This event of baptism, of circumcision, had manifested their unity with him in a new mode of
existence.[18] As those who had died and had been raised with him,
they must obey the injunction: " Put to death whatever is earthly in
you " (ch. 3:5). It was by putting off today the old nature (v. 9; here
the body of the flesh was made equivalent to the old Adam; cf.[56])
that the new nature was put on; each act of donning this new hu-

manity was an act of "being renewed" in the creator's image (v. 10). This continuing renewal was inseparable from the contemporary sharing in "Christ's afflictions." [14] The body of Christ participated in the circumcision (i.e., the crucifixion) of its head and thus shared in the love by which the head knitted the body together. By this sharing, solidarity "in the body of flesh" was overcome by solidarity in the body of Christ. This body was joined to its head by solidarity with the dead of whom he is the first-born. (Ch. 1:18.) It was related to its king by rejoicing in his redemption from the kingdom of sin. (Vs. 13-14.) All previous religious institutions had now become outmoded anticipations of this existence in the body. (Ch. 2:17.) [15] He had freed his body from all indebtedness to obey those regulations which have been dictated by the *stoicheia*, of which he is the head. In short, his body was the community whose life was "hid with Christ in God." This secret life was active wherever the forgiveness and the peace of the head were allowed to permeate its words and deeds. (Ch. 3:12-17.)

[94] The Unity of Jews and Gentiles

The Colossian church, as we have noted, was composed of men with diverse religious backgrounds. There were Greeks and Jews, barbarians and Scythians. Some of the Jews had probably embraced a type of Jewish Gnosticism; likewise some of the Greeks. Different segments of the church had been in touch with philosophical cosmologies, with ascetic regimentation, with Hellenistic mystery cults, with other manifestations of the human craving for salvation. Scholars can distinguish the separate components of this welter more easily than they can trace their dubious paternities. But for our purpose several points seem relatively dependable. The cleavages among the different religious heritages persisted within the church, and great importance and superiority were claimed by the competing heirs. The boundary between "the body of flesh" and "the body of Christ" had not been crossed in such a way as effectively to replace the boundary between Greek and Jew.

That this latter boundary survived was due to the stubborn refusal to accept Christ's victory over "elemental spirits." Such a boundary could not be erased so long as thrones and dominions remained potent, that is, so long as Christ was not recognized as the fullness of God, and his atonement as absolutely sufficient. One motif, therefore, in the assertion of Jesus' headship was the emancipation of his community from the ingrained division between Jews and Greeks. And the same motif was expressed by the assertion of the church's bodyhood. (Col. 3:9-13.) Because it was the one body of the one head, all types of societal divisions that had dominated "the old nature and its practices" must be surrendered, permanently and completely. To enter the body of Christ did not mean that a new set of practices should simply be superimposed upon the old. It did not vindicate the earlier patterns of behavior of one group against those of another group. The body of Christ was not rightly viewed as merely another society competing with other societies for a portion of man's allegiance. No, the body of Christ was as separate from the very practice of social divisioning (e.g., Christian versus non-Christian) as was the risen body of Christ separate from the "body of flesh." Only by dying to the entire pattern of drawing invidious distinctions among racial and cultural groups could the church rightly confess him as "the All in the All." (Vs. 9-11.) The image of the head and its body was thus used to attack at its deepest cosmic and psychic roots the perennial human habit of accepting as ultimate the world's way of dividing mankind into competing societies, whether religious, racial, cultural, or economic.

The image of the body of Christ thus served as a way of describing a social revolution. A new society had appeared that transformed the criteria of social judgment, the bases of social cohesion, and the structures of social institutions. This transformation did not take the form of giving to one human institution the position of dominance over all its competitors. No. The form of this body was the form of a servant whose task was that of proclaiming the reconciliation of all men to God and thus of freeing them from their allegiance to the "elemental spirits" whose tyranny was covertly channeled through the nationalisms, racialisms, and particularisms of existing societies. The truth embodied in Christ's headship and the church's bodyhood was an explosive force, designed to shatter all other conceptions of social organization and historical process. But it is clear that this explosive power has not been fully effective even within the church. As Professor Stauffer has written:

Paul had a multitude of important disciples. But none of them really understood Galatians until Luther. The Colossian legacy for the theology of history no one has really entered upon yet.[16]

[95]   The Growth of the Body

We have stressed the explosive power of the image of the head and the body. The author of Colossians stressed rather the inherent powers of growth — a motif much more compatible with the image itself. We should therefore examine the character of this growth. The author did not relate the picture of the growing body to the numerical expansion of the community through the addition of new members. Nor did he describe the believer's bodies as members of Christ's body as had been the case in I Corinthians. (Cf. [87]) He did not need to describe the various charismatic ministries as members of the body. (Cf. [89]) The only reference to members indicated those earthly instruments by which " the body of flesh " is sustained. Evil desires and covetousness were members by which that body solidified the dominion of darkness and death. (Col. 3:5.) Such members must be destroyed. But there is a strong emphasis upon the manner in which this body grows. It grows when men " hold fast to the head "; and it grows when from this head the whole body is " nourished and knit together." This growth, proceeding from the conjunction of the mutual obligations of the Lord and his community was viewed as " a growth from God " (ch. 2:19). Every item of nourishment, every tie by which the body was knit together, was seen as a merged activity of head and body. Thus, for example, the body grew whenever it allowed the word of Christ to dwell in it richly. The body grew as men obeyed the command of Christ to " teach and admonish one another," to " sing psalms and hymns and spiritual songs with thankfulness in your heart to God " (Ch. 3:15-16). In every genuine act of corporate thanksgiving the head was knitting the body together. But the process of growth also took place through many other forms of mutuality: compassion, patience, forgiveness, love. Each of these was seen as an activity of the head in nourishing the body and also the activity by which the body held fast to its head. Love was singled out as the perfect bond. But this kind of growth could not proceed except by renewed dying (v. 5) with the demand for individual renunciations which that symbol connoted. Nor could this kind of growth proceed apart from the daily work of each person in fulfilling his familial and economic obligations. (Chs. 3:18 to 4:1.) It is important to see in such activities as these the measure of the body's growth; it is also important to use them as indexes of the basic intent of the analogy of the head and the body. Always this growth was directed toward a particular end. The character of this end depended wholly upon the character of the head. As the author of Colossians wrote, " All things were created . . . for him." (Ch. 1:16.)

This idea of the head as the dominating purpose toward which everything moved was an important constituent in the total complex of meanings. It had several important corollaries. For example, the forgiveness that had become effective within the Christian community was seen as the beginning of a process that would continue until it had achieved its goal not only within the church but also throughout creation. (Vs. 20-23.) Those who to this end shared the redemptive sufferings of the Messiah were carrying out a ministry for the body, thus making God's word more fully known. (Vs. 24-28.)

Every act of Christian self-sacrifice, of vicarious suffering, and of loving service is something gained for the plērōma tou Christou, for the building up and perfecting of his body.[17]

This work of building up the body was designed to present every man as a whole Man, fully developed and mature in Christ; but all such work proceeded through the energies provided by the one Man who is the head. (Vs. 28-29.) The creation was thus viewed as inheriting the promise that when Christ appears his body also (all those whose life is his life) will be manifested in glory. (Ch. 3:4.) Herein appears to be expressed the faith that the church and the creation will ultimately become one body.

[96] The Fullness of God

In many ways the climax of New Testament reflections on the body of Christ is to be found in the letter to the Ephesians. Here may be observed the largest concentration of the key words: head, body, members. Here more than anywhere else the concern for understanding the character of the church dominates the discussion. Even so, it is difficult to locate any major novelty in the use of the image, although there are minor variations in accent. Every motif that has been noted in Colossians appears in Ephesians. We do not wish to interrupt the analysis of ideas to discuss the question of which of the two letters is earlier. Each of the motifs is more fully developed in Ephesians. This letter provides, therefore, an occasion for summarizing what has been said, for observing the interaction between this image and its cognates and for introducing our next objective: the comparative analysis and evaluation of the various ecclesiological pictures. We would be forced in any case to adopt a different approach here, inasmuch as this letter as it comes to us has lost its original address, and the specific occasions that prompted it cannot be recovered. It is less fruitful, therefore, to speculate concerning why the author emphasized one or another aspect of the total conception. In summarizing his exposition we will adopt a division of the data according to the earlier chapters of our study.

In Chapter III we surveyed the descriptions of the church that articulated the concrete historical heritage of nation, race, and cultus. One of the special values of Ephesians is the detailed use of the body image to express this heritage. Obviously addressed to communities of Gentile Christians, it described their new status vis-à-vis Israel. They had become " fellow heirs, members of the same body " (*sussōma*) (Eph. 3:6). This is the simple fact, and the term *sōma* indicated the completeness of the new communion. Moreover, the position of Christ as establishing this union was vigorously proclaimed:

For he is our peace, who has made us both one, and has broken down the dividing wall of hostility, by abolishing in his flesh the law of commandments and ordinances, that he might create in himself one new Man in place of the two, so making peace, and might reconcile us both to God in one body through the cross, thereby bringing the hostility to an end. (Ch. 2:14-16.)

It was in Christ Jesus that reconciliation had replaced hostility and separation. Further, the author explains the method by which Christ had accomplished this most spectacular of all fusions: he had reconciled the alien societies " to God in one body through the cross." It had been by his blood that the Messiah had broken down the dividing wall of hostility. He had made peace by a new act of creation in which two men became " one new Man." This required the abolition of the "law of commandments and ordinances," for hostility had been rooted in such laws. And this abolition took place " in his flesh." Here we discover again the essential role of Christ's body, a three-fold role: the solidarity had been achieved with all men by Christ's body of flesh, the reconciliation of all hatreds had been accomplished by the death on the cross, living membership in the risen body had been conferred on the two enemies, who in contemporary thought together represented the whole of mankind.

The paragraph in which the author so thoroughly expounded the role of the Messiah's body (chs. 2:11 to 3:6) was filled with other images as well. The author's mind moved freely from one to another as if all belonged necessarily together. We must be content with little more than seriatim mention. In his flesh Christ abolished the fleshly distinction between circumcision and uncircumcision, forcing upon Christians a new definition of both. (Ch. 2:11, 15; cf. [39]) Before his coming, alienation from the commonwealth of Israel had been equivalent to separation from the Messiah. In the Messiah both forms of alienation disappeared. Membership in his body was equivalent to membership in this commonwealth. (V. 12.) Here the two images (body-commonwealth) coincide. But the author shifted without any sense of contradiction from these nationalistic and racial categories to others that might be termed familial and liturgical. Members of the body were fellow citizens. (Cf. [27], [47], [81]) Together they constituted a building under construction (cf. [82]), which was identified as a holy temple in the lord. (Cf. [48]) Here as elsewhere the temple image was understood as God's dwelling place in the Spirit. There was not the slightest awkwardness in associating the body image with these others; in fact, the very processes by which the body was knit together were equally effective in constructing the commonwealth, the building, the household, the temple. One image was neither more central nor more ultimate than the others.

It is not alone the images of the people of God which are ex-pounded simultaneously with the body image and co-ordinated to it. We find woven into the same fabric the universal and cosmic images: the new creation, the new humanity of the one new Man, the primal purpose and promise of God and its final consummation. (Cf. [53],

[55], [56], [61]) Everything that God had "prepared beforehand" is now within reach of all men. (Ch. 2:10, 18.) The peace of God's eternal Kingdom is now something realized in the Messiah, something that must be announced to men, something that presses forward toward full enactment.

This eschatological unity of the whole creation under God, as an implicate of the body image, may be seen also in the summary of Eph. 4:1-16. Here the cosmic fullness of Christ was described in terms of the cosmic struggle with cosmic powers in which victory was achieved by a Messiah who "descended into the lower parts of the earth" and who in this descent "also ascended far above all the heavens." The captives that he took in this descent-ascent are almost certainly the principalities and powers, the rulers in heavenly places, including that "last enemy" death. (Cf. [58], [59], [65], [86]) The cosmic pleroma of God was here conferred upon the Messiah, through his ability "to fill all things" by demonstrating his victory over all other powers, in heaven, on earth, and under the earth. This victory, achieved in his death and resurrection, was the source of his grace and his gifts to men; it guaranteed the cosmic power and efficacy of those gifts as they operated in "building up the body of Christ" (ch. 4:12). It was also the ultimate source and guarantee of "the unity of the *Spirit* in the bond of peace." The unity of the body was here proclaimed as a fully ontological and a fully eschatological reality.

There is one body and one Spirit, just as you were called to the one hope that belongs to your call, one Lord, one faith, one baptism, one God and Father of us all, who is above all and through all and in all. (Vs. 4-6.)

Note the various ways in which this unity was announced. "There is one body and one Spirit." Here as everywhere in Pauline literature oneness in the body is fully complementary to oneness in the Spirit, and this oneness in the body is grounded in the truth that there can be but one body, but one Spirit. The body is a spiritual body. (Cf. [90]) This oneness is immediately expressed in terms of "the one hope of your calling." Where did the one hope begin? In God's foreknowledge, election, and call. To what end did the one hope extend? To the fulfillment of all the "covenants of the promise" (cf. chs. 4:4 and 2:12). Beginning and end are under the control of the one Lord who in faith and baptism was recognized and obeyed as Lord, both faith and baptism (cf. vs. 8-9) being modes of participation in his death, his resurrection, and his coming. Above all, through all, in all, the Father of all (n.b. the image of sonship; cf. [84]) was manifesting his one glory and filling all things with that glory. (Cf. [62])

This condensed summary of the oneness of the new creation should be viewed as a whole, each phrase being a different way of expressing the same reality. Each phrase was a corollary of the others. If one wishes to understand any one phrase, all the others constitute a definition. What constituted the one body as the body? The answers rush together: the body is what it is by virtue of " the unity of the Spirit and the bond of peace." It is constituted by a single calling and single hope. It is a realm inseparable from its lord, its faith, and its baptism. Finally, the body is defined by its one God whose rule extends without limit over, through, and in all. That the body included the specific human community was indicated by the distinctiveness and historical particularity of its call, it hope, its faith, its baptism. These factors exercised a constraint on specific individuals and congregations to lead a life " worthy of the calling " (ch. 4:1). But the cosmic inclusiveness of the body was also indicated, sharply and repeatedly, because the body was intrinsically the property and work of the Lord, the Spirit, and God. The fullness of the body was assured through the fullness of its head who had made captives of all other cosmic forces.

But if in this paragraph of Ephesians the accent fell upon the cosmic bonds between the body and the Godhead, in the paragraphs immediately succeeding, it fell upon those intrachurch relationships which we have surveyed in Chapter V.

And his gifts were that some should be apostles, some prophets, some evangelists, some pastors and teachers, for the equipment of the saints, for the work of ministry, for building up the body of Christ, until we all attain to the unity of the faith and of the knowledge of the Son of God, to mature manhood, to the measure of the stature of the fullness of Christ. (Ch. 4:11-13.)

Because Christians are the body, they are members of one another.[18] All have received Christ's gift of grace, a gift which, we noted, stemmed from his defeat of all demonic and angelic adversaries.

(Vs. 7-10.) The variety of gifts included different types of ministry, the emphasis here, as in I Cor., ch. 12, falling upon the forms of service rather than upon the individual servants. All the gifts together constituted a gift to the body from its head; together they were the means by which the whole body exercised a common ministry; their effective interaction produced growth within the body. This whole range of meanings operates within each act of ministry by any minister. For the work of service (Eph. 4:12) is the function of all the gifts, whether prophecy or teaching. (Cf. [89]) In one sense there was but one work and one ministry, a ministry designed to accomplish one end: "building up the body." A parallel statement of the goal was "a perfect man" whose stature is described as the fullness of Christ. As head he acts to join the body together, to supply it with food, to knit its sinews together. As the body, men grow up together into the head, into the measure of his fullness.

A single image, taken alone, is unable to bear the full weight of all these mutual interacting activities. It requires many separate injunctions to describe the communal character of this interaction. For example, "speaking the truth in love" is one of the means by which the knitting proceeds. (Eph. 4:15, 25.) On the other hand, such things as anger, theft, laziness, graceless talk, and bitterness are primary sins against the body. They create that kind of social integumentation which constitutes the "old nature," "the body of flesh." Alternatively expressed, every sin against the body is a denial that we are members of one another, a denial that "grieves the Holy Spirit." (Vs. 25, 30.) Christ's sacrifice for the body established love as the cohesive power of its growth and strength. Members consequently build up the body by walking in love toward one another. And this love is the sum and surrogate of all the modes of mutual action by which the body is knit together: righteousness, holiness, forgiveness. (Cf. [68])

A long paraenesis spelling out these works of love led to the statement of the mutual duties of husband and wife (Ch. 5:21) and this in turn prompted a long reference to the complex analogy that exists, on the one hand, between husband and wife in the new age, and, on the other, between the head and the body.

For the husband is the head of the wife as Christ is the head of the church, his body, and is himself its Savior. As the church is subject to Christ, so let wives also be subject in everything to their husbands. Husbands, love your wives, as Christ loved the church and gave himself up for her." (Ch. 5:23-25.)

As we have already explored the Adam-Eve and the bride idioms, (cf. [23], [56]) we will confine ourselves here to the specific relationships between head and body (v. 32). Christ acts as the head in various ways: he exercises Lordship and authority over his body, he loves it and gives himself for it, he sanctifies and washes it so that it may become glorious and holy. He nourishes and cherishes it. Together these constitute a complex definition of headship, one which draws more meaning from the Passion story than from the biological or the marital analogies. The life of the body is characterized in a correspondingly free fashion; it lives as body by its subjection to Christ's authority, by co-operating with his desire to present it in glorious perfection, by full acceptance of this mysterious union, by men treating one another as members of his body. Here again the anatomical analogy breaks down, while the marital analogy is more congruous. But neither analogy dictated the trend of thought, other than to stress the unity that is shared by head and body, by husband and wife. The real determinants of thought stem from the story of what Jesus Christ has done in saving the church and from the resulting relationships of dependence, obligation, and allegiance that qualify the life of the church as his body. The context gives but one example of the consequence: the full mutuality in love of every husband and wife, a mutuality, to be sure, that recognizes distinctions in authority and subjection.

This is a great mystery, and I take it to mean Christ and the church; however, let each one of you love his wife as himself, and let the wife see that she respects her husband. (Ch. 5:32-33.)

There is a "mystery" here, for the author asserts as an ultimate truth the inextricable conjunction of three imponderables: the unity of husband and wife expressed in daily attitudes, the unity of the church and its Savior, the unity of its Savior with God as "the fullness of him who fills all in all" (ch. 1:23). Each is a mystery of universal dimensions, but their compresence within the daily choices of ordinary saints is the greatest mystery of all. The use of the body image does not remove the mystery by reducing an unknown mathematical equation to a known formula. Rather the opposite. By making certain relationships explicit it transposes all of these recognizable relationships into the mystery of God's fullness. Or, to return to the Biblical text, only the power of the Spirit of the Christ to knit a community together in love can enable men to know the knowledge-surpassing dimensions of the fullness of God. (Ch. 3:19.)

We bring to a close the third stage of our project: the study of the character of the church as the body of Christ in the context of all the other images. We are ready now to examine the interrelations of the various ecclesiological pictures we have found.

VII

INTERRELATION OF THE IMAGES

W E COME NOW to the final stage of our inquiry, the appraisal of why and how the images as set forth in the New Testament are so intricately woven together and what strategic inferences may be drawn from that interweaving. This step will require more than a straight sequence of discussion of one passage after another or of one image after another. It requires at least three types of thinking, each quite difficult in itself. The first is synoptic thinking, by which I mean a thinking that embraces all of the images at once, seeing them together in a single panorama and reacting to them all. The second type is reciprocal thinking, by which I mean the effort to think one image into another, to make them almost yet not quite interchangeable, to see how the same meanings flow back and forth from one idiom to the other. The third type might be called retroactive or depth thinking. By this I mean the effort to recover what was in the mind of the author before he said " church " or " saints " or " body of Christ." [1] All three types of thinking, when employed rightly, should further our understanding of the communal imagination at work.

Let us begin simply by transposing into words a few of the cumulative reactions that may have been felt by the reader of this study as he has followed our meandering trail. What a profusion of images! This is due in part to the fact of sheer numbers, but also to the diverse origins of the analogies: in home life, in wedding customs, in farm and lake, in city streets and temple, in kitchen and in courtroom, in ancient legends and contemporary events. Moreover, we have not found in any writer the inclination to reduce the profusion to order, to weave the various strands into a single tapestry, or to arrange the kinds of figurative language into a neat pattern. At times it may seem that the writers did their perverse best to prevent later systematizations from succeeding. One consequence of this profusion is surely this: no one figure can be selected as the dominating base line of all thought about the church. The writers start their thinking not from one image, building upon its foundation a complex set of figurative constructions, but they seem to start from a reality that lies beneath and behind all the images. No writer makes any single image serve in a passage of any length as the only or the sufficient analogy for the community of faith.

There is, however, an equally significant corollary. If no figure dominates the stage, all figures gain in import by sharing that stage. Only after we have surrendered the futile effort to choose one image as the key to the others do we grasp the overwhelming synoptic impact of all the images. We may take as an example some minor images almost at random. " You are the salt of the earth. . . . You are a letter from Christ. . . . We are the aroma of Christ." In itself, in its frequency of appearance, in its affiliations of thought, none of these analogies commands attention for long. But when we see behind its use the full glory and shame of the church as reflected by all the other images, then we may be induced to reconsider our lowly evaluation of salt or letter or aroma. The same principle should apply to the appraisal of the body of Christ image. It matters not how low or high it may have ranked in our own scale of appreciations; what matters is that, interpreted in the context of all the other images, its pluriform implications for us should be enhanced. If all the images, thought together, provide a richer tapestry than any image, thought alone, then each image becomes richer in content when seen in context with the others.

Why is it that a synoptic thinking of all the images is more illuminating than any intensive view restricted to a single image? Why is it that each figure gains in force when viewed in the context of all? Surely the answer is this: through all the analogies the New Testament writers were speaking of a single reality, a single realm of activity, a single magnitude. The purpose of every comparison is to point beyond itself. The greater the number of comparisons, the greater the number of pointers. When so many separate pointers impel our eyes to look in one direction, our comprehension of the magnitude of what lies in that direction is enhanced. This is why in the New Testament we observe no sentimental fascination for the images themselves, such as a preacher or a poet feels for a symbol of his own devising. The overarching interest is that reality toward which they all point.

So effective are the pointers that we hardly need to ask concerning the identity of that reality. Image after image points beyond itself to a realm in which God and Jesus Christ and the Spirit are at work. It was of that work and of that realm that the New Testament writer was thinking as he spoke of Kingdom or temple or body. The study of images, therefore, reinforces the conviction that the reality of the church is everywhere anchored in the reality of God, the Holy Spirit, Jesus Christ. To be sure, if we limit our perception to the verbal form of the metaphors, sometimes one and sometimes another of the three Persons appears to displace the others. The image of the people of God, for example, appears to stress the work of the Father, whereas that of the body of Christ may encourage the " unitarianism of the Son," and that of the saints may focus thought upon the sanctifying Spirit. But we have seen that exposition of the meaning of any of these figures, when carried out in the contexts provided by the New Testament, inevitably leads the mind away from invidious contrasts among the three Persons. No important image retains its full range of reference unless the activity of God within the church is understood as an activity that operates in and through the Messiah and the Spirit. This is surely why the New Testament offers no definition of the church per se as a separate or autonomous entity.

Contemporary modern thought, by contrast, demands definitions that are church-centered in a way foreign to the New Testament. Often the stance from which our questions arise is a stance outside the church. What is this company of people? What distinguishes it from other institutions and societal groups? Such questions presuppose that we are not asking about the character of our own family from a position within that family. The presuppositions of the New Testament were quite different. There the images were forms of self-recognition adopted by a community whose sense of uniqueness stemmed from the fact that its thought was always centered beyond itself in the majestic activity of the One Father, the One Son, and the One Spirit. Through the diverse figures of speech, the early church recognized itself as a called community whose origin and boundaries and destiny were determined by the powerful promises of Him who sees the end from the beginning. It confessed itself to be a community in which the divine life, glory, and name were mediated afresh from the living "I am." Whatever the figure of speech, this society knew itself to be a Messianic community belonging to and dwelling in a living Jesus Christ whose sovereign rule marked the beginning and the goal of the new age. Whatever the figure of speech, the community saw itself as a charismatic reality knit together and empowered by the gifts of the Holy Spirit. Moreover, by the very plurality of parallels, the awareness of the inseparable unity of these heavenly components within the church's existence was deepened. By viewing the panorama of pictures synoptically, reciprocally, and retroactively, we are more than ever bound to acknowledge, with P. T. Forsyth, "the church as supernatural, as the society whose life is the Eternal and Holy Spirit." [2] Behind the images we sense the corporate awareness of a majesty that was at once heavenly and earthly, primal and final, corporate and cosmic.

It is the Referent behind all the references that explains why the same metaphors could be used for the life of the individual believer, for the life of the separate congregations, and for the total community of faith (e.g., temple). Rarely, if ever, have we encountered in the survey an analogy that was or could be limited to one of these "lives." Because of this interdependence of members, congregation, and church, the same figures of speech could apply alike to one or to all. Moreover, the cohesion of the entire society — past, present, and future — was such as to encompass in Christ the relations of every person to the whole of mankind. Oneness in Christ destroyed the barriers imposed by differences in time and place, in sex and race, in language and class; it destroyed even the conceptual barriers imposed by the various origins, histories, and nuances in the reservoir of images.

The common Referent behind all the references also explains why New Testament authors could confuse metaphors, with a nonchalance hardly to be equaled in any other literature. Paul, for example, could intentionally garble the figure of the body by combining it in a single paragraph with the figures of building, planting, nation, table, and temple. And John could without apparent incongruity visualize the bride as a city, a temple, a mother, a virgin, and a choir. Why this literary brigandage, this artistic mélange? It was made possible by a common perception of a reality that embraced all the images. The writer could presuppose an audience which to some degree had experienced a common field of force that freed them from verbalistic slavery to any description of that field. For such an audience each picture could be a channel for thought rather than a receptacle of ideas bearing an assigned weight. Such an audience would not be troubled by flagrant inconsistencies of logic or style. The reality to which each analogy applied was a mystery of such dimensions as to magnetize and control its use.

The character of this mystery was such that, although the analogies inspired by it could point effectively to it, they could never bound or limit it. For many moderns who crave an exact calculation of the boundaries of the church this is a distressing feature of the New Testament ecclesiological images. Those images are too elusive, too elastic, too ambiguous to satisfy their need. Often the initial recourse is to select one image, to concentrate upon it, to force it into a non-imagistic mold, and then to rely upon it for a definition of boundaries. Thus an image whose primary function had been the perception of reality or the self-recognition by the church of its depths and heights is forced to serve a quite different function, i.e., to enable modern Christians to illustrate their own prefabricated definition of the church and to provide them with a tool for securing agreement from churchmen who think otherwise. Doubtless this puts the matter too sharply, but it may serve as a reminder that an image does not remain the same when used to achieve an alien objective. Imagination used to foster self-recognition is one thing; used for rhetorical or dogmatic purposes it becomes quite another. In any case, it is clear that to give greater precedence and weight to the theological, Christological, and pneumatological elements in the life of the church is to move in the direction of recognizing that the church is a divine mystery that cannot be circumscribed by doctrinal or institutional measurement.

The fact that all the analogies point to a common Referent that has these dimensions does not, of course, degrade the various metaphorical constructions. We mentioned in the introduction the effort to distinguish between metaphors that are merely metaphorical and those which are ontological (cf. pp. 20 f.). What may we now say about that effort? First, the effort often presupposes the low value of a " mere metaphor." But if a mere metaphor like salt or first fruits is seen to refer clearly and directly to an ontological reality that is the same magnitude as that referred to by more impressive categories, such as temple or body, then the result may be not a degradation of the latter but an elevation of the former. To be sure, metaphors used simply as illustrations or literary embroidery are one thing and analogies used to explicate mysteries of God's being are quite another; but the test lies not in the metaphors themselves but in their function in the processes of the imagination. Secondly, those who appeal to the contrast between ontological and metaphorical statements are often motivated by the desire to safeguard the unique character of that eternal life which is embodied within and through the church. Our study should support the suggestion that this desire may be more effectively realized by other means than by insisting upon the " literal " character of the figure of the body of Christ. This insistence utilizes a linguistic distinction between the metaphorical and the nonmetaphorical as the basis for a theological distinction between what is central and what is peripheral. The motive may be right, but the method is, I think, self-defeating.

Perhaps an allegory of our own may be relevant to this issue. The child who has his first glimpse through a kaleidoscope is enchanted by the rapidly changing colors. He is fascinated when a slight turn of his wrist produces so great a change in the combinations of forms and colors. So too may a person be fascinated who tries to grasp the shapes of the ecclesiological images as they keep shifting from one dominant theme to another. The child, if he is normally inquisitive and destructive, will soon begin dismantling the instrument to see how it is put together. The child finds, as he separates the pieces of colored glass, that he had vastly exaggerated their number and brilliance. He finds that no piece by itself holds his full interest for long and that to study the various parts as parts soon loses its charm. The mystery when solved seems to be as simple as the scattered pieces of glass. It had been through the movement of the shifting pieces, as penetrated by a single shaft of light, that the life and color had been produced, a movement in which each piece had added to the richness of the other pieces. But now, dismembered and scattered on the desk, the pieces become rather dull. At an earlier moment he had been sure that red was the dominant color; later it had seemed to be the blue. But in the heap of separate fragments none retains its full luster. Then the parent explains to the child that the color had never been fully resident in the fragments themselves; they had merely refracted the clear light as it entered the kaleidoscope, breaking it up into the several colors of the spectrum. The kaleidoscope was more than a toy; it had served as a tool for studying the character of the light.

Admittedly, this allegory limps badly, but it may suggest the truth that what is perceived should not be identified with the mode of perception, that some realities are of such a nature that their perception is enhanced by the presence of pluriform modes of perception, and that these pluriform modes have an efficacy when used together that is destroyed by the reliance upon one mode alone. This is especially true, we may add, where thought is intended to move from the whole to a part rather than from a part to the whole.

By way of introduction to the task of studying interrelations we may make still a further observation. We have said that all the images point beyond themselves to the activity in time and space of God the creator, sustainer, and redeemer of human community. We have also stressed the double function of the images: the perception of this heavenly-earthly reality and the self-recognition by the congregation of its dependence upon it. The further observation springs from a factor that demanded endless repetition in the previous pages: self-recognition by the church of what it means to be the church is fostered by images that focus upon participation in the death and resurrection of the Messiah. It was perception of this event as central to the creation and redemption of the world which produced authentic self-knowledge on the part of the church. Oneness with the mysterious realm of God's glory was recognized by oneness in One who took upon himself the form of a servant. In him all die and all are made alive. Over and over again the communal imagination was centered upon the Passion story as a contemporaneous eschatological event. One consequence was this: no analogy drawn from ordinary occupations such as fishing or husbandry or housekeeping was wholly capable of bearing such a weight of meaning. Contrasts remained as essential as the correspondences. Contradictions and anomalies of a literary sort were inevitable.

If we remember these considerations, we will be helped to avoid a wrong formulation of the question. One should not ask how one image is superior to another. We would be on sounder grounds if we asked how one image benefited from its associations with another. Moreover, we should ask this question not alone in terms of the relative impact of the metaphors upon modern ears, but also in terms of the thinking of the New Testament writers. This is a point of some importance. Surely the study of the contextual meanings of the " body-members-head " complex has convinced us that this range of meanings is much wider than the current load of associations that these terms bear. Many efforts, some of them very impressive, have been made to delineate the total Pauline conception of the body of Christ. But to even the best of these books an inevitable reaction is that it does not do full justice to the variety and suppleness of Pauline thought. It is almost impossible to translate with complete fidelity an idiom so complex as that which embraces the body, its members and its head.

But we must turn from such generalizations to more limited examples. Let us select from each of the earlier chapters (III, IV, and V) a key picture. Let us ask how this term benefits from its association with the body image, and vice versa. Let us draw evidence for our answers from the Pauline passages in which the body idiom is central. We cannot expect to be exhaustive nor does the nature of the query permit precise or exact conclusions. We will be content if the study helps us to move a step or two beyond the sway of unrestrained conjecture and private prejudice.

The Body of Christ and the People of God

How, then, does the New Testament picture of the people of God profit from its association with the picture of the body of Christ? That the two pictures were cognate is indicated in Eph., ch. 2, where alienation from " the commonwealth of Israel " had been overcome by the reconciliation " in one body through the cross." Participation in this one body had brought " the hostility to an end." Here is good evidence, if we need it, to show that the author was referring to the same communal reality whether he spoke of the body of Christ or the household of God. In both cases he had in mind the work of God and the work of Christ on the cross, a single work producing a single reconciliation. But this reality prompted the use of two distinct images and the correlation of those images. So we are entitled to ask what the image of the body contributed to the image of the commonwealth.

Grounding our first observation in the discussion of the body in Rom., chs. 5 to 8 (cf. [86]), we may say that the picture of the body of Christ disclosed the full universality of God's people. The intended inclusiveness of this people became explicit in the correlation between the body of Christ and the inclusion of all men in this " one man's act of righteousness " (Rom. 5:18). Those who have known the law as a binding covenant have died to that law " through the body of Christ " (ch. 7:4) and thereby have been delivered from the Adamic body of sin and death to the body of life and righteousness in the last Adam. No longer could the image of God's people be considered as narrowly as it had been considered by Israel in the time of the promise. It must derive its meaning from the life of Israel in the time of fulfillment. As an image, the people of God lost, through its correlation with the Messiah's body, whatever particularistic connotation it may have carried.

By the same token the image of God's people became less collective and more corporate by becoming more personal. It was as a person, responding to the Messiah as a person, that a man died to the law through the body of Christ so that he might belong to another. The body image required for the individual a more intensely existential decision than was intimated by the people image. And it was by this existential act that he entered the corporate (not collective) life of Christ. The image of the people became genuinely corporate because every citizen entered this commonwealth through sharing in the death and resurrection of the Messiah. Thereafter the life of God's people could be defined more cogently as " the new life of the Spirit " (Rom. 7:6). It could no longer be defined by a collective law, but only by the corporate law of Christ, the law of Christ's body, which is love. Thus we can say that association with the body image produced a Christological definition of the people image that made the latter image more explicitly universal, more corporate, more personal, more existential, and more spiritual.

Still other inferences may be drawn from I Cor., ch. 6. (Cf. [87]) Paul appealed to the image of the Kingdom and to that of the temple in order to underscore the incongruity of a flagrant case of fornication. (I Cor. 6:9, 19.) But the stark identification of immorality as an idolatrous sin against the body and therefore as a blatant repudiation of the Lord of the body appeared to give a more compelling sense of the destructiveness of the sin. The picture of membership in the Lord's body was more effective at this point than the picture of membership in God's people. Every deed done in the body must now be scrutinized in the light of the Lord's redemption of that body and in the light of the death and resurrection of the Lord's body. Thus it appears that the body image enabled Paul to convey the truth that every believer's body is a temple of the Holy Spirit more readily than he could have done by using the people image. The command "Glorify God in your body" is grounded more directly in the body image than in the people image (v. 20), especially since the body image connotes "the price" with which every believer has been "bought."

Moving on all too quickly to another passage, we ask what nuances the image of the Eucharistic body may have added to the people image. (I Cor., chs. 10; 11; cf. [88]) Here we should not forget that the latter image was inseparable in content from the Passover festival and sacrifice, from the images of the bread and the wine, the altar and the prayers of thanksgiving. All these entered into the alembic of Paul's mind. Here we may surmise that the reference to Christ's body (v. 16) accented the cruciform character of the covenant. It also strengthened the sense of the corporate oneness of this people and the terrible jealousy of the people's Lord. (V. 22.) It made less marginal the concern for the conscience of the neighbor who eats from the same table. (V. 29.) Moreover, the revelation of schism *in the body* was more shocking than would have been that of a schism *in the people*. (Ch. 11:18-22.) The remembrance of the Lord's body and blood, the proclamation of his death by eating this bread and drinking this wine — all this made infinitely terrible the guilt of profanation, far more terrible than the comparable remembrance of the paschal lamb of the exodus saga. The use of the body image thus accented the truth that from its beginning the Mosaic community had drawn both its sustenance and its condemnation from the cruci-form presence of Christ. (Ch. 10:1-5.) The people of God from the beginning had been the body of Christ.

In the discussion of spiritual gifts in I Cor., chs. 12 to 14 (cf. [89]), Paul made no explicit use of the people image. We therefore pass over it with the single suggestion that the image of one body, one spirit, enabled Paul to stress the interdependence of members and gifts more evocatively than might have been possible by using the people image. "If one member suffers, all suffer together." (I Cor. 12:26.) This was, of course, true of the people of God. But the truth was more effectively expressed by the analogy that Paul adopts here.

In the discussion of the resurrection body in I Cor., ch. 15, the image of God's people was again so far in the background that the movement of Paul's mind from the one idiom to the other cannot be observed. And deductions drawn from the relative absence of the one are precarious indeed. We can, however, with some hesitation infer that some of the things said by Paul in this chapter could not have been said as cogently if they had been couched in the analogy of the people. Which things do I have in mind? One is this: the con-viction that the resurrection of Christ's crucified body had produced already a radically new situation for all men. Just as all men, both inside and outside the people of God, " bear the image of the man of dust," so the destiny of all men is encompassed by the " image of the man of heaven." Nothing could show more trenchantly that the one people of God is now living in the age of fulfillment. It is truly an eschatological community. Another point is this: the conviction that now this community, by virtue of its participation in the risen body of its Lord, bears within its own communal life (ch. 15:29-34, 56-58) the first fruits of the ultimate victory of God over the law, sin, and death. Its life as God's people is anchored already in the final subju-gation of all things to Christ. (V. 28.) Thus the personal, corporate bond that links the present earthly members both to the beginning and to the end of the age of fulfillment is signified more fully by the picture of Christ's body than by any comparable analogy that could be provided by the people idiom. At the same time, the miracle of the mortal nature putting on the immortal preserves the mysterious character of this bond. (Vs. 51 f.) A total transformation of the body is required, a transformation in personal and communal reality that conforms to the transformation in Christ's body. " It is sown a physical body, it is raised a spiritual body." (V. 44.) Self-recognition by the community that it participates already in the risen body presupposes a dual recognition: that it is participating now, by dying every day (v. 31), in the crucifixion and burial of the Messiah, and that it is the Messiah's victory over all his enemies that alone accomplishes this mystery: " sown a physical body, raised a spiritual body." To be in fact God's people, the church must ask itself whether its life testifies to this dual presupposition.

We have now suggested various benefits that the people image received from its association in Paul's thought with the body image. An extension of this survey to Colossians and Ephesians would be desirable, but this may suffice to illustrate our contentions that the benefits are various and significant. Too long have we suffered from the tendency to think of the two images in separation. They belong together. If they seem to be quite alien, this is a sign that we have not fully understood either. Why is it difficult for the modern Christian to think the body image into the people image? The reason may be found in a general misconception of the body. We tend to adopt modern connotations of the body which diminish the power and ·depth of the New Testament connotations; we tend to utilize an oversystematized, overdogmatized, and inflexible concept of the body. Moreover, our doctrinal obsessions often discourage that synoptic, reciprocal, and depth thinking which is so necessary if we are to grasp the subtle filiations of Paul's imagination.

We must now inquire concerning reverse influences. What benefits accrued to the body image from its association in Paul's thought with the people image? First of all, benefit was gained in stressing the concrete historical role of the Christ whose body is the church. The figure of the people of God preserved the understanding that the term " Christ " was not initially a personal name but the designation of an office (the *Messiah* of Israel) and that this Messiah must always be viewed as God's *Anointed*. We might indicate this connection, which even in Paul's day was likely to be obscured by Gentile Christians, by the phrase " the body of *the* Christ."

We noted earlier, in our discussion of I Cor., ch. 6, that the attitude toward the believer's body, expressed in the conception of

" members of Christ," was also expressed in the parallel conception of the " temple of the Holy Spirit." This conjunction served to bring to the consciousness of the believer, as he weighed the alternatives of moral choices, not alone the danger of sinning against the body but also the danger of blaspheming God's temple. The whole world of cultic and sacrificial practice in its symbolic Christian meaning (cf. [48]–[52]) here served to reinforce the moral imperatives expressed in the body image.

In the Pauline message of I Cor., ch. 10, we detect another place where the apostle supplemented the one image with others. He wanted to associate the hazards and the opportunities presented by " participation in the body and blood of the Lord " with something comparable. But where was anything comparable to be found? As one recourse he could shift from the image of the body to the altar sacrifices of Israel (I Cor. 10:18) with their power to unify and sanctify. He had another resource. Reminding his readers of the Scriptural accounts of the exodus (cf. [41]) he could help them picture other familiar instances in which participation in spiritual food had been followed by rebellion and destruction. (Vs. 1-5.) The body image did not immediately evoke the whole wealth of typological analogies provided by Israel's story. It was not easy, for example, to picture the fathers as sharing in this body. Some have felt that the apostle was forced into unwarranted exegesis to discern correspondences to Baptism and the Lord's Supper in the cloud and the sea, the manna and the rock. However that may be, his exegesis would have had to be even more elastic before he could discern in the Pentateuch narrative the participation in the body of Christ. (For some readers John, ch. 6, accomplished this typology.) We may infer that the warnings and instructions conveyed by these earlier events (I Cor. 10: 9-11) would not have been so accessible if Paul had relied wholly upon the image of the body.

This may suggest still a further value of the people image. Whenever Paul wanted to suggest the full solidarity of the Israel in the age of fulfillment with the Israel in the age of promise he combined the body image with others. By itself body did not connote the kinship between the sons and " our fathers " (v. 1) nor the connection in God's purposes between the new exodus and that accomplished under Moses. By itself the body image did not articulate the truth that

the church's enemy was the very destroyer who had tempted the
people from the beginning. (Vs. 9-12.) By itself it did not explicitly
relate the " new covenant in my blood " to that Passover covenant of
which it was the re-enactment and fulfillment. (Ch. 11:25.) Thus the
body image, considered by itself, did not serve to evoke in the
church's imagination the whole story of God's dealing with Israel in
the days before he sent the Messiah. Parenthetically, we may remark
that the later separation of the two images has enabled anti-Semitic
Christians to cherish the body image and to jettison the people image.
They can readily enough celebrate Communion in the Lord's body
with no inkling that this means participation in the Passover of
Israel from Egypt.

Racial and national analogies contributed another kind of value to
the discussion of the body in Colossians. These analogies provided
specific social, historical, and moral implications that otherwise
might have become obscured. Here the body of Christ was conceded
power to produce equality and unity between Jew and Greek, circumcized and uncircumcized. (Cf. [94]) Would this function of the
body have been so apparent apart from a high regard for the Jew and
from a specific mention of these two religious and racial categories?
Would the headship of Christ have carried such a concrete meaning
unless the power of the cross had been measured by such obstacles
as the law with its demands for righteousness? Would the symbols
of Baptism have been so directly applicable to all kinds of membership obligations had it not been declared to be a circumcision? By
showing that the law was one of the elemental forces, one of the
stoicheia, one of the principalities that had been overcome by this
head of the body, did not Paul make that headship apply all the more
effectively to other legal, political, and religious systems, even those
later called " Christian "? Consider, for example, Paul's assertion:
" You have *died to the law* through the body of Christ " (Rom. 7:4).
Surely the reference to the law aids in understanding the work of
this body. And surely that " law " included not only the Torah, for
which Paul had the highest respect, but also all other sets of religious
rules. (Col. 2:21.) When, then, by combining the two images of
body and law, Paul articulated the truth that all who belong to
Christ's body have died to the law, was he not defining the church
in terms of death to any legal system? And was he not applying this

to a specific congregation that had not fully died to law? From the confluence of the two key images, body and law, emerged a combined picture that preserved the truth that oneness in Christ's body means sharing in an event by which legal bonds of every sort have been " nailed to the cross " (v. 14). An ecclesiology that ignores this component of the body image ceases to be Pauline. Yet what prevents our ecclesiology from ignoring this component may be simply the fact that Paul's thought about the body was everywhere conditioned by specific references of this sort.

Consider now Eph. 2:11-22. (Cf. [96]) As we have previously noted, in one short paragraph a long parade of images is induced within the mind: circumcision, commonwealth of Israel, the blood of Christ, the abolition of the law, one new Man, reconciliation to God, citizens, saints, household of God, building, temple. The word " body " appears only once. (V. 16.) It is surrounded on all sides by analogies, all used with ontological seriousness. Through his one body Christ has reconciled two men and has created in himself one new Man. Here is the eschatological reality of a single man and a single community in which the final goal of peace is accomplished. But the references to circumcision and uncircumcision are absolutely necessary to make clear the kind of hostility and alienation which have been overcome in the one body. They are necessary if the reader, in hearing of the body, is to visualize something more than an endless number of anonymous individuals who enter a haven of peace. Rather, it was important, at least to Paul, that readers visualize two *men* becoming one, two men whose alienation had been religiously grounded and buttressed, two societies and two historical traditions whose hostility had attained the most massive kind of sociological inertia. This association gave to the miracle of the one body a tremendous social and historical weight. And it gave to the goal of unity also a tangible, earthy concreteness. The whole parade of analogies gave an immediate historical relevance to the " one body " of the cross, making clear the impact of this body on all the societal structures of the world. This welding of many images prevented the image of the body from being dissipated into esoteric Gnostic spirituality and from being lost in aeonic speculation. Because of this collocation of figures, the body image retained its gospel function of describing what God had done in fulfilling his covenants of promise to Israel by enabling strangers to live as citizens in his one household. Whether or not we have rightly appraised the value of the people image for the body image, one thing is clear: the apostle who developed the latter would not countenance the action of later disciples in repudiating the former. For him the description of how the Messiah made peace in his one body necessarily involved the picture of a commonwealth of Israel that should serve as a temple where God would dwell with all men.

The Body of Christ and the New Creation

We proceed now to analyze the complementary relations of the two master images: the new creation and the body of Christ. Our first need is to view each master image as a complex constellation of metaphors. As we have seen and must constantly remember, the new creation image involved the confluence of such pictures as the first fruits, the two Adams, putting on the new Man, the two kingdoms (of God and Satan), the two ages, the image and glory of God, his name and his life, his Spirit and his love. Similarly, the thought concerning Christ's body brings into orbit such pictures as the realm of life, the sovereignty of Christ over the bodies of believers, the unifying power of the Paschal and Eucharistic food, the interdependence of spiritual gifts, the contrast between physical and spiritual bodies, the headship of Christ over such elemental powers as the law and death, the reconciliation of two peoples (Jew and Gentile) in one, and the growth through love into mature manhood. It is no doubt difficult in the case of either master image to hold in mind all these subordinate pictures; but such an operation is necessary for this kind of analysis.

That Paul's mind itself was adept in such reciprocity is fully obvious. To summarize the evidence we may say that all but two of the images that we included in Chapter IV were common coin in Paul's vocabulary; more than this, all but two (the Son of Man, the Sabbath Rest) appear in Paul's letters in close conjunction with his discussions of *sōma*. In his thinking he thought all these other images into the *sōma;* conversely, his thinking of these other images was subtly conditioned by his understandings of the body. Stated in more abstract conceptual terms this observation becomes: the apostle's comprehension of universals was qualified and conditioned by his understanding of the body of a particular man, crucified at a particular time and place; likewise his comprehension of this crucified and glorified body was qualified and conditioned by his understanding of universals. Before he said " church," he was thinking of this particular body in its universal representativeness.

This frequent and ready coalescence of his thinking about Christ's body and God's creation makes difficult any separate analysis of the two. Before we can observe their interaction we must separate them from each other. But to separate them does violence to Paul's thought in which they have already been amalgamated. Yet unless we separate them we cannot appraise their mutual value to each other. We are aided by the fact that on occasion Paul wrote of the new creation without mentioning Christ's body, while in other contexts he wrote of the body without mentioning the new creation. His own practice therefore offers a precedent for separate analysis, even though his more typical practice is to present us with a complex conflation of the analogies.

How do the universal and cosmic images contribute to the body image? One point that may be noted is that the analogy of Adam's death (Rom. 5:12 f.) helps to underscore the inclusiveness of Christ's death and thereby of his body. The image of body, when linked to the thought of Adam, conveys the unlimited representative character of Christ's death. The Pauline discussion of the bondage of sin thus provided an illuminating antonym to the body of Christ. The latter was no less universal than the former. It is true that Paul nowhere referred to the *sōma* of Adam. Nevertheless, I think it is valid to infer that the solidarity and kinship of all men in the first Adam corresponded to the one body (the kinship and solidarity of all men) in Christ. His long discussion of the two representative men explicated the cosmic scope of the one act of disobedience and the one act of obedience. It was the cosmic scope of this one act of which Paul was thinking before he said " body of Christ."

This figure was also profoundly conditioned by the frequent cross references to the idea of the Holy Spirit. Christ's body reached as far but no farther than " the new life of the Spirit." " Spirit " was one of those terms which, as we have seen, expressed the ontological ultimacy of the new age. It was God's own life-giving Spirit, active everywhere in creation and in redemption. Considered in isolation, the image of the body need not involve the thought of oneness in the Holy Spirit. But Paul habitually thought these two into each other. For him the body was quite inseparable from " the Spirit of life in Christ Jesus." [3] Now this constant reference to the Spirit militated against misunderstanding the character of the body. The spiritual body was not a physical body. Such a combination of body with Spirit discouraged the tendency to confuse the term " body " with " flesh and blood." Again, the thrust of Paul's logic prevented a person from visualizing the body and the Spirit of Christ as though the physical and the spiritual were two separate realities, which, joined together, constituted the person of Christ. No, to be one body in Christ was nothing else but being one Spirit with him. Just as the presence of the nationalistic images preserved the understanding of this body as the body of the Messiah, so reference to the cosmic work of the Spirit preserved the understanding that this is the body of the eternal Son of God whose glory, life, and love fill the body with all the fullness of God.

Just as the image of the Second Adam found a useful antonym in the body of sin and death, so too other cosmic idioms provided other helpful antonyms. They enabled Paul, for example, to use the body image in a dynamic and militant way, as the antagonist of Satan. In some contexts membership in the body was shown to be a matter of global conflict, because the only alternative was partnership in demons or in idolatry. (I Cor., ch 10.) Jesus had been qualified as head by his victory in cosmic battle, by subduing all principalities and powers, including the Jewish law and cultus, the lords of the nations, and the mediatory aeons whom the Gnostics worshiped. This understanding of headship in turn gave great vitality to the concept of membership in his body, i.e., subjection to the authority of this head by using his weapons in the struggle against the same powers. (Eph., ch. 6.) Here again was a mode of thinking by which the body image as defined by *Christus Victor* became relevant to every significant battle line in heaven and on earth. The body of Christ was interpreted through this process of reciprocal thinking as the army of an all-powerful commander. And conversely, every significant battle with heavenly lords and their earthly subjects could be understood in terms of the broken, triumphant body of Christ, each battle

becoming an extension of that Gethsemane struggle in which a real
and final victory has been won in the " body of flesh."

The mutual interaction of the images may be detected by asking
a question that has been provoking some heat among New Testament scholars. Does the body image as Paul used it effectively express a powerful motivation for the church's mission in and for the
world? The usual answer has been yes. To cite but one exponent:

> The church is thus [as Christ's body] the means of Christ's work in the
> world; it is his hands and feet, his mouth and voice. As in his incarnate
> life, Christ had to have a body to proclaim his gospel and do his work, so
> in his resurrection life in this age he still needs a body to be the instrument
> of his gospel and of his work in the world.[4]

Another scholar, however, has recently rejected this use of the analogy. Ernest Best presents a carefully detailed argument to show that
Paul used this image solely to articulate obligations and functions
within the Christian community. As Best argues, Paul did not see
in the body idiom direct implications for the church's duties to the
world or its functions in the world. " The relationship of the church
to the world outside it is never discussed. . . . Body . . . was a
metaphor which looked inward and not outward." [5] It must be conceded that Dr. Best supports his position with vigor and persuasive-
ness. By contrast it is rather difficult to find any text in the Pauline
letters to corroborate the frequently quoted line: " He has no other
hands but our hands." Is this perhaps evidence that such a position
rests solely on extensions of an anatomical comparison that would
have been quite foreign to Paul's thought?

If we limited our answer to those Pauline texts in which the body
of Christ is directly identified with the church, we would be forced
to join Professor Best's side of the debate. Nowhere does Paul define
the church as the body in the sense that it becomes the sole means
by which the living Christ carries on his work in the world. But Professor Best's case loses force when we deal with the idiom of the body
of Christ as flexibly as Paul did and when we take into consideration
the way in which Paul combined this image with the cosmic images
that we surveyed in Chapter IV (excluding here such strategic categories as slaves, saints, and servants). Let us be specific. The Holy
Spirit provides gifts to the body as he wills. One of those gifts is
apostleship, which can even be considered a member of the body.

(I Cor., ch. 12; cf. [89]) Surely apostleship included a mission to the world and work in the world. "To make the word of God fully known" is a task that involves the apostle in suffering "for the sake of his body." (Col. 1:24 f.) Now this suffering *for* the church was not limited to suffering for the sake of those who already stood within the community; many of Paul's sufferings were a result of his apostleship to the Gentiles, for the sake of those destined by God for inclusion in the body. The suffering that could be compared and even identified with the Messiah's afflictions took place along a single battle line, the continuing warfare between Christ and Satan. It is in the framework of this warfare that we should interpret the references to the suffering, even in the verse "If one member suffers, all suffer together." This suffering, shared by the members with Christ, shared also with one another, was the continuing index of the Messianic vocation to the world. It is in this same sense that we must read the purpose of "dying to the law through the body of Christ." Paul makes the purpose very clear — "that we may bear fruit for God." (Rom. 7:4-6.) [6] So too the inclusion of Jew and Gentile as members of the same body defined the ministry of the church as one of making "*all men* see what is the plan of the mystery." (Eph. 3:6-9.) Moreover, the image of Christ as head (one of the pictures essential to the body) of all the "powers in heavenly places" made imperative for all members of the body the work of declaring this secret *to* all such powers. (Chs. 1:20-21; 3:10.) [7] How was the church to do this if not in terms of its faithful ministry of the gospel to the world? If behavior of husband and wife is an expression of membership in the body by acceptance of Christ's headship over all families, so too is the behavior of master and slave; so too is the use of God's armor against the wiles of the devil who deceives both the world and the church. (Eph., chs. 5; 6.) We conclude, therefore, that while the perception of the church as the body of Christ appears to connote only the internal cohesion of the church, this apparent fact is altered when we study all the activities of Christ in his body, when we adopt the Semitic view of the body's presence in the activity of its members, and when we *think into* the image of the body the other basic images that were present in Paul's mind.

Here as elsewhere is illustrated the strategic power of what we are thinking before we speak. Let me try to outline two different orders of priority that may dominate the process of thinking on this matter. The first order we shall call order A. If our mind works according to this order, before we say " church " we have already been thinking of something specific, of a certain company of people, others like ourselves and with ourselves within an organization that has very tangible boundaries. There follows an appropriation of the term " the body of Christ " as a way of saying something additional about this body of people. We do not detect the extent of the distance between the word "body " in the first instance and in the second. We can use the term " members of the body of Christ " as a commendatory way of expanding the significance of holding membership in the body of Christians. Then when we speak of Christ as the body's head our prior conception of this membership in the body of Christians determines the primary meaning of his headship. Of course we all do acknowledge this person as our Lord. Now because at the outset our prior conception of the church has been conditioning our thought and because this conception has subconsciously drawn a boundary between the church and the world, we accordingly assume that an equally sharp line separates Christ as head of the church from the heads of the other societies that compose the world. But now it becomes very difficult indeed to correlate the picture of Christ as head of his body, the church, with the picture of Christ who is simultaneously " the head over all things " (Eph. 1:22). Yet what is impossible for us was not only possible but absolutely essential for Paul. This is a sure sign that at some decisive point his order of thinking differed from ours.

Can we recover his order, calling it for the moment order B? Perhaps we can say that his thinking in this area began with the story of Jesus Christ, a story that reached its climax in the stark reality of his death and resurrection. *This* body which died and which was raised was Christ himself, who died and rose again. The event revealed that this Messiah had a decisive role in God's plan for the world. He was the last Adam, the first-born and first fruit of the dead. He was the King of God's eternal Kingdom, the eternal Son of God and image of God. He was the new creation and the One through whom and for whom all things were made. He had brought into subjection every heavenly force that opposes God — present and future, life and death, Satan and sin, the law and every angelic power. He descended into hell. He has been given a name above all other names. He sits at God's right hand. Thus all of the images that articulate the perception of the cosmic work and power of Jesus Christ throw light upon the image of Christ as head of all things, the light and life of all men. Wherever he rules, wherever he brings others into subjection by his victorious descent and ascent (Eph. 4:8-10), there is extended the Kingdom of life and the Spirit. This new realm, perceived as the sphere subjected to this head, is described by a range of images that parallel the perception of the head: the new creation, the new nature, the new Man, the Kingdom of Christ, life, light, glory, the Spirit, and all the others. The figure of the body of Christ now becomes a way of pointing to this reality which is one and the same, whatever the forms of speaking. The term " body " effectively describes this oneness: an inner interdependence of all its members; a reciprocal oneness of the members in Christ and Christ in the members; a hierarchical oneness in subjection and ministry, the head loving the body, the body giving glad subjection to the head. Thought moves, and so does the expression of that thought, from the perceived reality to the image. Through his death and resurrection Christ accomplished the reconciliation of Jews and Gentiles. Two men have become one: the body of Christ. By the same means Christ established his sovereignty over an individual's allegiance: that individual's body becomes a member of Christ's body. So, too, Christ nourishes men with his cup and his bread. Their participation at his table, proclaiming his death, establishes the covenant of the broken body. The Spirit gives gifts to those who are called into the common ministry; these gifts are members of the one body. Thus the perceptions of successive areas subjected by Christ elicit the various though cognate images of the one body. It is this inclusive and cumulative perception which finds expression finally in the idea of the church. The word for church now becomes invested with a tremendously large circle of meanings. But if we follow order B rather than order A, if before we say it the word " church " draws its meanings from the series of perceptions and self-recognitions that precede our saying it, certain connections that could not be absorbed into order A can now be absorbed and indeed become quite essential.

In order B one perceives a distance between world and church, but this distance must be expressed not by the reality of separate headships but by the reality of a single headship. Jesus Christ is head of all things because all things were made through him. He will be head because all things were made for him. And it is through the power of God active in his death and resurrection that this headship has been made manifest to his body (the area that participates in the subjection) and must be proclaimed by this body to every competing Lordship in heaven and on earth.

If a boundary exists between the church and the world, it is located and marked by the cross, viewed from one side as God's victory and from the other as scandalous and foolish. But as boundary the cross is also a bridge for constant two-way traffic. Whatever the distance between church and world, this distance must and can be crossed by the church because it has already been crossed by its head. In the church may be observed the present proleptic beginning of the end, when God will be all in all. The church is the first fruit of a resurrection whose power will be extended to all. The church now is the body where the head is fusing together the one new Man, a growing process in which *all* will attain " the stature of the fullness of Christ." (Eph. 4:9-13.) This process is carried on by Christ not through external extension, not by adding more and more members to his body, but through the inner transformation of life. But "the fullness of Christ," eschatologically perceived, includes all things, because it is participation in the body and blood of a Redeemer of all things. It is the body of life and righteousness, the bearer of promise, of judgment and mercy for all men. If this body is in truth the area where Christ the head carries on his work of subjecting all things to himself, then it is in truth the cosmic ministry of Christ, a body made up of members, that is, instruments of his love for all. If we follow this order of thinking, the earlier question of whether the church as Christ's body has an essential ministry to the world as Christ's body is answered before it is asked. For as the body of him who is head over all things, the church exists for the purpose of an ultimate erasure of the line between church and world. It follows that church-centeredness becomes world-centeredness, because the center of both church and world is the one new Man " in which there is neither Jew nor Greek, slave nor free, male or female." If it were otherwise, if Jesus Christ were not at once the head of the church and of the world but only of the church, he would merely be one of many cosmic lords and his body one of many worldly societies, and his church, in fact as well as in common assumption, one of many competing cultural religions with only a pathetically false claim to superiority. It is our conviction that synoptic and reciprocal thinking about all the Pauline images of the church is one of the strongest obstacles to this kind of misinterpretation of the body image.

Turning to the contribution of the body image to the other cosmic and universal idioms in the New Testament, we may suggest a single point, but one of tremendous power. The reference to Christ's body requires of us in using such images as the new creation to redefine them in terms of a single, once-for-all historical person and of a single, once-for-all event at a particular moment outside the walls of Jerusalem. And it forces upon those idioms the constant reference to a particular historic community that was in many ways no more obviously filled with the fullness of God than was the pathetic procession to Golgotha during the Passover.

The Body of Christ and the Fellowship in Faith

The analysis of the interaction between the body image and the images that stress the interdependence of life within the church (Chapter V) proceeds under somewhat different conditions. This is in part due to the fact that more clearly than any of the images surveyed in Chapter V the body image immediately and fully articulates the interdependence of the members. The body image offers the best single analogy of life-in-mutuality. The analogy of sonship and brotherhood stresses mutuality, but not so fully or so vividly. The analogy of the building articulates the integration of various stones within the structure and of various workers in its construction, but the relationships connote a less vital sort of growth. Growth is more native to the body than to the temple. Few images indeed provide a keener perception of the plural and the singular, the solidarity and the freedom, the integrity and mutuality, the dependence and interdependence of the church. This living polarity is implicit in the passages where the headship of Christ is stressed. It is in him as head that all things are held together. (Col. 1:1.) To him as head all authority has been given, so that a common subjection to him produces both equality and diversity among the members. Fullness of life in him who is " the head of all rule and authority " is possible because " the whole fullness of deity " dwells bodily in him. (Ch. 2:9-10.) From him as the head comes the power that knits the body together and that gives it growth toward maturity. (V. 19.) This accent incorporates the central thrust conveyed by the allusions to the company of slaves, disciples, servants, witnesses, and confessors. Common to all of these images is the recognition that it is by way of total obedience and subjection to the one Lord that participants in slavery become slaves of one another and that each member serves the body by serving others.

The same dynamic sense of solidarity is conveyed in the passages where, without reference to the head, the one body is simply identified with Christ himself. To put on Christ meant to put on love. The very purpose of being " called in the one body " is that the peace of Christ may " rule in your hearts " (ch. 3:15). To enter into this body is to become clothed with Christ's compassion for men, as well as to become so minded that one acts toward these men as toward Christ. (Vs. 12-17.) The body is a realm of mutual forgiveness and mutual concern in which each person gives priority to the others' needs.

But, as we have seen, there are passages where Paul's thought focuses upon the body's members, each person's body being viewed as a member of Christ. Each spiritual gift is a member. Gentiles together constitute a member. Participation in the Eucharist makes men sharers in the one body. The test of each member is what he does with his own life for the sake of other members. Every life must be presented to Christ as an instrument of his righteousness. Again the dominating function of the image is to produce that self-recognition by Christians which will remind them that they are slaves and servants of one another. All the subordinate accents, which are implicates of the one master image, elicit the sense of integrity and interdependence among the family of saints. Herein lies what is probably the major contribution of the body image to all the others. This contribution is at once so subtle and so massive that we may well doubt whether the other analogies for the interdependence of the church have any significant contribution to make to the body image. Yet the very fact that the apostle frequently shifts from the body image to the others should encourage us to conjecture why he should do so.

It would be fruitful, for example, to study what we have called the prepositions of mutuality in their bearing upon the body image. This should always be done in the context of Pauline passages where the body idiom is surrounded by such prepositions. For example, the first two chapters of Ephesians offer an instructive interplay of prepositions. Here it becomes quite obvious that what was meant by the body of Christ could be conveyed by the phrase *in Christ*. On the one hand, this prepositional phrase described a complex network of activities accomplished by God. It is in Christ that God has chosen us, blessed us, and shared with us his " glorious grace " (Eph. 1:3). In Christ, God has made known to us his purpose and has forgiven and redeemed us. (V. 12.) In Christ, God sealed us with the Holy Spirit and created us for good works. (Chs. 1:13; 2:10.) In Christ, God builds men into a single structure as his dwelling place. (Ch. 2:21.) But on the other hand *in Christ* indicates just as effectively the activity of the redeemed who hope and believe in him and who have access to the Father through him. Here, then, is the place where God's redemptive work and men's grateful response meet and are unified. God is in Christ; men are in Christ. The phrase " in Christ " thus contributes several helpful nuances to the figure of the body. It makes very clear the fact that in all contexts it is misleading to separate the body image from the Christ image. It discloses the truth that, when Paul said " body," he was, in fact, thinking of the whole range of Christ's activities rather than of an anatomical, biological, or sociological figure of speech. The phrase " in Christ " permits a greater flexibility in the description of those activities and preserves both the subjective and the objective aspects of each activity. For instance, such a verse as the following brings out several nuances in this relationship more clearly than if the thought were channeled through the body image alone: " We are his [God's] workmanship, created in Christ Jesus for good works, which God prepared beforehand, that we should walk in them " (V. 10). We should not overstress the contrast between these two modes of expression. This verse is an articulation of the meaning of existence as Christ's body. But the point is simply this: the alternate image *in Christ* sometimes leads one's mind beyond the usual limits of the body image. Whereas the body image focuses thought upon the member-member relationship, which derives from the head-body relationship, the prepositional phrase more subtly combines the multiform and cruciform activity of men.

The fruitful supplements which the prepositional phrases offer to the body image become more impressive when we survey all the major prepositions used. We have already seen how the use of the preposition " with " (*syn*) in compound verbs helped to connote the complex and intimate sharing of men in the death and resurrection of Christ. "God . . . made us alive together with Christ . . . and raised us up with him . . . and made us sit with him in the heavenly places." (Eph. 2:4-6; cf. [81]) This sequence of " *withs*," so typical of Paul's syntax, also discloses his perception of the same reality which elsewhere he describes as Christ's body. There is another Greek preposition usually rendered as " with " (*meta*). This word was employed more frequently to express God's presence in Christ with us. *Syn* thus expresses our solidarity with Christ and with one another; *meta* expresses God's solidarity through Christ with us.[8]

Still other prepositions articulated the multiple meanings of mutuality: through, into, for, from, to. Together they served to describe the total work of God in Christ and the total response of the new creation in him. They all indicate important aspects of that mutuality which is indicated by the one master image of the body. The fact that Paul relied on the prepositions more frequently and more fully than on the body image may suggest their basic importance. As a prism transforms a single ray of light into its component colors, so the prepositions break up the life of God in Christ into its diverse activities. And whether we are studying the composition of light or the structure of the body image, such prismatic diffusion is helpful. In fact, Paul was seldom betrayed by the temptation to allegorize the various anatomical functions, as if to ask what each muscle and each membrane represented and what functions were fulfilled by the stomach or the blood stream. Instead, his mind moved more easily from the figure of the body to verbs, prepositions, and conjunctions that did not correspond to bodily activities. These supplementary modes of speech served to deflect the mind from anatomical processes to that reality to which no figure, however elaborate, could do full justice. The prepositions (e.g., from and to) gave a stronger sense of the dynamic movement of divine potencies within the life of the church than could be given by any noun, however well chosen. (The noun *sōma* did not have a verbal form in New Testament Greek.) At times the nouns (commonwealth, peace, man, body, household, temple — Eph. 2:11-32) gave some idea of the fullness, the wholeness, the solidarity, the historicity of God's people. But at other times the primary carriers of meaning — the verbs, prepositions, and conjunctions — gave a better sense of the processes of inner transformation and of historical action through which men had come to share as a community in " the fullness of him who fills all in all " (ch. 1:23).

For an adequate conception of Pauline ecclesiology we should study almost every branch in the grapevine sentence with which Ephesians begins:

Blessed be the God and Father of our Lord Jesus Christ, who has blessed us in Christ with every spiritual blessing in the heavenly places, even as he chose us in him before the foundation of the world. (Vs. 3-4.)

Yet it is not until the very end of this sentence that he mentions church and body.

And he has put all things under his feet and has made him the head over all things for the church, which is his body, the fullness of him who fills all in all. (Vs. 22-23.)

This whole gargantuan sentence illustrates what the author thought before he said either of these nouns. He thought of God the Father, of his eternal and historical work begun " before the foundation of the world." He thought of " our Lord Jesus Christ " and of his eternal and historical love. He thought of the Holy Spirit given in fulfillment of the promise and as a guarantee of the inheritance. He thought of all that God had wrought by his power in exalting and enthroning Christ " above all rule and authority." He thought of a community of men and women believing and hoping, praying and loving, whom he normally addressed as " you " and with whom he identifies himself as " we." He perceived in the gospel a mysterious and majestic plan for the fullness of time, for the unification of things in heaven and things on earth. He perceived this and much more before he introduced the words for church and body as aids in helping his readers comprehend the greatness of the power that had grasped them. He adopted some images to express the nationalistic and cosmic dimensions of this power. He adopted other images to express the interdependence in love of God's sons "through Jesus Christ." The message dictated not alone the choice of nouns but the choice of pronouns, verbs, conjunctions, in fact, the whole syntax of his thought. His own example should become the stimulus and the guide for shaping the syntax of our thought about the church. If we would comprehend the same reality, we should make full use of the body image, but we should supplement it with many other images, and we should perceive the whole mystery of God's purpose in Christ before using either the term "body" or the term "church."

VIII

A POSTSCRIPT

A T THE TERMINATION of our survey it may be in order to recall the questions posed at the outset and to reflect on the character of the early Christian imagination. It would seem that this imagination was so flexible because it was so alive to the mystery of the church's participation in the creative and redemptive work of the Triune God. Perception of this mystery induced an almost endless variety of modes of describing it. Yet, if we are to believe the cumulative witness of the New Testament, every congregation was all too prone to blindness. It did not see itself either as it was or as it was meant to become. The images were normally used to cure this blindness. The cure required a rebirth of imagination that would enhance deeper perceptions and more authentic self-recognitions. They needed new eyes for seeing, and this change required a greater degree of " play " in their thinking.

To some extent, of course, all language is a product of the human powers of imagination. Or, as J. Huizinga has shown, language is an example of the play element in culture. Each word converts reality into sound by the aid of the imagination. Speech enables man to name things " and by naming them to raise them into the domain of spirit. . . . Behind every abstract expression there lies the boldest of metaphors, and every metaphor is a play on words." [1]

This process becomes " elaborate and ornate " when the imagination " seeks to account for the world of phenomena by grounding it in the Divine." Then the images become more weighty and more potent with symbolism. Thus the play element enters subtly into larger clusters of words and concepts. These larger clusters become embodied in poetry, mythology, and theology, all of which are dependent upon the use of complex living images.

The eternal gulf between being and idea can only be bridged by the rainbow of imagination. The word-bound concept is always inadequate to the torrent of life. Hence it is only the image-making or figurative word that can invest things with expression and at the same time bathe them in the luminosity of ideas: idea and thing are united in the image. But whereas the language of ordinary life — in itself a working and workmanlike instrument — is continually wearing down the image content of words and acquiring a superficial existence of its own (logical only in appearance), poetry continues to cultivate the figurative, i.e., image-bearing qualities of language, with deliberate intent.[2]

We may learn much from the insight of this great Dutch historian. To be sure, the New Testament writers should not be ranked with self-conscious poets or self-appointed mythmakers. Nor was it the ordinary " torrent of life " with which they were dealing. Nevertheless, the thought of the church was so illuminated by the " rainbow of imagination " that men were enabled to bridge the apparent gulf between the earthly forms of communal life and the heavenly ground. And it may be asserted that the church has not, during the centuries later, been able to improve on their panorama of pictures for expressing their self-awareness as the people of God, the fellowship of the Holy Spirit, and the body of Christ.

Even so, these and the other master images have their limitations. They are not themselves the reality to which they point. Confusion and distortion abound where this is not remembered. The reality has too much height and depth to permit a verbal idolatry of that sort. Yet when the contemporary church wishes to articulate its sense of an eternal origin and destiny it will do well to cultivate the image-bearing qualities of that language which it has inherited from the Bible. This cultivation requires no obsession with one image, but a new freedom in the use of many. The church should not seek a new understanding of itself merely by adding new and clever extensions to the primal images, a temptation that perennially entices theologians and homileticians. For example, it will not infer from the Biblical pictures of the building a set of rules for church architecture. Rather, it will discover the pertinence of archaic images by fresh contacts with its living Lord in the fullness of his glory. When it discerns again " the church's one foundation," it will draw further deductions from this truth concerning God's present power and purpose. Rare indeed is the passage in the New Testament in which the metaphor releases a series of secondary deductions. The metaphors themselves are the secondary deductions from the primal communal experience. This may result, as we have seen, in a profuse mixing of metaphors, but the mixture itself reflects not logical confusion but theological vitality. As K. Stendahl has said with regard to the idea of election:

Over against stringent logic (the way of thinking of later theology) stands Jewish thinking in images, where contradictory facts and conceptions can be put together in a kind of significant mosaic.[3]

In the light of the entire mosaic of ecclesiological images, we may now ask and answer two questions concerning the method of approach adopted for this study:

1. We began with a division between minor and major images. Is this division valid? Clearly no such distinction existed in the imagination of the New Testament writers. It is wrong to say that a major image is truer than a minor image when the latter gives expression to an authentic perception of the character and vocation of the church. Nor can we measure significance or authenticity by the number of appearances of the image or by the number of authors who use it. It is in the last resort quite impossible to draw a sharp line between one class of metaphors and another. For example, the picture of the Christian community as unleavened bread (cf. [6]) calls into play the associated figures of the Passover, the exodus, the table, the loaf, and the cup. It draws its full meaning not from a simple casual comparison (i.e., unleavened bread is sincerity and truth) but from the involvement of the congregation (" you really are unleavened ") in a communal heritage that is at once historical, cultic, corporate, eschatological, moral, and ontological. Or as another instance, we could take the symbol of circumcision. (Cf. [39]) Measured in terms of the frequency of direct application to the church, this analogy could well be classified as minor, and perhaps most modern readers would classify it thus. But it was manifestly so crucial an image in defining the Christian understanding of the people of God that it could not be omitted or discounted. No, the

character of the reality, the character of the imagination, and the re-sulting character of the images are such as to discourage the separation of minor pictures from major.

There remains, of course, the possibility that this separation has sufficient value to justify it merely as a matter of procedure. It has a negative logical value in that, by demonstrating the interdependence of minor and major, it has underscored the impossibility of making any such separation final. It has the dialectical value in that by classifying as minor certain idioms that have been cherished by some persons and as major certain idioms that have been discarded by others, it provokes us all to re-examine our prior classifications and to find better grounds for our evaluation than private or denominational habit. Furthermore it has a psychological value mentioned earlier, in that no mind can comprehend a large museum at a glance. We must visit it a room at a time, concentrating on one picture at a time, on one artist or on one school. It sometimes helps to decide in advance those canvases which seem to us the most important, even though before the visits are over we must look a second or a third time at several small and unpublicized paintings whose merit becomes clear only after studying larger and more famous canvases.

2. What can now be said about the distinctions we have drawn in Chapters III to VI among the so-called master images? Is it valid to separate images on the basis of the initial source and range of the analogy? It seemed obvious that Israel as an analogy had been drawn from the history of the nation, while a new humanity as an analogy had linked the church to a reality that transcended all national lines. So too the fellowship in faith had seemed to connote the texture of common life provided by belief in the same Lord, which linked men together without suggesting the national or cosmic scope of their fellowship. Such distinctions are inevitable, given the grain of our minds. But they do not fare well when dealing with New Testament writers. Time after time we have noticed that none of the master images could be restricted to the boundaries within which we have placed them. The pictures of the church as Israel and as the new humanity, as used by the New Testament writers, were not opposite but complementary. The first fruits was an analogy drawn from the pastoral, national, and cultic traditions of Israel, but it was used of the church to indicate a significant universal role and it was

equally evocative of the interdependence of members of the church. The analogy of sacrifice, Jewish and cultic in origin, served to articulate the final and inclusive adequacy of Jesus' death as well as the immediate duties and demands that bound Christians to one another. Most clearly of all, perhaps, the image of the family of God (to which we have given far too little attention) breaks through all barriers and is found in all quarters. Thus we must rule out the thought that the classification of pictures adopted in this study has merit other than as a method of procedure.

It has, I believe, some value in that regard. We have already spoken of the way in which the multiplicity of references to a common referent served to heighten its significance. That common Referent made central the crucifixion of Christ and the communion in his death. It was this communion in him which enabled men to perceive the fulfillment of God's promises to Israel, the beginning of the age of the Spirit, and the interdependence of men in a final dying and rising; and not only to perceive, but also to recognize themselves as participating therein. Every analogy, when it was applied to this reality, was stretched beyond its normal limits. This very elasticity served to underscore the utterly unique and utterly real life of the new creation. A vast number of idioms, used with multiple incongruities, were enlisted in the effort to describe such a creation. One result of this multiplicity is that it becomes quite impossible to reduce the images to a single, logically structured pattern. This fact suggests, however, that the reality of the church itself is such as to discourage a scholastic formulation of ecclesiological doctrine.

Can we now, looking backward over the whole panorama of pictures, say anything cogent about our initial questions: How can one distinguish between figurative and nonfigurative words and meanings? When must an image be taken in a merely metaphorical sense and when is it to be given an ontological sense? My own convictions, arrived at only near the conclusion of the study, are that none of these questions can be satisfactorily answered because they are wrongly formulated. Their pertinence diminishes steadily as one enters into direct conversation with the images themselves. Why is this so? Because the criteria for valid answers lie not in the images per se but in the reality to which they pointed and in the imagination that adopted them as pointers. The images that were most vital are those which combined both figurative and nonfigurative meanings, those which expressed both metaphorical and ontological seriousness. For this community had such a nature and Christian imagination had such a structure that both literal and figurative meanings were recognized as indispensable, however distressing that might prove to a more prosaic kind of logic. We might visualize a church that could be described adequately in literal terms only, with exact denotations that could be relied on to answer all ontological questions. Would that be the body of Christ? I do not think so. Or, if you prefer, visualize a church that could be defined adequately in nothing but figurative terms that carried no literal references and had no ontological Referent. Would that be His body? I do not think so. When we treat any of the New Testament figures for the church as merely literal or as merely metaphorical, we disclose all too clearly either the phantasmagorical or the pedestrian abnormality of our own minds. The glory of God in the church does not operate in such a way as to produce a communal mind that can be content with such abnormality.

The questions as stated do not always arise from abnormal minds, however, whether minds that rely only on literal definitions or those which love to roam in the stratosphere of imagistic speculation. Often these minds are engaged in the responsible burdens of church life, trying desperately to relate the New Testament faith to matters of urgent administrative decision. To such it must seem that the study of church images in the New Testament steadily makes those images less relevant to the practical ordering of the church's work.

To explain this very practical dilemma we may refer to an excellent summary of New Testament research during the years 1880 to 1930 by the Swedish scholar Olof Linton.[4] Dr. Linton shows clearly that since the First World War there has been, in works dealing with the early church, a steady turning away from questions of organization to questions of the ultimate significance of the church as a divine-human reality. As a result of this development, interest has shifted away from the political categories to the religious. Scholars have tended to replace the picture of the church as a building being constructed " from below up " with the picture of construction proceeding " from above down." The eschatological character of the church, its context and boundaries being defined by the Kingdom of

God, has been increasingly recognized. Theological categories have more and more displaced sociological and historical categories, for the church is seen as the realm for the operation of the Holy Spirit. Ever larger place has been given to the priority and power of the risen Christ in the idea of the church.

There is little doubt that the concentration of interest in the analogy of the body of Christ reflects this revolution. And there is little doubt that the "church idea" in the New Testament was everywhere dependent upon the miraculous mysterious presence of God and upon his powerful working through his Son and his Spirit. It may very well be that the church idea was so fully integrated with the God idea and the Christ idea that it is no longer possible to delineate a separate ecclesiology. In this respect the developments since Linton's survey corroborate his findings.

This increasing interest in the church idea has, however, created a host of problems. Some of these were apparent in 1932; some have emerged since then. How was the dominant idea of the church related to the actual history of the churches? How fully, for example, were Paul's images of the church as a building or as a temple actually descriptive of the turbulent congregation in Corinth? How concretely could they be related to its exercise of judicial powers over its members? (I Cor., ch. 6.) What specific guidance did the conception of the church as the new creation provide for the complex tasks of organizing the congregation or of determining its liturgical practice? How did the spiritual gifts help in governing the specific orders and offices? Many of these concerns are perennial, but questions of this sort become less answerable when full recognition is given to the theocentric and Christocentric structure of the church.

Still other questions have been provoked by the rapidly growing ecumenical mind among contemporary "church bodies." The various confessions and communions have been developing an uneasy conscience over the competing ecclesiologies that are embedded in their separate creeds and ministries. Their recovery of the church idea in the New Testament has revealed the essential unity of the church, a unity that is God-given and Spirit-nourished, "one body and one Spirit." It has also indicated the holiness, the catholicity, and the apostolicity of the church. No image can be found in the New Testament that does not, in context, bespeak the deep abiding

integrity, wholeness, and oneness of that reality which they called
"church." But what practical help is offered by the New Testament
to churches that, when they try to walk together in the movement
toward unity, find themselves more than ever frustrated by such
monumental obstacles as those which separate Catholic from Protes-
tant?

With the increasing tendency to exalt the central activity of Christ
and the Spirit in the life of the church, the lines that connect their
activity to the empirical behavior of the churches may become even
more difficult to appraise. Through exactly what channels does the
living Christ exert his Lordship over your congregation and mine,
your denomination and mine? Where are the marks of the Holy
Spirit's presence? What are the current forms taken by the gifts of
the Spirit? Do the images of the church offer help in the effort to
distinguish true from false apostles and prophets, or true from false
believers and congregations?

Again, the developing ecumenism of our time has posed with
growing insistence the question concerning the place of the laity in
the doctrine of the church. This is not due merely to the lay demand
for more power and authority nor to the traditional kind of anti-
clericalism. Nor is it explained by the perennial demand for theologians to produce a set of simplified dogmas for nonprofessionals.
Rather is it a matter of recovering an adequate theological understanding of the ecclesiological significance of the laity. What is their
role in the church idea? Their work is obviously essential to the
empirical operation of the churches; is it equally integral to the
status of the church as a heavenly realm?

Nothing more radically separates contemporary churches than
their evaluation of ministerial ordination and ministerial orders.
What role did these orders hold in the New Testament doctrines of
the church? The growing agreement with regard to the four marks
of the church — its oneness, its holiness, its catholicity, its apostolicity
— tends to accentuate rather than to solve these conflicts among the
churches over ministerial orders. In many areas there is agreement,
too, that the one essential ministry is the ministry of Christ to the
world and that the whole church participates in this one ministry.
But this agreement makes all the more intolerable (and perhaps insoluble) the divisions among the churches in this very area.

Still one further area may be cited. The recognition of the centrality of the divine mystery at the heart of the church's life has opened the way to a fruitful and necessary examination of the relation of the church to the world. A Christian picture of the world is as necessary as a Christian picture of the church, because the church's Lord is none other than the Lord of the world. A theology of the world is corollary to a theology of mission. What bearing does the understanding of New Testament ecclesiology have on the obligations of the church to the world in our time?

To suppose that our limited study of church images will provide satisfactory answers to such questions would, of course, be foolhardy. The deeper understanding of the body of Christ has been, as we have noted, among the factors that have made those questions both so urgent and so difficult. In a sense, the study of all the images increases perplexities in dealing with problems of this order. We guarantee our own later disillusionment when we rely upon a revised ecclesiology to solve such problems. We have seen reason to believe that church images exert their pristine power only when they are the genuine product of a vital communal imagination and when that imagination uses them to correct its own self-understanding, as a confession of its sin in not conforming to those images. The deficiencies in ecclesiological doctrine arise from the same rebellions that are expressed in countless other forms.

When we look back over our survey we note how few are the figures that in their New Testament usage reflect direct answers to such concerns. They seem to resist our efforts to use them to solve problems of organization or to smooth the path toward a reunion of the churches. They provide very dubious weapons either for partisan conflict or for reunion negotiations. For this reason the initial reactions to such a study as this are certain to be negative. " What can a recovery of the ecclesiological consciousness of the first congregations in the ancient Roman world contribute to the healing of Christian schisms which are now so deeply entrenched that they are accepted as normal? Obviously nothing."

Let me try to suggest in briefest summary why I think that this skepticism is as premature and as mistaken as is the contrary optimism. The New Testament images of the church may not be serviceable as tools for the eager hands of ecclesiastical trouble shooters, but they may, nevertheless, exert a power in their own right. If we may take as an example the first area mentioned — the agelong conflict between high-church and low-church views, a conflict that is not limited to a single tradition or to a traditional rivalry between two traditions — we see that these very epithets (high versus low) are metaphors or analogies that have been widely accepted as applicable to the current situation, even though anyone who has sought an agreed definition of these terms in the throes of an ecumenical conference will have learned how elastic they are. In this setting we venture two assertions, both supported by the findings of these chapters.

First of all, the New Testament conception of the church is higher (we must use this image in spite of its shortcomings) than any conception held by the so-called high churches. As evidence for this statement, I submit simply the full meaning of the four master images: the people of God, the new creation, the fellowship in faith, the body of Christ. In context these images point to a reality which is pre-existent and postexistent, which transcends the boundaries of time and space, of present and future, of life and death. This reality is as high as the Most High God who lives within it and moves through it to accomplish his eternal purpose. It is as high as the living Lord in whom and from whom the church receives the fullness of God's life and glory. It is as high as the Holy Spirit who leads the church into all truth and sanctifies it with his gifts. It is as high as the new humanity, as the resurrection body of Christ, as the Holy City, which comes down out of heaven. The dimension of height, suggested but not exhausted by these images, dwarfs to hill-like proportions the highest of the high churches. By comparison, rival ecclesiastical claims are little more than missiles shot into space; however high they go they do not reach an orbit in the heavenly places.

Second, the New Testament conception of the church is lower (again this image is hopelessly ambiguous) than any conception firmly believed and practiced by any low church. The evidence is amply provided by the same master images. The height of the people of God is accomplished by the depth of his condescension in love for those who are not his people. The new creation in its greatest power is introduced by a Messiah who humbled himself, who descended into hell, who took captivity captive by his death on a cross. The fellowship in faith is created by a God who in faithfulness to his promises suffered in man's suffering and thus created his people as a fellowship in faith, which by its suffering witnesses to the redemption of a suffering world. The body of Christ is a broken body, which produces by its very brokenness the unification of all things. Consequently, the reality of the church is slavery and servitude to him and this slavery is a mission to the lowest of men because it is a promise to them that love never fails. The church becomes the church through dying in the body of Christ to the law, to self, to sin, and to death. The true church is in actuality a cross-bearing Man. But can any of our churches think of themselves as being so low as this? By the definition of lowliness given to the church by its Servant, our most democratic pretensions seem shallow indeed. Our conception of high church has no universality, our conception of low church has no redemptive power. The New Testament images have both because they perceive in Jesus Christ the glory of God in his condescension to be wounded for our transgressions. It is his glory that provides the ontological ground of all the images of the church.

If these assertions are valid, have they the capacity to provide positive guidance for contemporary churches, whether low or high? Yes. It was the initial function of the images to promote self-recognition and freedom in this self-recognition. Nor was this self-recognition and freedom the fruit of self-commendation. We recall that it was individuals guilty of fornication whom Paul reminded that their bodies were members of Christ. It was a congregation torn by egoistic gluttony whom Paul reminded that in the Eucharist they became one body. It was a congregation that in practice denied the headship of Christ which provoked the apostle to affirm that very headship over both the world and the church. The image articulated a self-awareness that, just because it recognized the God-given fullness of the church, recognized also its own perfidy. Confessing its treacheries and receiving his grace, it became the channel of his mercy. The church was most really the church when it experienced in dying the transition from existence as " no people " to existence as " the people of God."

Is not this what happens when high church and low church are alike confronted by the true height and depth of God's people? Do they not discover that the distance between high and low, so great when measured by reference to the other, becomes no distance at all when compared with distances of another magnitude altogether? And does not this discovery, although not erasing ecclesiastical differences, impel churchmen to visualize those differences within a new framework? Framework is of course too static and formal an image. The New Testament images are more vital in their reiterated suggestion that the only framework is that provided by Him to whom the church belongs. " You are Christ's and Christ is God's." If in their deepest self-awareness high and low churches could recognize this being possessed by Christ as the framework within which their conflicts proceed, those conflicts which measure alienation might begin to represent a mutual alienation from Christ, a mutual condemnation by him, and a mutual election to serve as his people.

This same series of observations may be germane to the second problem: How does the living Christ operate through the current empirical forms in the life of the church? Can we detect the particular channels through which the heavenly powers sustain the work of the church on our street? The images, it must be confessed, are not very helpful here in any direct way. They suggest that no systematic objective answer can be given. They suggest that the channels are so diverse, so intricately woven into the fabric of social and personal decisions, so pervasive of all " the joints and sinews " of the one body, that any attempt to limit the marks of Christ's presence to a manageable and identifiable list is to mistake the character of the body's cohesion. One could point to particular answers, such as the Pauline insistence that the growth of the body is accomplished by love, a love that flows from the head and knits together every membrane and muscle. But answers of this sort do not provide the kind of help desired. One could point to the cardinal importance of the Eucharist and yet be appalled by the likelihood that " this is not the Lord's supper which you eat." In his references to the body Paul insisted that " discernment of the Spirits " is necessary and possible, but he insisted also that such discernment is in itself a spiritual gift. The mind of Christ is capable of discerning the marks of his presence, but his humility, although shared freely with his brothers, does not enable them to formalize those marks. The images therefore suggest that our desire to codify the marks of the church may itself be due to our sin, or at least to the poverty of our imagination.

What, now, may a consideration of the church images contribute to a better understanding of the intended functions of laymen and of ministerial orders within the church? At this point we are embarrassed by the potency of the answers, so long, that is, as we are not judging these answers in terms of our own prejudices and pressures. Another volume could well begin at this point. Here we must content ourselves with a few conclusions that the panorama of pictures suggests. This panorama is dependent upon another panorama, the portraits of the Messiah. The story of Jesus as Messiah defines the church as his people. The picture of him as priest, as sacrifice, as shepherd, as king, as man, as servant, as witness, as holy one — these pictures are absolutely primary in the definition and redefinition of the corresponding pictures of the church. Thus the whole panorama of images confirms the conclusions of Alan Richardson:

Because Christ is the apostle, the church is apostolic; because he is the High Priest, the church is sacerdotal; because he is Servant, the church is ministerial.[5]

So too when we shift attention from the Christological to the ecclesiological facet of the images. Almost without exception the pictures of the church are not pictures of a part of the church, a group of select Christians or congregations or a particular ministerial order, but pictures of the church as a whole.

The whole church is apostolic . . . just as the whole church is priestly and is ministerial.[6]

It is amazing to analyze the extent to which this observation applies to the entire parade of analogies: the people, circumcision, sons of Abraham, family, flock, temple, sacrifice, saints, slaves, stewards, body. The images as a whole fuse together the ministry of Christ, variously conceived, with the ministry of his people as a whole. In that single, corporate ministry every individual as a lamb or as a disciple has an essential share. Shareholders (*koinōnoi*) in the Spirit are shareholders in the manifold vocation that the Spirit assigns. No image can be legitimately construed as excluding "one of the least of these my brethren" from kingship or priesthood, stewardship or army, sainthood or slavery. The analysis of the master images thus supports the inference that ecclesiology is nothing more nor less than the theology of the laity. In this connection it is important to note that the nexus between Christ and church is everywhere provided by Baptism and the Eucharist, in which all believers share.

Baptism is, as it were, the ordination of a new member of the royal priesthood; it is the making of a layman in the church of Christ. A layman in the New Testament sense, i.e., a member of the *laos* is certainly not . . . a church member who has no ministerial responsibility, one who has handed over his functions of evangelism and pastoral care to certain professional Christians who are paid to perform them. All the laity . . . are priests and ministers . . . and all the "ministers" are equally "laymen." [7]

Such observations do not solve modern dilemmas concerning the laity, but they do support the conviction that none of those dilemmas is insoluble if we allow our thinking to be permeated by the images of Christ and by the images of the church. Can the same thing be said of the tangled issues raised by the diverse ministerial orders within the church? In certain respects the latter problem seems the more intransigent. And it must be said that the gamut of New Testament images is less extensive and less helpful here.

There are some sixteen images which in the New Testament contexts refer more or less directly to the distinctive functioning of a special order of ministers within the church. In most cases the order mentioned is that of the apostles. Here is the list: a letter of Christ, the fish net, the boat, the aroma, the planting, the building, the pillars, the wedding feast, ambassadors, the twelve tribes, the shepherds, the city, the sacrifice, the disciples, the stewards, the diversity of gifts in the one body. In some of these the apostles are singled out as a separate group, usually dependent on the apostolate of Christ and with a mission representative of the whole church. On the other hand, many images by implication offer no place for a differentiation of the ministry, for example, the images related to the family permit only the distinction between the first-born son and the other sons. (Cf. also the images reviewed in Chapter IV.) Even so, we must conclude that the images corroborate other evidence that the New Testament assumed that the apostles carried on a work intrinsic to the church's life. The images also corroborate the legitimacy, as spiritual gifts, of prophecy, of teaching, of administration, of service, of speaking with tongues. They intimate a distinctness in degree of importance of these various offices. The image that throws the greatest light upon this area is the image of the one body and the one spirit. Yet the three passages where the members of the body are described as the variety of gifts (I Cor., chs. 12 to 14; Rom., ch. 12; Eph., ch. 4) do not list these gifts in the same order. Moreover, different ministries are mentioned by the three lists as examples of the gifts. We may infer that Paul was not outlining (by way of metaphor) an existing hierarchy of neatly separated orders. Rather was he simply illustrating the plurality and unity of the ministries of the church by referring to many distinct activities within the congregation, some of which could and some of which could not be " ordered."

The three lists together hardly give us a coherent picture of the ministry of the apostolic church. They were not intended to do so; each was written in the course of a practical instruction in the duties of churchmanship as these were to be performed by the laity.[8]

It appears to be a fact therefore that we " can obtain from the New Testament only a very indistinct picture of these ministries." The New Testament does not even allow us to distinguish between orders and functions, since the whole church participated so fully in the functions of the separate orders. There are quite naturally contrary opinions as to why this should be so, and insufficient evidence for adequate explanations. Our survey of images might intimate that the reason for New Testament indistinctness stems from the truth that the writers perceived a different reality as truly constitutive of the church and, accordingly, the powers of their imagination worked toward different goals. Is it fortunate or unfortunate that these pictures of the ministerial orders are so indistinct? Professor Richardson, whose excellent analysis I have followed closely, answers " Unfortunate." Here I disagree. I believe it is fortunate. It is a good thing that scholars cannot agree on the pattern that the ministry actually had in the first century. It is good that the documents do not allow us to determine " archaeologically " the original polity of the church. This makes it necessary for every Christian community, however it may be ordered today, to ask not whether its ordering of the ministry accords with a primitive archetype but whether this community as a whole manifests the threefold character of the New Testament church — its apostolic, priestly, and ministerial character. How is the essential vocation of the apostolic church "manifested or obscured both in the total laity and in the particular ministerial organization?" These are the questions formulated by Canon Richardson, and I agree wholeheartedly. This is the type of question that the ecclesiological images of the New Testament provoke, and when the question is presented in this form those images give their own very cogent answers.

If our churches were prompted by the images to ask themselves this question, some deadlocks among contemporary communions might yield. It is the suspicions that the high churches have of the low, often quite justified, that impels them to defend the ontological realism of the body of Christ and therefore to maintain as essential the inherited ministerial orders, including episcopal succession. These suspicions might be undermined to the extent that the low churches actually adopted as their dominant ecclesiology the full height of the New Testament images. On the other side, the suspicions, equally justified, that the low churches have of the high prompt them to defend the metaphorical character of the body of Christ and, accordingly, to treat as temporary and limited the necessity of ministerial orders. These suspicions would be undermined to the extent that the high churches should actually appropriate the full lowliness of the New Testament images. And if mutual suspicions were undermined by a mutual appreciation of the height and depth of Christ's ministry through the church, these alienated churches might be reconciled. That very reconciliation would express the vitality of the images, for it was initially the reality of reconciliation that produced the images and made them vehicles of God's work.

This leads us to the final area of urgent and vocal contemporary concern — the need for a truer comprehension of the relationship between the church and the world. Do the church images help us here? Three comments suggest a positive answer. (1) As already noted, the images were not initially shaped by the tendency to define the church by contrasting it to the world. The images did not grow out of a basically sociological, psychological, or moral comparison-

and-contrast between the church and its surrounding societies, nor out of a "ghetto-consciousness" on the part of Christian leaders. They grew primarily from the revolution experienced by the coming of the Kingdom of God in the Messiah. The images were elicited to function as positive witnesses to this revolution. The Christological and soteriological images were determinative of the ecclesiological. (2) In their major connotations the Christological images expressed in varying ways and degrees Christ's headship over *the world* under the dominion of Alpha and Omega. They articulated a new understanding of God's judgment and mercy for *all* men. They transformed the meaning of such cosmic terms as sin and death. Early Christian pictures *of the world* were shaped in conformity to the gospel. In other words, as Lord of the world the Son of God vindicated his right to define what is world and what is church, where the world is to be found within the church and where the church within the world. Both ontologically and eschatologically the existing wall between church and world became subject to Christ's power to destroy all walls. (3) We have noted the degree to which the gallery of images was cruciform in construction. The Christological images centered in the Passion of the Servant of God. So too did the ecclesiological. So too did the pictures of the world. The images that expressed the contrast between church and world found that contrast illuminated by the cross. Likewise the images that expressed the mission of the church to the world pointed to the world by pointing to this death and this resurrection. The images that expressed the final assurance of salvation for all men drew their inspiration from this event which happened once upon a time, yet once for all time. But these same images expressed the actuality of judgment for all men. Thus if we take seriously the cumulative impact of all the images, if we think of them reciprocally and retroactively, our minds will begin again with the gospel proclamation of the death and resurrection of this Man, of the death and resurrection of all men in this Man, and of the communion realized among members of his body. Beginning there and then looking afresh at the church and the world in our own day, we may find that a revolution has taken place and that the images have again fulfilled their function of helping us to perceive this mystery and to recognize in it not only our own sins but also the sins of the whole world, not only God's glory in the church but also God's glory throughout the world. Such a restoration of the Christian imagination may enable the church to use again the whole medley of New Testament images with an authentic comprehension of their meaning, freed from the idolatry and tyranny of words by the sovereignty of the Word made flesh.

APPENDIX

ANALOGIES DISCUSSED IN THE TEXT

Chapter II

[1] the salt of the earth
[2] a letter from Christ
[3] fish and fish net
[4] the boat
[5] the ark
[6] unleavened bread
[7] one loaf
[8] the table of the Lord
[9] the altar
[10] the cup of the Lord
[11] wine
[12] branches of the vine
[13] vineyard
[14] the fig tree
[15] the olive tree
[16] God's planting
[17] God's building
[18] building on the rock
[19] pillar and buttress
[20] virgins
[21] the Messiah's mother
[22] the elect lady
[23] the bride of Christ
[24] the wedding feast
[25] wearers of white robes
[26] the choice of clothing
[27] citizens
[28] exiles
[29] the Dispersion
[30] ambassadors
[31] the poor
[32] hosts and guests

Chapter III

[33] the people of God
[34] Israel
[35] a chosen race
[36] a holy nation
[37] twelve tribes
[38] the patriarchs
[39] circumcision
[40] Abraham's sons
[41] the exodus
[42] house of David
[43] remnant
[44] the elect
[45] flock
[46] lambs who rule
[47] the Holy City
[48] the holy temple
[49] priesthood
[50] sacrifice
[51] aroma
[52] festivals

Chapter IV

[53] the new creation
[54] first fruits
[55] the new humanity
[56] the last Adam
[57] the Son of Man
[58] the Kingdom of God
[59] fighters against Satan
[60] Sabbath Rest
[61] the coming age
[62] God's glory
[63] light
[64] the name
[65] life
[66] the tree of life
[67] communion in the Holy Spirit
[68] the bond of love

Chapter V

[69] the sanctified
[70] the faithful
[71] the justified
[72] followers
[73] disciples

[74] road
[75] coming and going
[76] witnessing community
[77] confessors
[78] slaves
[79] friends
[80] servants
[81] "with . . ."
[82] edification
[83] household of God
[84] sons of God
[85] brotherhood

Chapter VI

[86] the body of life
[87] members of Christ
[88] the body and the blood
[89] the diversities of ministries
[90] spiritual body
[91] head of cosmic spirits
[92] head of the church
[93] the body of this head
[94] the unity of Jews and Gentiles
[95] the growth of the body
[96] the fullness of God

NOTES

Chapter I. The Scope and Method of Study

1. Among the books that have thus far appeared are the following: Nels F. S. Ferré, *Christ and the Christian* (Harper & Brothers, 1958); John Knox, *The Early Church and the Coming Great Church* (Abingdon Press, 1955); Paul S. Minear, *Jesus and His People* (Association Press, 1957) and *Horizons of Christian Community* (The Bethany Press, 1959); Anders Nygren, *Christ and His Church* (The Westminster Press, 1956); W. Norman Pittenger, *The Church, The Ministry and Reunion* (The Seabury Press, Inc., 1957) and *The Word Incarnate* (Harper & Brothers, 1959); Thomas F. Torrance, *Royal Priesthood* (Oliver & Boyd, Ltd., Edinburgh, 1955); Claude Welch, *The Reality of the Church* (Charles Scribner's Sons, 1958).

2. For the purpose of this discussion, Amos Wilder has provided a good definition of imagination as " that synthesizing function of the mind in dealing with experience at all levels whereby we objectify for ourselves realities with regard to which we have rather clues than controlled evidence" (*New Testament Faith for Today*, p. 63; Harper & Brothers, 1955).

3. Cf. E. Best, *One Body in Christ*, pp. 98 ff. (S.P.C.K., London, 1955); E. L. Mascall, *Christ, the Christian and the Church*, pp. 110–112 (Longmans, Green & Co., Ltd., London, 1955); J. A. T. Robinson, *The Body*, pp. 49–55 (Henry Regnery Company, 1952).

4. Cf. Welch, *op. cit.*, pp. 181 f.

5. Alan Richardson, *Introduction to the Theology of the New Testament* (S.C.M. Press, Ltd., London, 1958), p. 257.

6. We must all beware of what Amos Wilder calls " the stultifying axiom that genuine truth or insight or wisdom must be limited to that which can be stated in discursive prose, in denotative language stripped as far as possible of all connotative suggestion . . ." (*op. cit.*, p. 60).

7. Wilder, *op. cit.*, p. 93.

Chapter II. MINOR IMAGES OF THE CHURCH

1. This, with many other sayings, illustrates a distinction between an "additive plural" and a "social plural," a distinction made clear in Best, *op. cit.,* pp. 1, 2.

2. Cf. E. Hoskyns, *The Fourth Gospel* (S.P.C.K., London, 1947), pp. 552–556.

3. The version of the parable in the *Gospel of Thomas,* 81:28 ff., appears to be entirely free from implicit references to the church. It is also to be noted that Christian art of the second century made a prominent use of the fish symbol.

4. Cf. Bo Reicke, *Disobedient Spirits and Christian Baptism* (Einar Munksgaard, Copenhagen, 1946), pp. 126–136.

5. Cf. A. Maillot, in J. J. von Allmen, *Vocabulary of the Bible* (Lutterworth Press, London, 1958), pp. 41 f.

6. Cf. Richardson, *op. cit.,* pp. 378 f.; S. Hanson, *The Unity of the Church in the New Testament* (Uppsala, 1946), pp. 31–33.

7. Cf. A. J. Rawlinson, *The Gospel According to St. Mark* (Methuen & Co., Ltd., London, 1925), p. 32.

8. Cf. C. H. Dodd, *Interpretation of the Fourth Gospel* (Cambridge University Press, Cambridge, 1953), pp. 287 ff.

9. For a convenient summary, cf. A. Corell, *Consummatum Est* (S.P.C.K., London, 1958), pp. 92 f.

10. Ps. 80:8; Jer. 2:21; Hos. 10:1; Ezek. 15:2-6; 19:10; Isa. 5:1-7; 27:2-3. For a forceful summary of this tradition, cf. Jean Danielou, *The Lord of History* (Longmans, Green & Co., Ltd., London, 1958), pp. 168 f.

11. Corell, *op. cit.,* pp. 27 f.

12. Dodd, *Interpretation of the Fourth Gospel,* pp. 136, 196, 410–412, 418.

13. Cf. Danielou, *op. cit.,* pp. 172–178.

14. In this connection it should be observed that the figures implied in the verbs "to give" and "to give the increase" are more important to Paul's emphasis than the noun for "planting." Moreover, in the case of these verbs there are many parallel passages both in Paul and in other writers. For *didonai* as referring simultaneously to God, Christ, and community, cf. Rom. 15:5-6; Eph. 3:14-19; John 3:34-36; 17:2-24; for *auxanein,* cf. Acts 6:7; 12:24; 19:20; II Cor. 9:9-15; Eph. 2:19-22; 4:15-16; Col. 1:6-10; 2:19 (in Ephesians and Colossians there is a similar conjunction of growth and building); Mark 4:8; Matt. 13:32; I Peter 2:2 (here there is a similar conjunction of milk and growth).

15. Cf. Best., *op. cit.,* pp. 160–169.

16. Cf. Oscar Cullmann, *Peter* (The Westminster Press, 1953), pp. 155–212.

17. Cf. Acts, ch. 15; Gal., ch. 2; Matt. 18:15-20; John, chs. 20; 21. Also the *Gospel of Thomas,* 82:30 to 83:14.

18. Hos., ch. 3; Jer. 2:1; Ezek. 16:23.

19. Cf. Lohmeyer, *Die Offenbarung des Johannes* (Mohr, Tübingen, 1926), *ad loc.*

20. Cf. Minear, *Horizons of Christian Community* (The Bethany Press, 1958), pp. 90 ff.

21. 1 Baruch 4, 5; Gal. 4:25; Rev., ch. 12. Cf. Wilder, in *The Interpreter's Bible*, Vol. 12, 1957, pp. 209 f., 302. (Abingdon Press.)

22. Cf. Welch, *op. cit.*, pp. 131–138; H. de Lubac, *The Splendour of the Church* (Sheed & Ward, Inc., 1926), pp. 41 ff.; C. Chavasse, *The Bride of Christ* (Faber & Faber, Ltd., London, 1940), pp. 49–98; Mascall, *op. cit.*, pp. 124 ff.; Richardson, *op. cit.*, pp. 256 f.; Best, *op. cit.*, pp. 169–183.

23. Cf. also John 2:1-11; [11]; Dodd, *op. cit.*, pp. 297 ff.

24. Danielou, *op. cit.*, p. 216.

25. Cf. Danielou, *op. cit.*, pp. 214–240; also cf. [8], [32].

26. The symbolism of clothing enters prominently into the Gospel stories of the transfiguration (Mark 9:2-8) and of the crucifixion (Mark 15:16-24). So too, the theme of nakedness recurs often in the New Testament. Cf. Minear, *Christian Hope and the Second Coming* (The Westminster Press, 1954), pp. 139–148.

27. Col. 3:10-11; Eph. 4:22-25; cf. [55].

28. In a recent essay, W. C. van Unnik has demonstrated the rarity of direct allusions to the church as the Diaspora, and the danger of exaggerating this element in early Christian thinking. Cf. *Ecclesia*, Aangeboden aan J. N. Bakhuizen van den Brink (Martinus Nijhof, The Hague, 1959), pp. 33–45.

29. Cf. John 17:8-18; 20:21; Hanson, *op. cit.*, pp. 33-37.

30. Matt. 11:5; Luke 7:22; 4:18.

31. Cf. II Cor. 8:9; Rev. 2:9; Luke 18:22; 19:8.

32. Matt 10:40. Cf. Danielou, *op. cit.*, pp. 64–71.

Chapter III. THE PEOPLE OF GOD

1. The importance of this image for New Testament ecclesiology may be briefly indicated by reference to the frequency of its appearance. It is to be found in fourteen New Testament writings. In seven others, equivalent expressions are used, such as Israel, the circumcision, the twelve tribes, the household of God (Galatians, Ephesians, Philippians, Colossians, I and II Thessalonians, James). In three others, the absence of the term is probably not significant (I and II Timothy, Philemon). There are three others from which the term is missing I, II, and III John). When this absence is linked with a rare use in the Gospel of John (John 11:50 is an important exception), we may conclude that the Johannine tradition found this concept uncongenial, while in all other major New Testament traditions it was a natural and important mode of thought. A selected list of passages where the people (*laos*) of God has a marked significance for the self-consciousness of the Christian church follows:

Matt. 1:21; 2:6; 4:16, 23　　　　Acts 3:23; 7:34; 13:17-31; 15:14;
John 11:50; 18:14　　　　　　　　18:10
Rom. 9:25-26; 11:1 f.; 15:10　　II Cor. 6:16
Titus 2:14　　　　　　　　　　　Heb. 2:17; 4:9; 8:10; 10:30; 13:12

I Peter 2:9-10   Rev. 18:4; 21:3
Luke 1:17, 77; 2:10, 31-32; 7:16

2. In this regard, the New Testament continues the practice of the LXX. Cf. Strathmann, in Kittel, TWNT IV, 29-37. The chief exceptions are provided in the Lucan writings. Ibid., p. 50.

3. II Cor. 6:16; Heb. 8:10; Rev. 21:3; cf. Ex. 19:5; Deut. 7:6; 14:2; Ps. 135:4.

4. Matt. 2:6; Luke 2:31-32; John 11:50; Acts 15:14; Rom. 15:10; Titus 2:14; Heb. 2:12; 13:12.

5. Cf. W. Gutbrod, "Israel," in Kittel, TWNT III, 385-395.

6. James 1:1; Rev. 7:4; Matt. 19:28. We should not overlook the double name of the father of the twelve: Jakob-Israel.

7. John 8:39; James 2:21; Heb. 11:17 f.

8. Rom. 9:8; Acts 7:2; Rom. 4:9-10; Heb. 11:8-12. Cf. Hanson, *op. cit.*, pp. 70 f.

9. R. L. Calhoun, in Minear, ed., *The Nature of the Unity We Seek* (The Bethany Press, 1958), p. 76.

10. A judicious but comprehensive study of exodus typology in Paul is provided by H. Sahlin, "The New Exodus of Salvation" in *The Root of the Vine*, ed. A. Fridrichsen (The Dacre Press, London, 1953), pp. 81 ff. Sahlin rightly concludes that the thought of "the entire Primitive Church" was thoroughly conditioned by the understanding of the church as engaged in "the new exodus of salvation" (p. 94). Too little theological attention has been given to this mode of perceiving the character of the church, although scholars in many countries are becoming alive to its importance. Cf. also Danielou, *op. cit.*, pp. 204–213.

11. Matt. 1:1, 6, 17; Luke 3:23-31; Rom. 1:3; II Tim. 2:8; Rev. 3:7; 5:5; 22:16.

12. Luke 1:32-33, 69-73; Acts 13:22-26.

13. Rom. 11:13 ff. Compare Isa. 6:13; 11:1; 37:31. Cf. also the discussion of the olive tree [15].

14. In this judgment I part company, somewhat unwillingly, from many British and Swedish scholars. T. W. Manson, for example, was an outstanding exponent of the centrality of the remnant idea. Cf. *The Teaching of Jesus* (Cambridge University Press, Cambridge, 1945): "Whether we begin with the religion of the Old Testament and work our way forward through prophecy and apocalyptic, or whether we start from the fact of the early church and try to trace it to its beginnings, the idea of the faithful remnant is the Ariadne thread that leads us to the center of the labyrinth. There we find the crucified . . ." (p. 236). The best contemporary Swedish scholarship is represented in a symposium edited by Fridrichsen, *The Root of the Vine*. In his essay, G. A. Danell sees the two concepts of election and remnant as interdependent (pp. 24 ff.). But this forces him to illustrate the remnant ideology by reference to the election of Abraham, the preference given to Jacob, the protection accorded to Joseph and to the people of Israel in Egypt. It is a dubious procedure

to extend the concept of the Babylonian remnant to all the earlier exiles. Yet it is only by such an extension that one can find important parallels in the New Testament for the remnant ideology.

15. Luke 6:13; John 6:70; 13:18; 15:6, 19; Acts 1:2; 9:15.

16. James 2:5; I Cor. 1:27; I Thess. 1:4; II Peter 1:10.

17. Mark 13:20-22; Matt. 22:22-31; Luke 18:7; Rom. 8:23; Eph. 1:4; Col. 3:12; II Tim. 2:10; Rev. 17:14.

18. In my previous note I criticized certain Swedish scholars for unjustifiably broad definitions of the remnant. Here I hasten to approve their stress on the centrality of election. Two essays in *The Root of the Vine* are especially noteworthy: those of Danell and K. Stendahl. Danell's work is valuable in showing how the election of Israel in the Old Testament was set in a universal context. "The God who created heaven and earth and mankind, who replenished the earth and divided it among many peoples, is the same God who chooses Abraham and Isaac. . . . As the Election in the story of Moses presupposes that Yahweh is a universal, creative God, the one true God, so the Election itself has a universal purpose" (pp. 24, 27). Stendahl gives a penetrating analysis of the force of Matt. 22:14 and effectively counteracts any interpretations of predestination or of communal solidarity in election that would negate personal responsibility. "Election in Christ not only constitutes a new society; its meaning is to be found in a new society, and not in the status of individuals." (P. 69.) "A collective election in Christ, which is not at the same time an individual election to Christ and the church, does not do justice to the text. 'For many are called, but few are chosen.'" (P. 80.) These comments may well warn us not to view the more "nationalistic" images as if they contradicted either a genuine universalism or a personal responsibility for communal and individual righteousness. Cf. also Corell, *op. cit.,* pp. 186–193.

19. Paul's conception of both Israel and the world had been revolutionized by God's revelation in Christ. By contrast, rabbinic Judaism, although appealing to God's election of Israel, allowed its primal perceptions of what constituted Israel to be determined by the biological and institutional differences between Jews and Gentiles. Yahweh protected Israel from evil, while the gods of the Gentiles were seductive idols. Holiness was defined by its opposite: Gentile wickedness. The world had been created for the sake of Israel. Gentiles were permanently excluded from God's favor. Thus particularism triumphed by the building of a wall between Jews and Gentiles, a wall that coincided with identifiable marks such as birth and circumcision (cf. R. Meyer, "*laos,*" in Kittel, TWNT IV, 39–49). But Paul saw this complex of notions as a fundamental perversion of God's purpose in creating Israel for the sake of the world. The visible line between Jew and Gentile was not so frozen that men could confine Israel within fixed bounds. No. "All Israel will be saved" but only after "the full number of Gentiles come in" (Rom. 11:25). Israel is not to be defined by the contrast to Gentiles. But Israel, the Gentiles, and the provisional line between are to be understood in terms of an inclusive sovereignty.

20. Matt. 26:31; Luke 2:8; 12:32; John 10:16; Acts 20:28-29; I Cor. 9:7;

I Peter 5:2-3; although this view of Luke 2:8 could be challenged. Cf. below, p. 88.

21. Matt. 7:15; 9:36; and parallels; 10:6, 16 and parallels; 15:24; 25:32; John 10:1-27; 21:16-17; Rom. 8:36; Heb. 13:20; I Peter 2:25.

22. John 10:1-16; Acts 20:28-29; I Peter 5:1-3.

23. E.g., Ps. 23; 77; 78; 80; Isa., ch. 40; Jer., ch. 23; Ezek., ch. 34; Zech., chs. 7 to 14.

24. Matt. 7:15; Luke 10:3; Acts 20:29; John 10:12.

25. Acts 20:28; Heb. 13:20; Acts 8:32; I Peter 2:25.

26. Rev. 7:17. Cf. Ezek. 34:23; Ps. 23:2; Isa. 25:8.

27. Cf. P. W. Meyer, *Journal of Biblical Literature,* Vol. 35, 1956, pp. 232 f.

28. Cf. I Peter 1:19; 2:25; Acts 8:32; Matt. 8:17; Luke 22:37.

29. J. Robert Nelson, in the *Ecumenical Review,* IX, 1957, p. 110; F. W. Dillistone, *Structure of the Divine Society* (The Westminster Press, 1957), pp. 47-85.

30. Von Allmen, *Vocabulary of the Bible,* p. 281.

31. *Ibid.,* p. 284.

32. I use the term "inner history" in the same sense as H. R. Niebuhr in his *Meaning of Revelation* (The Macmillan Company, 1941), pp. 73-90.

33. Von Allmen, *op. cit.,* p. 284.

34. Hanson, *op. cit.,* p. 12.

35. John 2:19-21; cf. Mark 15:29; Matt. 22:61.

36. But cf. Corell, *op. cit.,* pp. 49-53.

37. Eph. 2:21; I Peter 2:7; Mark 12:10.

38. I Peter 2:5, 9; Rev. 1:6; 5:10; 20:6.

39. M. Bouttier, in von Allmen, *op. cit.,* p. 340.

40. *Ibid.,* p. 342; Phil. 2:17.

41. Richardson, *op. cit.,* pp. 295-303.

42. Von Allmen, *op. cit.,* p. 125.

43. Cf. C. K. Barrett in W. D. Davies and D. Daube, eds., *The Background of the New Testament and Its Eschatology* (Cambridge University Press, Cambridge, 1956), pp. 366-373.

44. Cf. Hanson, *op. cit.,* pp. 13 f.

Chapter IV. The New Creation

1. Cf. G. Lindeskog, *Studien zum neutestamentlichen Schöpfungsgedanken* (Uppsala, 1952), pp. 217-251.

2. James 1:18; cf. also Rev. 14:4; II Thess. 2:13. Cf. also Best, *op. cit.,* p. 38.

3. I Tim. 4:4; I Cor. 10:26; Rev. 4:11; 10:6.

4. Cf. Hanson, *The Unity of the Church* (Uppsala, 1946), pp. 65-70, 73; Best, *op. cit.,* pp. 34-42.

5. U. Simon, *Heaven* (Harper & Brothers, 1958), Chapter 3.

6. Richardson, *op. cit.,* p. 139.

7. Dodd, *op. cit.,* pp. 246 f.

8. This fusion of images that have different roots is described by G. Linde-

skog: "Creation in the Old and New Testaments," in *The Root of the Vine,* ed. Fridrichsen, Chapter 1. "Jesus gives this image, which he gets from Daniel, a totally new meaning by fusing it with another Scriptural image, the Suffering Servant of Isaiah 53. . . . Christ is the New Man, the second Adam; as Son of Man he is also the perfect man." (pp. 15.) Cf. also Hanson, *op. cit.,* pp. 18 f., 28 f., 37.

9. For a fuller development of this picture of the army, see my *Horizons of Christian Community,* Chapter 2; cf. also Hanson, *op. cit.,* pp. 18-23; R. Leivestad, *Christ the Conqueror* (The Macmillan Company, 1954), pp. 272–285.

10. Heb. 4:1-11; John, ch. 5; Mark 2:23 to 3:6; Luke 13:6-21; [52]. Cf. Danielou, *op. cit.,* pp. 4, 22ln; cf. C. K. Barrett, *loc. cit.,* pp. 363–392.

11. The inner substance of the new and the old age is indicated in the following contrasting characterizations:

> this age . . . the coming age (Mark 10:3; Matt. 12:32; Eph. 1:21)
> sons of this age . . . sons of light (Luke 16:8)
> sons of the evil one . . . sons of the Kingdom (Matt. 13:38)
> sons of this age. . . sons of the resurrection (Luke 20:34-36)
> the works of darkness . . . the armor of light (Rom. 13:11-13)

12. Gal. 5:21; I Cor. 6:9-10; Rom. 14:17.

13. Luke 6:20-23; Matt. 5:3-10; James 2:5; I Cor. 1:26-30.

14. Whether or not the idea of glory should be classed as an image is problematic. I have included it for several reasons: (1) It is clearly cognate with other terms which are readily listed as images: e.g., Kingdom, light. (2) It is used in the New Testament in such a way as to define what constitutes the church as sons and heirs of glory. (3) Its history is crowded with empirical analogies: e.g., the thunder and lightning, the wealth and grandeur of imperial offices, the fame and power of great men. (4) In many contexts the reality in mind is hidden behind external shame. The explication of the invisible and the paradoxical reality therefore virtually requires metaphorical language.

15. J. Pedersen, *Israel,* I (Oxford University Press, London, 1926), pp. 237–339.

16. *Ibid.,* pp. 234–235.

17. Minear, *Horizons of Christian Community,* Chapter 1.

18. E. Stauffer, *New Testament Theology* (The Macmillan Company, 1955), pp. 120–122. Cf. Rom. 1:18 ff.

19. II Cor. 4:6; Col. 1:13; I Peter 2:9.

20. I John 2:9; Rom. 13:12-14; Eph. 5:9; Phil. 2:14-16; I Thess. 5:8-11.

21. Richardson, *op. cit.,* pp. 67–72; Dodd, *op. cit.,* pp. 201–212, 297–389; Rudolf Bultmann, *Theology of the New Testament* (Charles Scribner's Sons, 1955), Vol. II, pp. 15–69.

22. The references to light enable the reader to detect many correlations with other ecclesiological images. Each corollary becomes an index to the meaning of light, and light in turn adds meanings to the corollary. In the following list may be found some of the more important, explicit corollaries:

God's life	John 1:4	[65]
God's Kingdom	Col. 1:12-13	[58]
God's people	I Peter 2:9-10	[33]
God's city	Rev. 21:23 to 22:5	[47]
God's glory	Eph. 1:18	[62]
The new creation of a new humanity	II Cor. 4:6	[55]
The sons of God	John 1:9, 13	[84]
The army fighting the devil	Eph. 5:9-13	[59]
Fellowship with one another	I John 1:1-10	[81]
The temple	Rev. 1:9 to 2:7	[48]

23. It is not perhaps convincing or cogent to classify *name* with the more visual images such as salt or building. Yet its meaning in the Bible almost forces us into such a classification. The word itself is a symbolic pointer to a reality that is invisible and inaudible. The word therefore belongs more closely to the figurative vocabulary of the Bible than to the more prosaic currency of everyday modern speech. Our thought should be alerted to its multiple nuances, for we are dealing not with a telephone book but with the hidden substance of selfhood. If the idea is valid that to enter the new humanity is to receive a new name, one is justified in inferring that the words "name" and "humanity" are in this context equally figurative.

24. Cf. Minear, *Jesus and His People,* Chapter 2.; cf. also C. Biber, in von Allmen, *op. cit.,* pp. 278–281.

25. Cf. J. Burnier, in von Allmen, *op. cit.,* pp. 234–237.

26. I am indebted for some of these observations to my student Miss Marianne Micks.

27. Cf. Danielou, *op. cit.,* pp. 46–55.

28. *Doctor Zhivago,* p. 42. Pantheon Books, Inc., 1958.

Chapter V. The Fellowship in Faith

1. John 17:17-19 (verb); Acts 9:31-32; Rom. 15:25-26; Heb. 2:10-12 (verb); I Peter 2:9-10; Jude 3; Rev. 20:9.

2. Perhaps the reader will allow us to waive the question whether or not the designation *saints* is rightly listed as an image. In such a listing there are obvious difficulties: the term by itself does not convey a visual or auditory impression, nor does it originate as a literary analogy, like that of salt. Yet in its complex associations when applied to the community, it suggests ranges of meaning which reach far beyond the obvious denotation and which call for an active imagination if the play of divine and human forces is to be perceived.

3. The use of the verb *pisteuein* more clearly indicates the basic components of this belief: trust, confidence, commitment. It more clearly indicates the interdependence of believing with hoping and loving. It more often shows that the object of faith determines the basic content of faith (e.g., to believe in (*eis*) the Lord Jesus Christ).

4. The virtual interchangeability of idioms may be observed in at least six writers:

The Gospel of John — 1:12; 3:15; 5:24; 17:20-21
The Acts — 2:44; 4:4, 32; 5:14
Paul — Rom. 3:22; I Cor. 14:22; Eph. 1:19
Hebrews — 4:3
I Peter — 2:7
The Revelation — 17:14

5. I Cor. 1:9; 10:13; II Cor. 1:18; I Thess. 5:24; Heb. 10:23; 11:11;.I Peter 4:19.

6. Heb. 2:17; 3:2; I John 1:9; Rev. 1:5; 3:14; 19:11.

7. Cf. A. Schlatter, *Gottes Gerechtigkeit* (Stuttgart, 1952), pp. 363–380.

8. John 17:25; Rom. 3:26; Heb. 12:23; Rev. 16:5.

9. Acts 3:14; 13:38-39; 22:14; II Tim. 4:8; I John 1:9; 2:1, 29.

10. Rom. 1:17; 5:19; Heb. 10:38; I Peter 3:12; 4:18; Acts 13:38-39; Matt. 10:41; 25:37, 46; I Cor. 6:11.

11. Matt. 13:17; 23:35; Heb. 11:4; 12:23; Rom., ch. 4.

12. E.g., Matt., chs. 5 to 7; 10:24-25; 19:23-30; Luke 9:57-61; 14:26-33; John 8:12; 10:4-5; 13:24-26.

13. Cf. Acts 6:1-2, 7; 9:1, 19, 25-26, 38; 11:26, 29; 14:20-22, 28; 18:23, 27; 19:9, 30; 20:1, 30; 21:4, 16.

14. Luke 14:33; Mark 8:34; Matt. 10:37 f.; Luke 9:57 f.; 14:26-33.

15. Cf. K. Stendahl, *The Scrolls and the New Testament* (Harper & Brothers, 1957), pp. 6–8.

16. A somewhat parallel use of the image of the Way as access to God through the cross may be found in Heb. 9:8-14; 10:19-25.

17. Cf. Minear, *Jesus and His People*, pp. 31–40; *Horizons of Christian Community*, pp. 76 f., 95 ff.

18. Luke 24:48; Acts 1:8, 22; 2:32; 3:15; 5:32; 10:39; 13:32; 22:15; 26:16.

19. "All do not die for their faith, but all suffer for it." Leivestad, *op. cit.*, p. 215.

20. Cf. Matt. 10:32; John 9:22; Acts 24:14; Rom. 10:9; I Tim. 6:12-13; Heb. 3:1; 10:23; 13:15; I John 2:23; Rev. 3:1-6.

21. Some paragraphs which follow have appeared in the *South East Asia Journal of Theology* (Oct., 1959, pp. 7 f.). They are used here by permission of the editor.

22. Cf. the opening verses of Romans, Philemon, Titus, James, II Peter, Jude, Revelation.

23. Rom. 6:22; 14:18; Acts 2:18; 4:29; I Cor. 7:22; I Thess. 1:9; I Peter 2:16; Rev. 7:3; 11:18.

24. Matt. 6:24; 10:24; 20:27; Mark 10:44; Luke 17:10; John 13:16.

25. Matt., chs. 13; 18; 22; 24; 25; Mark, ch. 12; Luke, chs. 14; 15; 20.

26. Matt. 10:24; John 13:16; 15:20; Mark 10:44-45. There is an extensive literature on the Servant Messiah and the Servant People. Cf. Manson, *The Servant Messiah* (Cambridge University Press, Cambridge, 1953); E. Schweizer, *Erniedrigung und Erhöhung bei Jesus und seinen Nachfolgern* (Zwingli,

Zürich, 1955); K. Barth, *Church Dogmatics* (T. & T. Clark, Edinburgh, 1958), IV, 2, pp. 690 ff.; M. D. Hooker, *Jesus and the Servant* (S.P.C.K., London, 1959); L. S. Mudge, *Scottish Journal of Theology* (June, 1959, pp. 113–128).

27. Rom. 6:18; 8:12-15; Gal. 4:3, 24-25; 5:1; Heb. 2:15.

28. I Cor. 7:22; Eph. 6:6; Col. 3:24; I Peter 2:16.

29. Luke 11:5-8; 14:10-12; 15:6, 9, 29.

30. Rom. 16:1; Phil. 1:1; I Tim. 3:8-13; 4:6.

31. Matt. 20:26; Luke 22:26-27; Rom. 15:8.

32. I Cor. 12:5; Luke 12:37; 22:26-27; Matt. 25:44.

33. Other words were used to refer to Christians as stewards and attendants. They are not of such significance as to demand separate attention. John 18:36; I Cor. 4:1.

34. James M. Robinson, *The Problem of History in Mark* (Alec. R. Allenson, Inc., 1957), pp. 79–80, has shown how the church consciousness of Mark was expressed in the formula of those who were with Jesus.

35. Ernest Best, in his study of the formula *syn christō (op. cit.,* pp. 44-64), gives a more thorough analysis of that phrase than we can here give. Our conclusions generally support his, except at two points. Professor Best observes that Paul never speaks of " Christ with the believer " and that therefore we are dealing " with a very one-sided relationship " (p. 50). This conclusion should be modified in terms of W. C. van Unnik's penetrating study of *Dominus Vobiscum,* in *New Testament Studies in Honor of T. W. Manson* (Manchester University Press, Manchester, 1959), pp. 287 ff. Professor van Unnik shows that the usual preposition for indicating Christ's presence with the believer is *meta.* In the second place, Professor Best deduces from the Pauline formula the conclusion that there is very little evidence that the phrase " with Christ " suggested " an interrelationship of believers." I think that a full study of the compound verbs would lead to a modification of this judgment.

36. Phil. 1:27; 4:3; I Cor. 16:16; 3:9; II Cor. 1:24.

37. I Cor. 3:1-19; II Cor. 10:8; 12:19; 13:10.

38. Probably the most thorough exegetical treatment is the monograph by P. Vielhauer, *Oikodome* (1939); the most far-reaching theological discussion is K. Barth, *Church Dogmatics,* IV, 2 (English translation), pp. 626–641.

39. I Peter, ch. 2; Eph., ch. 2; Acts 7:48-49; II Cor., ch. 5.

40. In at least four other New Testament books the association of the church as the house of God with the house of Israel appears as an entirely natural and accepted convention. With *oikos:* Luke 1:32-33; Acts 2:36, 39; with *oikia:* John 8:31-47; with *oikeios:* Eph. 2:12-22.

41. Pedersen, *op. cit.,* p. 49.

42. *Ibid.,* p. 14.

43. *Ibid.,* p. 48.

44. *Ibid.,* p. 49.

45. *Ibid.,* p. 51.

46. *Ibid.,* pp. 56, 57.

47. Luke 10:6; 7:35; 16:8; John 12:36; Eph. 5:8 f.; I Thess. 5:5; Matt. 8:12; 13:38; II Peter 2:14; Eph. 2:3; John 17:12; Matt. 23:15; I John 3:10; Acts 13:10; Matt. 13:38.

48. Pedersen, *op. cit.*, p. 54.

49. Theodorus Christiaan Vriezen, *Outline of Old Testament Theology* (Basil Blackwell & Mott, Ltd., Oxford, 1958), p. 142.

50. Ex. 4:22; Hos. 11:1; Deut. 14:1; Isa. 1:2; 30:1; Jer. 3:14; Deut. 32:6; Jer. 3:4; Isa. 63:16; 64:8; Mal. 1:6.

51. Vriezen, *op. cit.*, pp. 145-147.

52. Cf. H. F. D. Sparks in D. E. Nineham, ed., *Studies in the Gospels* (Oxford University Press, London, 1955), pp. 241 ff.

53. Matt. 5:24; 18:15, 21, 35; I Cor. 6:1-6; I John 2:9 f.

54. The inner fabric of brotherhood was also indicated by the strong emphasis on brotherly love. Cf. Rom. 12:10; I Thess. 4:9; Heb. 13:1; I Peter 1:22; 3:8; II Peter 1:7.

Chapter VI. THE BODY OF CHRIST

1. Mark 14:22 and parallels; John 2:19-21; Heb. 10:5, 10; 13:3, 11-12; I Peter 2:24.

2. We should indicate the fact that Paul does not in this passage explicitly use the term *sōma* (body) to refer to the realm of life in Christ. I have done so to make explicit the contrast on which, as it seems to me, the whole argument of Paul is based. The contrast would remain essential to Paul's thought and relevant to our inquiry even though this phrase, " the body of life," were to be deleted.

3. Best, *op. cit.*, pp. 52, 53.

4. This extreme form of equivalence, against which Dr. Best argues, seems to be defended in a rather unguarded way by Bishop John Robinson. Cf. *The Body*, pp. 46 f.

5. J. A. T. Robinson, *op. cit.*, p. 80n.

6. We observe in passing that in this chapter, Paul thinks of the head (*kephalē*) as one of the members of the body and not as the unique role of Jesus Christ. Only in Colossians and Ephesians does headship become a central accent in the picture.

7. Cf. Knox, *The Death of Christ* (Abingdon Press, 1958), pp. 123 f.; J. A. T. Robinson, *op. cit.*, pp. 78-83; Richardson, *op. cit.*, pp. 255 f.

8. Markus Barth, *The Broken Wall* (The Judson Press, 1959), p. 57.

9. J. A. T. Robinson, *op. cit.*, pp. 81-83.

10. If we should look for those passages outside of I Corinthians in which the reference of *sōma* is most closely related to that in ch. 15 and throws most light upon it, we would study again Rom., chs. 5 to 8; 14:7-9, and we would carry through a detailed exegesis of II Cor., chs. 4; 5, and of Phil., ch. 3.

11. Markus Barth, *op. cit.*, p. 118.

12. P. T. Forsyth, *The Church and the Sacraments* (Independent Press, London, 1947), p. 6.

13. It has been all too easy for the church to make its doctrine and practice of baptism into a kind of legal requirement, a necessitous bond with its demands, an arbitrary requirement of self-abasement (Col. 2:10-19), which, in effect, becomes another sign of the " worship of angels." So too, any ordinance, rule, or sacrament of the church can readily become a form for donning again the clothes of the " old man."

14. This is a very difficult verse to interpret. I have stressed what I take to be a conservative and minimal accent which can be supported by parallel expressions elsewhere.

15. Col. 2:17 is another very difficult verse. The relation of the shadow to the body remains problematical, but in this context we cannot exclude all interest in the church from the term " body " (RSV: " substance ").

16. Stauffer, *op. cit.*, p. 39.

17. Richardson, *op. cit.*, p. 254.

18. Eph. 4:25; cf. I Cor. 12:25; Rom. 12:5; [89].

Chapter VII. INTERRELATION OF THE IMAGES

1. This type of thinking is illustrated well in an essay by J. de Zwaan, in which he contrasts what the churchman of the second century thought before he said " church " with what the churchman of the first century thought. To the latter " saying ' church ' meant having said ' Christ,' and saying that as the last word." In *Aux Sources de la Tradition Chretienne, Essays in Honor of M. Goguel*, p. 271.

2. Forsyth, *op. cit.*, p. 32.

3. I Cor. 6:17 — " He who is united to the Lord becomes one spirit with him."

  I Cor. 12:13 — " By one Spirit we were all baptized into one body."

  I Cor. 15:44 — " It is raised a spiritual body."

  I Cor. 15:45 — " The last Adam became a life-giving spirit."

  Eph. 2:18 — " Through him we both have access in one spirit to the Father."

  Eph. 2:22 — " A dwelling place of God in the Spirit."

  Eph. 4:4 — " There is one body and one Spirit."

4. Richardson, *op. cit.*, p. 256.

5. Best, *op. cit.*, p. 188; also pp. 113, 137, 157 f.

6. Professor Best denies that the church is in Paul's mind in this passage (pp. 52-54). I believe that this denial presupposes a modern conception of the church which must be rejected.

7. Professor Best grants this idea as a possible exception to his conclusion (p. 189n) but radically underestimates its importance.

8. Cf. W. C. van Unnik, *Dominus Vobiscum, loc. cit.*, pp. 270-303.

Chapter VIII. A POSTSCRIPT

1. J. Huizinga, *Homo Ludens,* English edition, 1955, p. 4.

2. Huizinga, *op. cit.*, p. 133.

3. Stendahl, *The Root of the Vine,* p. 67.

4. Olof Linton, *Das Problem der Urkirche in der Neuer Forschung.* Uppsala, 1932.

5. Richardson, *op. cit.,* pp. 291–306.

6. *Ibid.*

7. *Ibid.,* pp. 301, 302.

8. *Ibid.,* pp. 334, 335.

INDEX

Scripture References